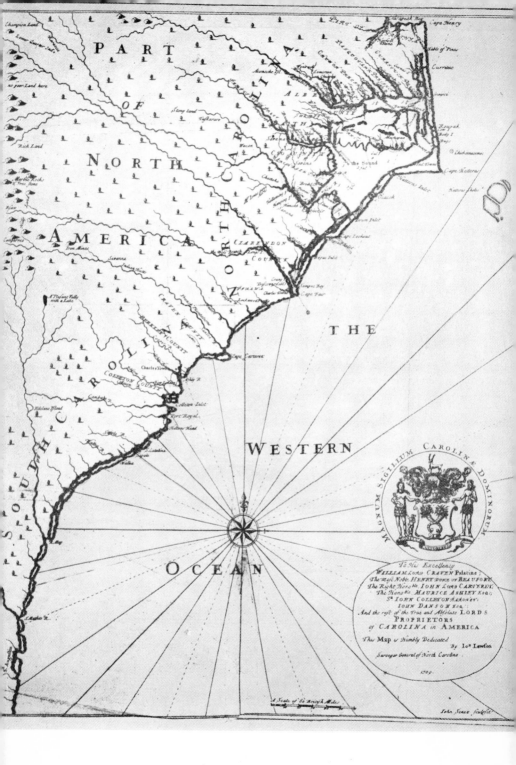

Lawson's History of North Carolina

CONTAINING THE EXACT DESCRIPTION AND
NATURAL HISTORY OF THAT COUNTRY, TO-
GETHER WITH THE PRESENT STATE THEREOF
AND A JOURNAL OF A THOUSAND MILES
TRAVELED THROUGH SEVERAL NATIONS OF
INDIANS, GIVING A PARTICULAR ACCOUNT
OF THEIR CUSTOMS, MANNERS, ETC., ETC.

By JOHN LAWSON, Gent.
Surveyor-General of North Carolina

LONDON:
Printed for W. Taylor at the Ship, and F. Baker at the
Black Boy, in Pater-Noster Row, 1714.

MCMLI
GARRETT AND MASSIE · PUBLISHERS
RICHMOND ·VIRGINIA

EDITED BY
FRANCES LATHAM HARRISS

Contents

Illustrations

Foreword

MANY of Lawson's guesses in regard to his route through practically unexplored country are misleading. His route has been carefully traced by Mr. James Mooney, of the Bureau of Ethnology.

"Starting from Charleston, South Carolina, he went by water to the mouth of the Santee, which he ascended twenty or thirty miles to the French settlements. Then taking the trail from Charleston, which came in near the present railroad crossing, he followed the eastern side of the Santee, Wateree, and Catawba rivers, passing in succession through the territories of the Sewee, Santee, Congaree, Wateree, and Waxhaw tribes, until he came to the Catawba (Esaw and Kadapaw), on the boundary between South Carolina and North Carolina. Here he took the great trading path from Virginia to Georgia and followed it into North Carolina as far as Occaneechi village, about the present Hillsboro, North Carolina. On this part of the journey he encountered the Sugeree, Saponi, Keyauwee, and Occaneechi, and crossed several rivers and small streams. His 'Sapona' River supposed by him to be a branch of the Cape Fear, is the Yadkin, which he crossed at the traders' ford near the site of Salisbury. Here was the Saponi village, the name being still commemorated in a small station on the northern side of the river. His 'Rocky' River, miles farther on, is probably Abbott (s') Creek, and his 'Haw or Reatkin' is the Haw, which he forded about at the present railroad crossing at Graham. In fact, the Richmond and Danville Railroad (North Carolina Railroad, branch of Southern), from Hillsboro, N. C. through Greensboro, Salisbury, and Charlotte, into South Carolina, is laid out almost exactly on the line of the old Occaneechi trail along which Lawson traveled. It is evident that he was not aware of the existence of the Yadkin or Pedee as a distinct stream, as in crossing it he supposes it to be a branch of the Cape Fear River, and later on confounds it under the name of

'Reatkin' with the Haw or main upper portion of the same stream. At the Occaneechi village, near Hillsboro, commemorated in the 'Occaneechi hills' at that town, he left the trading path and struck off in a southeasterly direction (turned from his course by the report of an invasion of the Iroquois from the North) toward the English settlements on the coast. His general course was down along the western bank of Eno and Neuse rivers until he crossed over to the northern bank about the falls near the railroad crossing at Wake Forest, where he entered the territory of the Tuscarora. He then continued down between the main Neuse and the Contentnea, probably passing near the site of Goldsboro, until he turned northward and crossed the latter stream about the present railroad crossing at Grifton, afterwards continuing across the Tar or Pamlico at Greenville or lower down, and finally coming out at the English settlements, after a trip of about seven weeks, on the 'Pamticough River, in North Carolina, where, being well received by the inhabitants and pleased with the goodness of the country, we all resolved to continue.'" (*Siouan Tribes of the East,* pp. 38, 41. By James Mooney.)

Lawson's classification of alligators, snakes, terrapins, lizards, etc. as "insects" sounds remarkably ignorant to modern ears. It appears the word was used in his day as a synonym of strange, unknown, and is still used colloquially in certain parts of England to indicate anything that crawls.

Lawson's description of North Carolina appeared first as a part of John Steven's *A New Collection of Voyages and Travels: With Historical Accounts of Discoveries and Conquests in all Parts of the World,* begun in London in 1708 and completed in 1710 and 1711. In 1709 Lawson's work appeared alone, in small quarto, with map and plate under title of *A New Voyage to Carolina; Containing the Exact Description and Natural History of that Country: Together with the Present State thereof and a Journal of a Thousand Miles, Travel'd thro' several Nations of Indians, Giving particular Account of their Customs, Manners, &c.* By John Lawson, Gent.,

Surveyor General of North Carolina. London: Printed in the Year 1709. Tyler, *History of American Literature*, 11, 282-289, speaks of it as an "uncommonly strong and sprightly book." Other editions appeared in 1714 and 1718. A German edition of Lawson was printed in Hamburg in 1712, another issue being brought out in 1722. The North Carolina Legislature brought out an edition in 1860, but this was unfortunately very poorly done. This present reprint of Lawson's History is a true copy of the original containing the original map and plate (The Beastes of Carolina). It contains also six black and white prints of the John White paintings, made by him in 1585. The originals are now in the British Museum. The prints in this volume were copied from de Bry's woodcuts of the White pictures illustrating his publication of Hariot's *History of Virginia*, in 1588. These pictures illustrate so perfectly descriptions of Indian life as given by John Lawson more than a century later, that they seemed not out of place, but adding interest to, this volume.

The editor wishes to acknowledge with appreciation her debt to the scholarly researches of Dr. Stephen B. Weeks, and to Mr. Marshall DeLancey Haywood, for the valuable records they have left us of Lawson and his work. Mrs. Charles A. Cannon placed at our disposal her interesting library of North Carolina literature and rare works of the colonial period, which enabled us to achieve what we believe to be accuracy in every detail of this edition of a book whose unstrained and vivid style brings the past to life under our eyes. All editions of this book are extremely rare; the 1709 edition is priceless and almost unobtainable. The State Library owned a copy of the 1718 edition which in 1820 was considered a unique possession, and which perished when the Capitol at Raleigh burned in 1831. Its place was supplied by James Madison with a 1714 copy. It is said that Wake Forest College owns a 1709 edition, and the State Library now owns both the 1714 and 1718 editions. There are less than a dozen of these early and accurate copies listed in this country.

FRANCES LATHAM HARRISS, Editor.

Biographical Sketch of John Lawson

THE proprietory period in North Carolina produced only one volume as its contribution to American colonial history, John Lawson's *History of North Carolina,* though, strictly speaking, it is not a history at all in the usually accepted sense. In offering a reprint of this book the editor believes that Americans are being given an opportunity to learn and understand the difficulties and dangers, the primitive luxuries and beauties of the wild which were endured and enjoyed by the men and women of high courage who met and overcame them, not to be found within the covers of any other one volume in such clear and complete detail. The narrative is enlivened constantly by a hearty and vivid humor and betrays in every line Lawson's youthful zest in the adventure, but this joyous current which carries the reader rapidly along from page to page does not conceal from his eyes the hardships and perils accompanying the daily life of the white man in the land of the Indian.

Of John Lawson himself little is known with certainty prior to his life in North Carolina. He appears to have flashed like a meteor across our ken, leaving behind him only this illuminating record of his presence and the tragic memory of his death. Where he was born, who were his parents, and where he was educated have not thus far been brought to light, though much scholarly effort has been expended upon the subject. Stephen B. Weeks, Ph.D., of the United States Bureau of Education (1896) formed this definite conclusion from his extensive researches into the subject, that John Lawson came from the family of the Lawsons of Brough Hall, Yorkshire, England, and was probably "the son of that Lawson who was such a faithful adherent of the King in the civil war that he suffered the sequestration of his estates under the Commonwealth." In 1665, during the Restoration, his estates were returned to him, and he received Knighthood for his loyalty.

All we know of John Lawson indicates beyond doubt that he was a gentleman by birth, that he was well educated, his tastes cultured, and that he possessed ample means to indulge them, and was free to choose the course of his life and steer it where he would. Being of a mind, as he tells us, to travel and see the world, he started to journey with the human mass crowding toward Rome to witness the pageant of the Pope's Jubilee, in the year 1700. But he "met a gentleman who had been abroad, and was very well acquainted with the ways of living in both Indies," and the course of his life was changed. The gentleman fired his imagination with the possibilities of adventure in the New World, so Lawson deserted the well known path across the old, familiar world, to pit his youthful strength and ardor against the mystery and unknown hazards of the new.

Five years after his arrival in the colony we find him one of the incorporators of Bath Town, the first town established in North Carolina. He remained in the colony for eight years before returning to England, during which time he was engaged in surveying and encouraging colonization, as well as writing his *History of North Carolina*. In recognition of his valuable services he was appointed Surveyor-General of the Colony by the Lords Proprietors. His intimate associates at Bath were Christopher Gale, who became the first Chief Justice of North Carolina, and Captain Lionel Reading, who was apparently a cultured man as we find him appointed Trustee of Bath Library, a valuable collection of books provided by the celebrated Dr. Bray, and the first public library in North Carolina.

In 1709 Lawson was in London, evidently attending to the publication of his book which made its first appearance in that year. With him on that visit were Christopher Gale and Lionel Reading. These two gentlemen are generally believed to have been endeavoring to straighten out with the home government the violent quarrel in progress at that time between Colonel Thomas Carey and William Glover, President of the Council. This quarrel was incited by the oath of allegiance to Queen Anne which the Quakers considered an unwarranted burden placed on their consciences which they refused to bear, and resulted in the uprising known as "Carey's Rebellion." While Lawson appears to have been tolerant and liberal in his attitude toward others, there is no evidence that he interested himself in the Carey troubles, or ever took part in political disputes. He was a very busy man, more interested in his orchards than in matters of colonial policy. His book is singularly free from allusion to political or personal affairs. It was while on this visit to England that Lawson was called upon by the Lords Proprietors to assist DeGraffenreid, a Swiss adventurer, in the settlement of his colony of Palatines in North Carolina. That connection proved to be a most unfortunate one for John Lawson.

During January of the year 1710 the party of North Carolina gentlemen with seven hundred Palatines returned to America. De-Graffenreid remained in England. The misfortunes of the Palatines, with Lawson's struggles to assist them, their appeal to the Lords Proprietors against the injustices of DeGraffenreid, and the latter's scurrilous accusations against Lawson after his death, form too long a story for this sketch.

It was in September, 1711, that Lawson started on his last trip of exploration. With him went DeGraffenreid, two negroes, and two trusted Indians. Christopher Gale had intended joining the expedition but, as he himself expressed it later, "the happy illness of my wife prevented me." The purpose of the trip was to discover how far up the Neuse River was navigable, and if it was possible to locate a better road in that direction to Virginia. At that time the Indian tribes had become encouraged to believe that the constant quarrels of the whites among themselves were an opportunity offered them to put up a fight to regain their lost lands and hunting grounds. Led by the savage Tuscaroras, they had been stealthily organizing their forces for some time. Lawson must have been aware to some extent of this condition of affairs, but the strength of the movement was a monstrous surprise to everyone. Conscious of his kindness and fair dealing with the Indians, and being an absolutely fearless man, he evidently saw no danger to himself in moving freely about the Indian country attending to his own affairs. He had, however, been appointed an associate of Edward Mosely in surveying the disputed boundary line between North Carolina and Virginia. His work as surveyor brought him into constant contact with the Indians. Stirred as they were by bitter thoughts of their losses and watching him at work, they mistook him for the cause of their despoiling, ignorant of the truth that he was only an agent. Apparently the possibility of such a feeling against him had not occurred to his mind.

The only account we have of this fatal trip up the Neuse River is from the pen of DeGraffenreid, when he was trying to explain his conduct of affairs to the Lords Proprietors. He does not fail to use that pen entirely to his own advantage and in cold disparagement of a man forever silenced by a cruel death. DeGraffenreid recounts at length how the little party slowly made their way up the river. Suddenly they were surrounded and seized by a number of Indians who led them away to King Hencock's town of Catechna, where they were tried, acquitted, and ordered set at liberty next day. Meantime other prominent Indians arrived who wanted to know why these white men were being set at liberty. DeGraffenreid asserts that at this critical time Lawson ruined their prospects by quarreling with the King of the Corees. This is difficult to understand, because it is so entirely out of keeping with what we know of Lawson's character. However, they were tried again and sentenced to death. Many indignities were heaped upon them, their periwigs torn from their heads and thrown in the fire. Finally they were led away under heavy guard. Many pages are filled by DeGraffenreid in explaining how he escaped the result of this death sentence, and shifting all the blame and responsibility for Lawson's death upon the shoulders of Lawson himself. Presumably the negro slaves suffered death with Lawson, though DeGraffenreid does not mention them at all. He informs us that he declared himself to the Indians as being under the particular care and protection of the Great White Queen, who would terribly avenge him if any harm came to him. Why no such consideration prevented the awful slaughter of her subjects visited upon the white settlements by these Indians a few days later the Baron does not attempt to explain.

John Lawson was left alone to face torture and death. In what manner, no one knows. Christopher Gale believed that he died after the manner described in his *History of North Carolina,* with the pitch pine splinters stuck all over his body and lighted as torches, a living column of fire until released by the mercy of death. The offices of trust which he held, the character of the men who were his friends, the records of his dealings given in the Colonial Records of North Carolina, and the Minutes of the Lords Proprietors, the kindly tolerance for the savages as expressed in his book, his sympathy for their ignorance and desire for fair dealing towards them on the part of the "Christians" are clear evidence of the manner of man he was. We may be sure that he died as he had lived, a gallant gentleman.

FRANCES LATHAM HARRISS.

Wilmington, North Carolina
    November, 1937

Preface

'TIS a great Misfortune that most of our Travelers, who go to this vast Continent in America, are Persons of the meaner Sort, and generally, of a very slender Education; who being hired by the Merchants to trade amongst the Indians, in which Voyages they often spend several Years, are yet, at their Return, uncapable of giving any reasonable Account of what they met withal in those remote Parts; though the Country abounds with Curiosities worthy a nice Observation. In this Point, I think the French Outstrip us.

First: By their Numerous Clergy, their Missionaries being obedient to their Superiors in the highest Degree, and that Obedience being one Great Article of their Vow, and strictly Observed amongst all their Orders.

Secondly: They always send abroad some of their Gentlemen in Company of the Missionaries, who, upon their Arrival, are ordered out into the Wilderness, to make Discoveries, and to acquaint themselves with the Savages of America; and are obliged to keep a strict Journal of all the Passages they meet withal, in order to present the same not only to their Governors and Fathers, but likewise to their Friends and Relations in France; which is industriously spread about that Kingdom, to their Advantage. For their Monarch being a very good Judge of Men's Deserts, does not often let Money or Interest make Men of Parts give Place to others of less Worth. This Breeds an Honorable Emulation amongst them, to outdo one another, even in Fatigues and Dangers; whereby they gain a good Correspondence with the Indians, and acquaint themselves with their Speech and Customs; and so make considerable Discoveries in a short time. Witness their Journals from Canada to the Mississippi, and its several Branches, where they have effected great Matters in a few years.

Having spent most of my Time, during my eight Years Abode in Carolina, in travelling, I not only surveyed the Sea-Coast, and those

Parts which are already inhabited by the Christians, but likewise viewed a spacious Tract of Land lying betwixt the Inhabitants and the Ledges of Mountains, from whence our noblest Rivers have their Rise, running towards the Ocean, where they water as pleasant a Country as any in Europe; the Discovery of which being never yet made Public, I have, in the following Sheets, given you a Faithful Account thereof; wherein I have laid down Everything with Impartiality, and Truth, which is indeed, the Duty of every Author, and Preferable to a smooth Stile, accompanied with Falsities and Hyperboles.

Great part of this pleasant and healthful Country is inhabited by none but Savages, who covet a Christian Neighborhood, for the Advantage of Trade, and enjoy all the Comforts of Life, free from Care and Want.

But not to amuse my Readers any longer with the Encomium of Carolina, I refer 'em to my Journal, and other more particular Description of that Country and its Inhabitants, which they will find after the Natural History thereof, in which I have been very exact, and for Method's sake arranged each Species under its distinct and proper Head.

Dedication

TO HIS EXCELLENCY
William Lord Craven, Palatine;
The most Noble, Henry Duke of Beaufort;
The Right Honorable John Lord Carteret;
The Honorable Maurice Ashley, Esq.;
Sir John Colleton, Baronet,
John Danson, Esq.;
And the rest of the true and Absolute
Lords Proprietors
of the
Province of Carolina in America

My Lords,

As debts of gratitude ought most punctually to be paid, so, where the Debtor is uncapable of Payment, Acknowledgments ought, at least to be made. I cannot, in the least, pretend to retaliate Your Lordships Favors to me, but must farther intrude on that Goodness of which I have already had so good Experience, by laying these Sheets at your Lordships' Feet, where they beg Protection, as having nothing to recommend them but Truth; a Gift which every Author may be Master of, if he will.

I here present Your Lordships with a Description of your own Country, for the most part, in her Natural Dress, and therefore less vitiated with Fraud and Luxury. A Country, whose Inhabitants may enjoy a Life of the greatest Ease and Satisfaction, and pass away their Hours in solid Contentment.

Those Charms of Liberty and Right, the Darlings of an English Nature, which Your Lordships grant and maintain, make you appear Noble Patrons in the Eyes of all Men, and we a happy People in a Foreign Country; which nothing less than Ingratitude and Baseness can make us disown.

As Heaven has been liberal in its Gifts, so are your Lordships favorable Promoters of whatever may make us an easy People, which, I hope, Your Lordship will continue to us and our Posterity; that we and they may always acknowledge such favours, by banishing from among us every Principle which renders Men factious and unjust; which is the hearty Prayer of,

My Lords,

Your Lordships most obliged,

most humble and

most devoted servant,

JOHN LAWSON.

Introduction

IN the Year 1700, when People flocked from all Parts of the Christian World, to see the Solemnity of the Grand Jubilee at Rome, my Intention at that Time being to travel, I accidentally met with a Gentleman, who had been Abroad, and was very well acquainted with the Ways of Living in both Indies; of whom having made Inquiry concerning them, he assured me that Carolina was the best Country I could go to; and, that there then lay a Ship in the Thames in which I might have my Passage. I laid hold on this Opportunity, and was not long on Board, before we fell down the River and sailed to Cowes; where, having taken in some Passengers, we proceeded on our Voyage, 'till we sprung a-leak, and were forced into the Islands of Scilly. Here we spent about ten Days in refitting; in which Time we had a great deal of Diversion in Fishing and Shooting on those rocky Islands. The Inhabitants were very courteous and civil, especially the Governor, to whose good Company and Favour, we were very much obliged. There is a Town on one of these Islands, where is good Entertainment for those that happen to come in, though the Land is but mean, and Flesh-meat not Plenty. They have good Store of Rabbits, Quails and Fish; and you see at the poor Peoples Doors, great Heaps of Periwinkle-shells, those Fish being a great Part of their Food. On the first Day of May, having a fair Wind at East, we put to Sea, and were on the Ocean (without speaking to any Vessel, except a Ketch, bound from New England to Barbadoes, laden with Horses, Fish, and Provisions), till the latter End of July, when the Winds hung so much Southerly, that we could not get to our Port, but put into Sandy-hook-bay, and went up to New York, after a pinching Voyage, caused by our long Passage. We found at the Watering-Place, a French Man-of-War, who had on Board Men and Necessaries to make a Colony, and was intended for the Mississippi river, there to settle. The Country of New York is very pleasant in Summer, but in the Winter very cold, as all the Northern Plantations are. Their chief Commodities are Provisions, Bread, Beer, Lumber, and Fish in abundance: all which are very good, and some Skins and Furrs are hence exported. The City is governed by a Mayor (as in England), is seated on an Island, and lies very convenient for Trade and Defence, having a regular Fort, and well mounted with Guns. The buildings are generally of a smaller Sort of Flemish Brick, and of the Dutch Fashion (excepting some few Houses). They are all very firm and good Work, and conveniently placed, as is likewise the Town, which gives a very pleasant Prospect of the neighboring Islands and Rivers. A good part of the Inhabitants are Dutch, in whose Hands this Colony once was. After a Fortnight's Stay here, we put out from Sandyhook, and in fourteen Days after arrived at Charles-Town, the Metropolis of South Carolina, which is situate in 32.45 North Latitude, and admits of large Ships to come over their Bar up to the Town, where is a very commodious Harbor about five Miles distant from the Inlet, and stands on a Point very convenient for Trade, being seated between two pleasant and navigable Rivers. The Town has very regular and fair Streets, in which are good Buildings of Brick and Wood; and since my coming thence, has had great Additions of beautiful large Brick-buildings, besides a strong Fort and regular Fortifications made to defend the Town. The Inhabitants, by their wise Management and Industry, have much improved the Country, which is in as thriving Circumstances at this Time as any Colony on the Continent of English America, and is of more Advantage to the Crown of Great Britain, than any of the other more Northerly Plantations (Virginia and Maryland excepted). This Colony was at first planted by a genteel Sort of People, that were well acquainted with Trade, and had either Money or Parts, to make good use of the Advantages that offered, as most of them have done, by raising themselves to great Estates, and considerable Places of Trust, and Posts of Honour, in this thriving Settlement. Since the first Planters abundance of French and others have gone over and raised themselves to considerable Fortunes. They are very neat and exact in Packing and Shipping of their Commodities; which Method has got them so great a Character Abroad, that they generally come to a good Market with their Commodities; when oftentimes the Product of other Plantations, are forced to be sold at lower Prices. They have a considerable Trade, both to Europe and to the West Indies, whereby they become rich, and are supplied with all Things necessary for Trade and genteel Living, which several other Places fall short of. Their cohabiting in a Town has drawn to them ingenious People of most Sciences, whereby they have Tutors amongst them that educate their Youth a-la-mode.

Their Roads, with great Industry, are made very good and pleasant. Near the Town is built a fair Parsonage house, with necessary Offices, and the Minister has a very considerable Allowance from his Parish. There is likewise a French Church in Town, of the Reformed Religion, and several Meeting-houses for dissenting Congregations, who all enjoy at this day an entire Liberty of their Worship; the Constitution of this Government allowing all Parties of well-meaning Christians to enjoy a free Toleration and possess the same privileges, so long as they appear to behave themselves peaceably and well. It being the Lords Proprietors Intent that the Inhabitants of Carolina should be as free from Oppression as any in the Universe, which doubtless they will, if their own Differences amongst themselves do not occasion the contrary.

They have a well disciplined Militia; their Horse are most Gentlemen and well mounted, and the best in America, and may equalize any in other Parts. Their Officers, both Infantry and Cavalry, generally appear in scarlet Mountings, and as rich as in most Regiments belonging to the Crown, which shows the Richness and Grandeur of this Colony. They are a Fronteer, and prove such troublesome Neighbors to the Spaniards, that they have once laid their Town of St. Augustine in Ashes, and drove away their Cattle, besides many Encounters and Engagements, in which they have defeated them, too tedious to relate here. What the French got by their Attempt against South Carolina, will hardly ever be ranked amongst their victories; their Admiral Mouville, being glad to leave the Enterprize, and run away, after he had suffered all the Loss and Disgrace he was capable of receiving. They are absolute Masters over the Indians, and carry so strict a Hand over such as are within the Circle of their Trade, that none does the least Injury to any of the English, but he is presently sent for and punished with Death, or otherwise, according to the Nature of the Fault. They have an entire Friendship with the neighboring Indians of several Nations, which are a very warlike People, ever faithful to the English, and have proved themselves brave and true on all Occasions; and are a great Help and Strength to this Colony. The Chief of the savage Nations have heretofore groaned under the Spanish Yoke, and having experienced their Cruelty have become such mortal Enemies to that People, that they never give a Spaniard Quarter; but generally, when they take any Prisoners (if the English be not near to prevent it), scalp them, that is, to take their Hair and Skin of their Heads, which they often flee away while the Wretch is alive. Nothwithstanding the English have used all their Endeavors, yet they could never bring them to leave this Barbarity to the Spaniards, who as they alledge, use to murder them and their Relations, and make Slaves of them to build their Forts and Towns.

This place is more plentiful in Money than most, or indeed any of the Plantations on the Continent; besides, they build a considerable Number of Vessels of Cedar, and other Wood, with which they trade to Cuirassau and the West Indies; from one they bring Money, and from the other the Produce of their Islands, which yields a necessary Supply of both to the Colony. Their Stocks of Cattle are incredible, being from one to two thousand Head in one Man's Possession. These feed in the Savannahs, and other Grounds, and need no Fodder in the Winter. Their Mutton and Veal is good, and their Pork is not inferior to any in America.

As for Pitch and Tar, none of the Plantations are comparable for affording the vast Quantities of Naval Stores, as this Place does. There have been, heretofore, some Discoveries of rich Mines in the mountainous Part of this Country: but being remote from the present Settlement, and the Inhabitants not well versed in ordering Minerals, they have been laid aside till a more fit Opportunity happens. There are several noble Rivers, and spacious Tracts of rich Land in their Lordships Dominions, lying to the Southward, which are yet uninhabited, besides Port Royal, a rare Harbour and Inlet, having many Inhabitants thereon, which their Lordships have now made a Port for Trade. This will be a most advantageous Settlement, lying so commodiously for Ships coming from the Gulph, and the Richness of the Land, which is reported to be there. These more Southerly Parts will afford Oranges, Lemons, Limes, and many other Fruits, which the Northerly Plantations yield not.

The merchants of Carolina are fair, frank Traders. The Gentlemen seated in the Country, are very courteous, live very nobly in their Houses, and give very genteel Entertainment to all Strangers and others that come to visit them. And since the Produce of South and North Carolina is the same, unless Silk, which this place produces great Quantities of, and very good, North Carolina having never made any Tryal thereof as yet, therefore I shall refer the natural Produce of this Country, to that Part which treats of North Carolina, whose Productions are much the same. The Christian Inhabitants of both Colonies pretty equal, but the Slaves of South Carolina are far more in Number than those in the North. I shall now proceed to relate my Journey through the Country from this Settlement to the other, and then treat of the natural History of Carolina, with other remarkable Circumstances which I have met with, during my eight Years Abode in that Country.

A JOURNAL of a thousand miles travel among the Indians *from South to North Carolina*

ON December the 28th, 1700, I began my Voyage (for North Carolina), from Charles-Town, being six English-men in Company, with three Indian-men and one Woman, Wife to our Indian-Guide, having five Miles from the Town to the Breach, we went down in a large Canoe, that we had provided for our Voyage thither, having the Tide of Ebb along with us, which was so far spent by that Time we got down, that we had not Water enough for our Craft to go over, although we drew but two Foot, or thereabouts. This Breach is a Passage through a Marsh lying to the Northward of Sullivans Island, the Pilots having a Look-out thereon, lying very commodious for Mariners (on that Coast), making a good Land-Mark in so level a Country, this Bar being difficult to hit, where an Observation hath been wanting for a Day or two; North-East Winds bringing great Fogs, Mists and Rains, which, towards the cool Months of October, November, and until the latter End of March, often appear in these Parts. There are three Pilots to attend and conduct Ships over the Bar. The Harbour where the Vessels generally ride, is against the Town on Cooper's River; lying within a Point which parts that and Ashley-River, they being Land-locked almost on all Sides.

At four in the Afternoon (at half Flood), we passed with our Canoe, over the Breach, leaving Sullivans Island on our Starboard. The first Place we designed for was Santee River, on which there is a Colony of French Protestants, allowed and encouraged by the Lords Proprietors. At Night we got to Bell's Island, a poor Spot of Land, being about ten Miles round, where lived (at that Time), a Bermudian, being employed here with a Boy, to look after a Stock of Cattle and Hogs, by the Owner of this Island. One Side of the Roof of his House was thatched with Palmeto-trees, the other open to the Heavens, thousands of Musketoes, and other troublesome Insects, tormenting both man and Beast inhabiting these Islands. The Palmeto-trees, whose Leaves growing only on the top of the tree, in the shape of a Fan, and in a Cluster like a Cabbage; this Tree in Carolina, when at its utmost Growth, is about forty or fifty Foot in Height, and two Foot through. It is worth mentioning, that the Growth of the Tree is not perceivable in the Age of any Man, the Experiment having been often tried in Bermudas and elsewhere, which shows the slow Growth of this Vegetable, the Wood of it being porus and stringy, like some Canes; the Leaves thereof, the Bermudians make Women's Hats, Bokeets, Baskets, and pretty Dressing boxes, a great deal being transported to Pensilvania, and other Northern Parts of America, (where they do not grow,) for the same Manufacture. The People of Carolina make of the Fans of this Tree, Brooms, very servicable to sweep their Houses withal.

We took up our Lodging this Night with the Bermudian; our Entertainment was very indifferent, there being no fresh Water to be had in the Island.

The next Morning we set away through the Marshes; about Noon we reached another Island, called Dix's Island, much like to the former, though larger; there lived an honest Scot who gave us the best Reception his Dwelling afforded, being well provided of Oat-meal, and several other Effects he had found on that Coast; which Goods belonged to that unfortunate Vessel, the Rising Sun, a Scotch Man-of-War, lately arrived from the Isthmus of Darien, and cast away near the Bar of Ashley River, the September before, Capt. Gibson of Glasco then commanding her, who, with above an hundred Men then on Board her, were every Soul drowned, in that terrible Gust, which then happened; most of the Corps being taken up, were carefully interred by Mr. Graham, their Lieutenant, who happily was on Shore during the Tempest.

After Dinner we left our Scotch Landlord, and went, that Night, to the North-East Point of the Island. It being dark ere we got there, our Canoe struck on a Sand near the breakers, and were in great Danger of our Lives, but (by God's Blessing) got off safe to the Shore, where we lay all Night.

In the Morning we set forward on our intended Voyage. About two o'Clock we got to Bulls Island, which is about thirty Miles long, and hath a great Number of both Cattel and Hogs upon it; the Cattel being very wild and the Hogs very lean. These two last Islands belong to one Col. Cary, an Inhabitant of South Carolina. Although it were Winter, yet we found such Swarms of Muske-toes, and other troublesome Insects, that we got but little Rest that Night.

The next Day we intended for a small Island on the other Side of Sewee-bay, which, joining to these Islands, Shipping might come to victual or careen: but there being such a Burden of those Flies that few or none, cares to settle there; so the Stock thereon are run wild. We were gotten about half Way to Racoon Island, when there sprung up a tart Gale at N. W., which put us in some Dan-ger of being cast away, the Bay being rough, and there running great Seas between the two Islands, which are better than four Leagues asunder, a strong Current of a Tide setting in and out, which made us turn Tail to it, and got our Canoe Right before the Wind, and came safe into a Creek that is joining to the North End of Bulls Island. We sent our Indians to hunt, who brought us two Deers, which were very poor, and their maws full of large Grubs.

On the Morrow we went and visited the Eastern-most Side of this Island, it joining to the Ocean, having very fair, sandy Beeches, paved with innumerable Sorts of Curious pretty Shells; very pleas-ant to the Eye. Amongst the rest, we found the Spanish Oyster-Shell, whence come the Pearls. They are very large, and of a Dif-ferent Form from other Oysters; their Colour much resembles the Tortoise-Shell, when it is dressed. There was left by the Tide, Several strange Species of a Mucilaginous, slimy Substance, though living, and very aptly Moved at their first Appearance; yet, being left on the dry Sand, (by the Beams of the Sun,) soon exhale and vanish.

At our Return to our Quarters, the Indians had Killed two more Deer, two wild Hogs, and three Raccoons, all very lean except the Raccoons. We had great Store of Oysters, Conks, and Clanns, a large Sort of Cockles. These Parts being very well furnished with Shell-Fish, Turtle of several Sorts, but few or none of the green, with other Sorts of Salt-water Fish, and in the Season good Plenty of Fowl, as curleus, Gulls, Gannets, and Pellicans, besides Duck and Mallard, Geese, Swans, Teal, Widgeon, &c.

On Thursday morning we left Bulls Island, and went through the Creeks, which lie between the Bay and the main Land. At Noon we went on Shore, and got our Dinner near a Plantation, on a Creek having the full Prospect of Sewee-Bay. We sent up to the House, but found none at Home but a Negro, of whom our Messenger purchased some small Quantity of Tobacco and Rice. We came to a deserted Indian Residence, called Avendaugh-bough, where we rested that Night.

The next Day we entered Santee River's Mouth, where is fresh Water, occasioned by the extraordinary Current that comes down continually.—With hard Rowing, we got two Leagues up the River, lying all Night in a swampy Piece of Ground, the Weather being so cold all that Time, we were almost frozen ere Morning, leaving the Impression of our Bodies on the wet Ground. We set forward very early in the Morning to seek some better Quarters. As we Rowed up the River we found the Land towards the Mouth, and for about sixteen Miles up it, scarce any Thing but Swamp and Percoarson, affording vast Ciprus-Trees of which the French make Canoes that will carry fifty or sixty barrels. After the Tree is moulded and dug they saw them in two Pieces, and so put a Plank betwixt and a small Keel to preserve them from the Oyster-Banks, which are innumerable in the Creeks and Bays between the French Settlement and Charles-Town. They carry two Masts and Bermudas Sails, which makes them very handy and fit for their Purpose; for although their River fetches its first Rise from the Mountains and continues a Current some hundreds of Miles ere it disgorges itself, having no sound, bay or Sand-Banks betwixt the Mouth thereof and the Ocean. Notwithstanding all this, with the vast Stream it affords at all Seasons, and the repeated Freshes it so often alarms the Inhabitants with, by laying under Water great Part of their Country, yet the Mouth is barred affoarding not above four or five Foot Water at the Entrance. As we went up the River we heard a great Noise as if two Parties were engaged against each other; seeming exactly like small Shot. When we approached nearer the Place we found it to be some Sewee Indians firing the Cane Swamps, which drives out the Game, then taking their particular Stands, kill great Quantities of both Bear, Deer, Turkies, and what wild Creatures the Parts afford.

These Sewees have been formerly a large Nation, though now very much decreased, since the English hath seated their Land, and all other Nations of Indians are observed to partake of the same Fate, where the Europeans come, the Indians being a People very apt to catch any Distemper they are afflicted withal. The Small-Pox has destroyed many thousands of these Natives who, no sooner than they are attacked with the violent Fevers and the Burning which attends that Distemper, fling themselves over-Head in the Water, in the very Extremity of the Disease, which, shutting up the Pores, hinders a kindly Evacuation of the pestilential Matter, and drives it back, by which Means Death most commonly ensues; not but in other Distempers which are epidemical, you may find among them Practitioners that have extraordinary Skill and Success in removing those morbific Qualities which afflict them, not often going above one hundred Yards from their Abode for their Remedies, some of their chiefest Physicians commonly carrying their Compliment of Drugs continually about them, which are Roots, Barks, Berries, Nuts &c., that are strung upon a Thread. So like a Pomander, the Physician wears them about his Neck. An

Indian hath been often found to heal an Englishman of a Malady for the Value of a Match-Coat, which the ablest of our English Pretenders in America, after repeated Applications, have deserted the Patient as incurable; God having furnished every Country with specific Remedies for their peculiar Diseases.

Rum, a Liquor, now so much in Use with them that they will part with the dearest Thing they have, to purchase it; and when they have got a little in their Heads, are the impatientest Creatures living, till they have enough to make them quite drunk, and the most miserable Spectacles when they are so, some falling into the Fires, burn their Legs or Arms, contracting the Sinews, and becoming cripples all their Lifetime; others from Precipices break their Bones and Joints, with abundance of Instances, yet none are so great to deter them from that accursed Practice of Drunkenness, though sensible how many of them (are by it) hurryed into the other World before their Time, as themselves oftentimes will confess. The Indians I was now speaking of, were not content with the common Enemies that lessen and destroy their Country-men, but invented an infallible Stratagem to purge their Tribe, and reduce their Multitude into far less Numbers. Their Contrivance was thus, as a Trader amongst them informed me.

They seeing several Ships coming in, to bring the English Supplies from Old England, one chief Part of their Cargo being for a Trade with the Indians, some of the craftiest of them had observed that the Ships came always in at one Place, which made them very confident that Way was the exact Road to England; and seeing so many Ships come thence, they believed it could not be far thither, esteeming the English that were among them, no better than Cheats, and thought, if they could carry the Skins and Furs they got, themselves to England, which were inhabited with a better Sort of People than those sent amongst them, that then they should purchase twenty times the Value for every Pelt they sold Abroad, in Consideration of what Rates they sold for at Home. The intended Barter was exceeding well approved of, and after a general Consultation of the ablest Heads amongst them it was *Nemine Contradicente* agreed upon, immediately to make an addition of their Fleet, by building more Canoes, and those to be of the best Sort and bigest Size, as fit for their intended Discovery. Some Indians were employed about making the Canoes, others to hunting, every one to the Post he was most fit for, all Endeavors tending towards an able Fleet and Cargo for Europe. The Affair was carried on with a great deal of Secrecy and Expedition, so as in a small Time they had gotten a Navy, Loading, Provisions, and Hands, ready to set Sail leaving only the Old, Impotent and Minors at Home, 'til their successful Return. The Wind presenting, they set up their Mat-Sails, and were scarce out of Sight, when there rose a Tempest, which it is supposed carryed one Part of these Indian Merchants by Way of the other World, whilst the others were taken up at Sea, by an English Ship, and sold for Slaves to the Islands. The Remainder are better satisfied with their Imbecilities in such an Undertaking, nothing affronting them more than to rehearse their Voyage to England.

There being a strong Current in Santee-River, caused us to make small Way with our Oars. With hard Rowing we got that Night to Mons. Eugee's House, which stands about fifteen Miles up the River, being the first Christian dwelling we met withal in that Settlement, and were very courteously received by him and his Wife.

Many of the French follow a Trade with the Indians, living very conveniently for that Interest. There is about seventy Families seated on this River, who live as decently and happily as any Planters in these Southward Parts of America. The French being a temperate industrious People, some of them bringing very little of Effects, yet, by their Endeavors and mutual Assistance, amongst themselves (which is highly to be commended) have outstripped our English, who brought with them larger Fortunes, though (as it seems) less endeavor to manage their Talent to the best Advantage. 'Tis admirable to see what Time and Industry will (with God's

Blessing) effect. Carolina, affording many strange Revolutions in the Age of a Man, daily Instances presenting themselves to our View, of so many from despicable Beginnings, which, in a short Time, arrive to very splendid Conditions. Here Propriety hath a large Scope, there being no strict Laws to bind our Privileges. A Quest after Game being as freely and peremptorily enjoyed by the meanest Planter, as he that is the highest in Dignity, or wealthiest in the Province. Deer and other Game that are naturally wild, being not immured, or preserved within Boundaries, to satisfy the Appetite of the Rich alone. A poor Laborer that is Master of his Gun, &c., hath as good a Claim to have continued Coarses of Delicacies crouded upon his Table, as he that is Master of a great Purse.

We lay all that Night at Mons. Eugee's, and the next Morning set out farther, to go the Remainder of our Voyage by Land. At ten a Clock we passed over a narrow, deep Swamp, having left the three Indian Men and one Woman, that had piloted the Canoe from Ashley-River, having hired a Sewee-Indian, a tall lusty Fellow, who carried a Pack of our Cloaths of great weight; notwithstanding his Burden, we had as much a do to keep pace with him. At Noon we came up with several French Plantations, meeting with several Creeks by the Way. The French were very officious in assisting with their small Dories, to pass over these Waters, (whom we met coming from their Church) being all of them very clean and decent in their Apparel; their Houses and Plantations suitable in Neatness and Contrivance. They are all of the same Opinion with the Church of Geneva, there being no Difference amongst them concerning the Punctilios of their Christian Faith; which Union hath propagated a happy and delightful Concord in all other Matters throughout the whole Neighborhood, living amongst themselves as one Tribe or Kindred, every one making it his Business to be assistant to the Wants of his Countryman, preserving his Estate and Reputation with the same Exactness and concern as he does his own, all seeming to share in the Misfortunes, and rejoice at the Advance and Rise of their Brethren.

Towards the Afternoon we came to Mons. L'Jandro, where we got our Dinner; there coming some French Ladies while we were there who were lately come from England, and Mons. L'Grand, a worthy Norman, who hath been a great Sufferer in his Estate by the Persecution in France, against those of the Protestant Religion: This Gentleman very kindly invited us to make our Stay with him all Night, but we being intended farther that Day took our Leaves, returning Acknowledgements of their Favors.

About four in the Afternoon, we passed over a large Ciprus run in a small Canoe; the French Doctor sent his Negro to guide us over the Head of a large Swamp. So we got that Night to Mons. Gallian's the elder, who lives in a very curious contrived House built of Brick and Stone, which is gotten near that Place. Near here comes in the Road from Charles-Town and the rest of the English Settlement, it being a very good Way by Land, and not above thirty-six Miles, although more than one hundred by Water; and I think the most difficult Way I ever saw, occasioned by Reason of the multitude of Creeks lying along the Main, keeping their Course through the Marshes, turning and winding like a Labyrinth, having the Tide of Ebb and Flood twenty Times in less than three Leagues going.

The next Morning very early we ferried over a Creek that runs near the House; and after an Hour's Travel in the Woods, we came to the River-side, where we staid for the Indian who was our Guide, and was gone round by Water in a small Canoe to meet us at that Place we rested at. He came after a small Time, and ferried us in that little Vessel over Santee-River, four Miles and eighty-four Miles in the Woods, which the overflowing of the Freshes, which then came down, had made a perfect Sea of, there running an incredible Current in the River, which had cast our small Craft and us away, had we not had this Sewee Indian with us; who are excellent Artists in managing these small Canoes.

Santee river at this Time, (from the usual Depth of Water,) was risen perpendicular thirty-six foot, always making a Breach from her

Banks about this Season of the Year. The general Opinion of the Cause thereof, is supposed to proceed from the overflowing of fresh Water-Lakes that lie near the Head of this River, and others, upon the same Continent. But my Opinion is, that these vast Inundations proceed from the great and repeated Quantities of Snow that falls upon the Mountains, which lie at so great a Distance from the Sea, therefore they have no Help of being dissolved by those saline, piercing Particles as other adjacent Parts near the Ocean receive, and therefore lies and increases to a vast Bulk, until some mild Southerly Breezes coming on a sudden, continues to unlock these frozen Bodies, congealed by the North-West Wind, dissipating them in Liquids, and coming down with Impetuosity, fills those Branches that feed these Rivers and causes this strange Deluge, which oft times lays under Water the adjacent Parts on both Sides this Current, for several Miles distant from her Banks; though the French and Indians affirmed to me, they never knew such an extraordinary Flood there before.

We all, by God's Blessing and the Endeavors of our Indian Pilot, passed safe over the River, but was lost in the Woods, which seemed like some great Lake, except here and there a Knowl of high Land which appeared above Water.

We intended for Mons. Gallian's jun., but was lost, none of us knowing the Way at that Time, although the Indian was born in that Country, it having received so strange a Metamorphosis. We were in several Opinions concerning the right Way, the Indian and myself supposed the House to bear one Way, the rest thought to the contrary; we differing, it was agreed on amongst us, that one-half should go with the Indian to find the House, and the other part to stay upon one of these dry Spots, until some of them returned to us and informed us where it lay.

Myself and two more were left behind, by Reason the Canoe would not carry us all; we had but one Gun amongst us, one Load of Ammunition and no Provision. Had our Men in the Canoe miscarried, we must, (in all Probability), there have perished.

In about six Hours' Time from our Men's Departure, the Indian came back to us in the same Canoe he went in being half drunk, which assured us they had found some Place of Refreshment. He took us three into the Canoe telling us all was well: Padling our Vessel several miles through the Woods, being often half full of Water; but at length we got safe to the Place we sought for, which proved to lie the same Way the Indian and I guessed it did.

When we got to the House, we found our Comrades in the same Trim the Indian was in, and several of the French Inhabitants with them, who treated us very courteously, wondering at our undertaking such a Voyage, through a Country inhabited by none but Savages, and them of so different Nations and Tongues.

After we had refreshed ourselves, we parted from a very kind, loving and affable People, who wished us a safe and prosperous Voyage.

Hearing of a Camp of Santee Indians not far off we set out intending to take up our Quarters with them that Night. There being a deep Run of Water in the Way, one of our Company being top heavy, and there being nothing but a small Pole for a Bridge, over a Creek, fell into the Water up to the Chin; myself laughing at the Accident, and not taking good Heed to my steps, came to the same Misfortune. All our Bedding was wet. The Wind being at N. W. it froze very hard, which prepared such a Night's Lodging for me, that I never desire to have the like again; the wet Bedding and freezing Air had so qualified our Bodies, that in the Morning when we awaked we were nigh frozen to Death, until we had recruited ourselves before a large Fire of the Indians.

Tuesday Morning we set towards the Congerees leaving the Indian Guide Scipio, drunk amongst the Santee-Indians. We went ten Miles out of our Way to head a great Swamp, the Freshes having filled them all with such Quantities of Water that the usual Paths were rendered impassible. We met in our Way with an Indian Hut, where we were entertained with a fat boiled Goose,

Venison, Raccoon and ground Nuts. We made but little Stay: about Noon we passed by several large Savannahs', wherein is curious Ranges for Cattel, being green all the Year; they were plentifully stored with Cranes, Geese, &c., and the adjacent Woods with great Flocks of Turkies. This Day we traveled about thirty Miles, and lay all Night at a House which was built for the Indian Trade, the Master thereof we had parted with at the French Town, who gave us Leave to make use of his Mansion. Such Houses are common in these Parts, and especially where there is Indian Towns and Plantations near at hand, which this Place is well furnished withal.

These Santee-Indians are a well humored and affable People; and living near the English, are become very tractable. They make themselves Cribs after a very curious Manner, wherein they secure their Corn from Vermin, which are more frequent in these warm Climates than Countries more distant from the Sun. These pretty Fabrics are commonly supported with eight Feet or Posts about seven Foot high from the Ground, well daubed within and without upon Laths, with Loom or Clay, which makes them tight and fit to keep out the smallest Insect, there being a small Door at the gable End, which is made of the same Composition, and to be removed at Pleasure, being no bigger than that a slender Man may creep in at, cementing the Door up with the same Earth when they take Corn out of the Crib, and are going from Home, always finding their Granaries in the same Posture they left them: Theft to each other being altogether unpracticed, never receiving Spoils but from Foreigners.

Hereabouts the Ground is something higher than about Charles-Town, there being found some Quaries of brown, free Stone, which I have seen made Use of for Building, and hath proved very durable and good. The Earth here is mixed with white Gravel, which is rare, there being nothing like a Stone to be found of the natural Produce, near to Ashley-River.

The next Day about Noon, we came to the Side of a great Swamp, where we were forced to strip ourselves to get over it, which, with much Difficulty, we effected. Hereabouts the late Gust of Wind, which happened in September last, had torn the large Ciprus-Trees and Timbers up by the Roots, they lying confusedly in their Branches, did block up the Way, making the Passage very difficult.

This Night we got to one Scipio's Hutt, a famous Hunter. There was no Body at Home, but we having (in our Company) one that had used to trade amongst them, we made ourselves welcome to what his Cabin afforded, (which is a Thing common) the Indians allowing it practicable to the English Traders to take out of their Houses what they need in their Absence, in Lieu whereof they most commonly leave some small gratuity of Tobacco, Paints, Beads, &c. We found great Store of Indian Peas (a very good Pulse) Beans, Oyl, Thinkapin Nuts, Corn, barbacued Peaches, and Peach-Bread, which Peaches being made into a Quiddony, and so made up into Loaves like Barley-Cakes, these cut into thin Slices, and dissolved in Water, makes a very grateful Acid, and extraordinary beneficial in Fevers, as has often been tried, and approved on by our English Practitioners. The Wind being at N. W., with cold Weather, made us make a large Fire in the Indian's Cabin; being very intent upon our Cookery, we set the Dwelling on Fire, and with much a do put it out, though with the Loss of Part of the roof.

The next Day we traveled on our Way, and about Noon came up with a Settlement of Santee Indians, there being Plantations lying scattering here and there, for a great many Miles. They came out to meet us, being acquainted with one of our Company, and made us very welcome with fat barbacued Venison, which the Woman of the Cabin took and tore in Pieces with her Teeth, so put it into a Mortar, beating it to Rags, afterwards stews it with Water, and other Ingredients, which makes a very savoury Dish.

At the Cabins came to visit us the King of the Santee Nation. He brought with him their chief Doctor, or Physician, who was warmly and neatly clad with a Match-Coat, made of Turkies Feathers, which makes a pretty Shew, seeming as if it was a garment of the deepest silk Shag. This Doctor had the Misforune to lose his Nose by the Pox, which Disease the Indians often get by the English Traders that use amongst them; not but the Natives of America have for many Ages (by their own Confession) been afflicted with a Distemper much like the Lues Venerea, which hath all the Symptoms of the Pox, being different in this only, for I never could learn, that this Country-Distemper, or yawes, is begun or continued with a Gonorrhœa, yet is attended with noctural Pains in the Limbs, and commonly makes such a Progress as to vent Part of the Matter by Botches, and several Ulcers in the Body, and other Parts, oftentimes Death ensuing. I have known mercurial Unguents and Remedies work a Cure, following the same Methods as in the Pox, several white People, but chiefly the Criolos, losing their Palates and Noses by this devouring Vulture.

It is epidemical, visiting these Parts of America which is often occasioned through the immoderate drinking of Rum, by those that commonly drink water at other Times, cold Night's Lodging, and bad open Houses, and more chiefly, by often wetting the Feet and eating such Quantities of Pork as they do, which is a gross Food, and a great Propagator of such juices as it often meets withal in human Bodies, once tainted with this Malady, which may differently (in some Respects) act its Tragedy, the Change being occasioned by the Difference of Climates and Bodies as in Europe. We being well enough assured that the Pox had its first Rise (known to us) in this new World, it being caught of the Indian Women by the Spanish Soldiers that followed Columbus in one of his Expeditions to America, who after their Arrival in Old Spain, were hastened to the Relief of Naples, at that Time besieged by the French. Provisions growing scarce, the useless People were turned out of the City, to lesson the Mouths; amongst these the Curtesans were one Part, who had frequently embraced the Spaniards, being well fraught with Riches by their new Discovery. The Leager Ladies had no sooner lost their Spanish Dons, but found themselves as well entertained by the French, whose Camp they traded in, giving the

Monsieurs as large a Share of the pocky Spoils within their own Lines, as the Spaniards had, who took the Pains to bring it in their Breeches as far as from America; the large Supplies of Swine's Flesh which that Army was chiefly victualed withal, made it rage. The Siege was raised; the French and Spaniards retreating to Flanders, which was a Parade of all Nations; by which Means this filthy Distemper crowded itself into most Nations of the known World.

Now to return to our Doctor, who, in the Time of his Affliction, withdrew himself (with one that labored under the same Distemper) into the Woods. These two perfected their Cures by proper Vegetables, &c., of which they have Plenty, and are well acquainted with their specific Virtue.

I have seen such admirable Cures performed by these Savages, which would puzzle a great many graduate Practitioners to trace their Steps in Healing, with the same Expedition, Ease and Success; using no racking Instruments in their Chirurgery, nor nice Rules of Diet, and Physic, to verify the Saying, *qui Medice vivit, misere vivit*. In Wounds which penetrate deep and seem mortal, they order a spare Diet, with drinking Fountain water; if they perceive a White Matter or Pus to arise, they let the Patient more at large, and presently cure him.

After these two had performed their Cures at no easier Rate than the Expense of both their Noses, coming again amongst their old Acquaintance so disfigured, the Indians admired to see them metamorphosed after that manner, enquired of them where they had been all that Time, and what were become of their Noses? They made Answer That they had been conversing with the white Man above, (meaning God-Almighty,) how they were very kindly entertained by that Great Being; he being much pleased with their Ways, and had promised to make their Capacities equal with the white People in making Guns, Ammunition, &c., in Retaliation of which they had given him their Noses. The Verity of which they yet hold, the Indians being an easy, credulous People, and most notoriously cheated by their Priests and Conjurers, both

Trades meeting ever in one Person, and most commonly a Spice of Quackship added to the other two Ingredients, which renders that cunning Knave the Impostor to be more relied upon; thence a fitter Instrument to cheat these ignorant People; the Priest and Conjurers being never admitted to their Practice, till Years and the Experience of repeated Services hath wrought their Esteem amongst the Nations they belong to.

The Santee King, who was in Company with this No-nosed Doctor is the most absolute Indian Ruler in these Parts, although he is Head but of a small People, in Respect to some other Nations of Indians, that I have seen. He can put any of his People to Death that hath committed any Fault which he judges worthy of so great a Punishment. This Authority is rarely found amongst these Savages, for they act not (commonly) by a determinative Voice in their Laws towards any one that hath committed Murder, or such other great Crime, but take this Method; him to whom the Injury was done, or if dead, the nearest of his Kindred, prosecutes by Way of an actual Revenge, being himself if Opportunity serves his Intent, both Judge and Executioner, performing so much Mischief on the Offender or his nearest Relation, until such Time that he is fully satisfied. Yet this Revenge is not so infallible but it may be bought off with Beads, Tobacco, and such like Commodities that are useful amongst them, though it were the most sable Villainy that could be acted by Mankind.

Some that attended the king presented me with an odoriferous balsamic Root, of a fragrant Smell and Taste, the Name I know not; they chew it in the Mouth, and by that simple Application heal desperate Wounds both green and old; that small Quantity I had was given inwardly to those troubled with the Belly-ache, which Remedy failed not to give present Help, the Pain leaving the Patients soon after they had taken the Root.

Near to these Cabins are several Tombs made after the manner of these Indians; the largest and the chiefest of them was the Sepulchre of the late Indian King of the Santees, a Man of great

Power, not only amongst his own Subjects, but dreaded by the neighboring Nations for his great Valour and Conduct, having as large a Prerogative in his Way of Ruling, as the present King I now spoke of.

The manner of their Interment is thus: A Mole or Pyramid of Earth is raised, the Mould thereof being worked very smooth and even, sometimes higher or lower, according to the Dignity of the Person whose Monument it is. On the Top thereof is an Umbrella, made Ridgeways, like the Roof of an House, this is supported by nine Stakes, or small Posts, the Grave being about six or eight Foot in Length and four foot in Breadth; about it is hung Gourds, Feathers, and other such like Trophies, placed there by the dead Man's Relations, in respect to him in the Grave. The other Part of the Funeral-Rites are thus: As soon as the Party is dead, they lay the Corps upon a Piece of Bark in the Sun, seasoning or embalming it with a small Root beaten to Powder, which looks as red as Vermillion; the same is mixed with Bear's Oil to beautify the hair, and preserve their Heads from being lousy, it growing plentifully in these Parts of America. After the Carcass has laid a Day or two in the Sun, they remove and lay it upon Crotches cut on purpose, for the Support thereof from the Earth, then they annoint it all over with the forementioned Ingredients of the Powder of this Root and Bear's Oil. When it is so done, they cover it very exactly over with Bark of the Pine, or Ciprus Tree to prevent any Rain to fall upon it, sweeping the Ground very clean all about it. Some of his nearest of Kin brings all the temporal Estate he was possessed of at his Death, as Guns, Bows and Arrows, Beads, Feathers, Match-Coat, &c. This Relation is the chief Mourner, being clad in Moss and a Stick in his Hand, keeping a mournful Ditty for three or four Days, his Face being black with Smoak of Pitch Pine mingled with Bear's Oil. All the while he tells the dead Man's Relations, and the rest of the Spectators, who that dead Person was, and of the great Feats performed in his Lifetime; all what he speaks, tending to the praise of the Defunct. As soon as the Flesh grows mellow and will cleave from the Bone, they get it off and burn it, making all the Bones very clean, then annoint them with the Ingredients aforesaid, wrapping up the Skull (very carefully) in a Cloath artificially woven of Possom's Hair. (These Indians make Girdles, Sashes, Garters, &c., after the same Manner.) The Bones they carefully preserve in a wooden Box, every Year oiling and cleansing them. By these Means preserve them for many Ages, that you may see an Indian in Possession of the Bones of his Grand-father, or some of his Relations of a larger Antiquity. They have other Sorts of Tombs as where an Indian is slain, in that very Place they make a Heap of Stones, (or Sticks where Stones are not to be found) to this Memorial, every Indian that passes by, adds a Stone to augment the Heap, in Respect to the deceased Hero.

We had a very large Swamp to pass over near the House, and would have hired our Landlord to have been our Guide, but he seemed unwilling, so we pressed him no farther about it. He was the tallest Indian I ever saw, being seven Foot high, and a very straight compleat Person, esteemed on by the King for his great Art in Hunting, always carrying with him an artificial Head to hunt withal. They are made of the Head of a Buck, the back Part of the Horns being scrapt and hollow for Lightness of Carriage. The Skin is left to the setting on of the Shoulders, which is lined all around with Small Hoops, and flat Sort of Laths, to hold it open for the Arm to go in. They have a Way to preserve the Eyes, as if living. The Hunter puts on a Match-coat made of Deer's Skin, with the Hair on, and a Piece of the white Part of the Deer's Skin that grows on the Breast, which is fastened to the Neck-End of this stalking Head, so hangs down. In these Habiliments an Indian will go as near a Deer as he pleases, the exact Motions and Behaviour of a Deer being so well counterfeited by them, that several Times it hath been known for two Hunters to come up with a stalking Head together, and unknown to each other, so that they have killed an Indian instead of a Deer, which hath happened sometimes to be a Brother or some Dear Friend; for which Reason they allow not of that Sort of Practice where the Nation is populous.

Within half a Mile of the House we passed over a prodigious wide and deep Swamp, being forced to strip stark-naked, and much a-do to save ourselves from drowning in this Fatigue. We with much a-do got through, going that Day about five Miles farther, and came to three more Indian Cabins, called in the Indian Tongue, Hickerau, by the English Traders, the black House, being pleasantly seated on a high Bank, by a Branch of Santee-River. One of our Company that had traded amongst these Indians told us, That one of the Cabins was his Father's-in-law; he called him so by Reason the old Man had given him a young Indian Girl, that was his Daughter, to lie with him, make Bread, and to be necessary in what she was capable to assist him in, during his Abode amongst them.

When we came thither first there was no Body at Home, so the Son made bold to search his Father's Granary for Corn and other Provisions. He brought us some Indian Maiz and Peas, which are of reddish Colour, and eat well, yet colour the Liquor they are boiled in as if it were a Lixivium of red Tartar. After we had been about an Hour in the House where was Millions of Fleas, the Indian Cabins being often fuller of such Vermin, than any Dog-Kennel, the old Man came in to us, and seemed very glad to see his Son-in-Law.

This Indian is a great Conjuror, as appears by the Sequel. The Seretee or Santee Indians were gone to War against the Hooks and Backbooks Nations, living near the Mouth of Winyan-River. Those that were left at Home, (which are commonly old people and children,) had heard no News a long Time of their Men at Arms. This Man, at the Entreaty of these People, (being held to be a great Sorcerer amongst them,) went to know what Posture their fighting Men were in. His Exorcism was carried on thus: He dressed himself in a clean white dressed Deer-Skin, a great Fire being made in the Middle of the Plantation, the Indians sitting all around it, the Conjuror was blindfolded, then he surrounded the Fire several Times, I think thrice; leaving the Company he went into the Woods, where he stayed about half an Hour, returning to them surrounded the Fire as before; leaving them, he went the second Time into the Woods; at which Time there came a huge Swarm of Flies, very large, they flying about the Fire several Times, at last fell all into it, and were visibly consumed. Immediately after the Indian-Conjuror made a huge Lilleloo, and howling very frightfully. Presently an Indian went and caught hold of him, leading him to the Fire. The old Wizzard was so feeble and weak, being not able to stand alone, and all over in a Sweat, and as wet as if he had fallen into the River. After some Time he recovered his Strength, assuring them that their Men were near a River, and could not pass over it till so many Days, but would, in such a time, return all in Safety to their Nation, All which proved true at the Indians' Return, which was not long after. This Story the Englishman, his Son-in-Law, affirmed to me.

The old Man staid with us about two Hours, and told us we were welcome to stay there all Night, and take what his Cabin afforded; then leaving us, went into the Woods to some Hunting-Quarter not far off.

The next Morning early we pursued our Voyage, finding the Land to improve itself in Pleasantness and Richness of Soil. When we had gone about ten Miles one of our Company tired, being not able to travel any farther; so we went forward, leaving the poor dejected Traveler with Tears in his Eyes to return to Charles-Town, and travel back again over so much bad Way, we having passed through the worst of our Journey, the Land here being high and dry, very few Swamps and those dry and a little way through. We traveled about twenty Miles, lying near a Savanna that was overflown with Water; where we were very short of Victuals, but finding the Woods newly burnt, and on fire in many Places, which gave us great Hopes that Indians were not far off.

Next Morning, very early, we waded through the Savanna, the Path lying there; and about ten a Clock came to a hunting Quarter of a great many Santees. They made us all welcome, showing a great deal of Joy at our coming, giving us barbecued Turkeys, Bear's Oil and Venison.

Here we hired Santee Jack, (a good Hunter, and a well humored Fellow) to be our Pilot to the Congeree Indians. We gave him a Stroud-water-Blew to make his Wife an Indian Petticoat, who went with her Husband. After two Hours Refreshment we went on, and got that Day about twenty Miles; we lay by a small, swift Run of Water, which was paved at the Bottom with a Sort of Stone much like to Tripoli, and so light that I fancied it would precipitate in no Stream, but where it naturally grew. The Weather was very cold, the Winds holding Northerly. We made ourselves as merry as we could, having a good Supper with the Scraps of Venison we had given us by the Indians, having killed three Teal and a Possum, which Medly, all together, made a curious Ragoo.

This Day all of us had in Mind to have rested, but the Indian was much against it, alleging, That the Place we lay at was not good to hunt in, telling us if we would go on, by Noon he would bring us to a more convenient Place, so we moved forwards, and about twelve a'Clock came to the most amazing Prospect I had seen since I had been in Carolina; we traveled by a Swamp-side which Swamp I believe to be no less than twenty Miles over, the other Side being as far as I could well discern, there appearing great Ridges of Mountains bearing from us N.N.W. One Alp with a Top like a Sugar-loaf, advanced its Head above all the rest very considerably. The Day was very serene which gave us the Advantage of seeing a long Way; these Mountains were clothed all over with Trees which seemed to us to be very large timbers.

At the Sight of this fair Prospect we staid all Night; our Indian going about half an Hour before us, had provided three fat Turkeys ere we got up to him.

The Swamp I now spoke of, is not a miry Bog as others generally are, but you go down to it through a steep Bank, at the Foot of which begins this Valley, where you may go dry for perhaps two hundred Yards, then you meet with a small Brook or Run of Water about two or three Foot deep, then dry Land for such another Space, so another Brook, thus continuing. The Land in this pocoson, or Valley, being extraordinary rich, and the Runs of Water well stored with Fowl. It is the Head of one of the Branches of Santee-River; but a farther Discovery Time would not permit; only one Thing is very remarkable, there growing all over this Swamp a tall, lofty Bay-tree, but is not the same as in England, these being in their Verdue all the Winter long; which appears here, when you stand on the Ridge, (where our Path lay,) as if it were one pleasant, green Field, and as even as a Bowling-green to the Eye of the Beholder, being hemmed in on one Side with these Ledges of vast high Mountains.

Viewing the Land here, we found an extraordinary rich, black Mould, and some of a Copper-colour, both Sorts very good, the Land in some Places is much burthened with Iron Stone, here being great store of it, seemingly very good. The eviling Springs, which are many in these Parts, issuing out of the Rocks, which Water we drank of, it coloring the excrements of Travelers, by its Chalybid Quality, as black as a Coal. When we were all asleep in the Beginning of the Night, we were awakened with the dismalist and most hideous Noise that ever pierced my Ears. This sudden Surprizal incapacitated us of guessing what this threatening Noise might proceed from: but our Indian Pilot, (who knew these Parts very well,) acquainted us, that it was customary to hear such Music along that Swamp side, there being endless Numbers of Panthers, Tygers, Wolves, and other Beasts of prey, which take this Swamp for their Abode in the Day, coming in whole Droves to hunt the Deer in the Night, making this frightful Ditty till Day appears, then all is still as in other Places.

The next Day it proved a small drisly Rain, which is rare, there happening not the tenth Part of Foggy falling Weather towards these Mountains as visits those Parts near the Sea-board. The Indian killed fifteen Turkeys this Day, there coming out of the Swamp, (about Sun-rising), Flocks of these Fowl, containing several hundred in a Gang, who feed upon the Acorns, it being most Oak that grow in these Woods. There are but very few Pines in those Quarters.

Early the next Morning, we set forward for the Congeree-Indians, parting with that delicious Prospect. By the Way our Guide killed more Turkeys and two Polecats, which he eat, esteeming them before fat Turkeys. Some of the Turkeys which we eat whilst we stayed there, I believe weighed no less than forty Pounds.

The Land we passed over this Day was most of it good, and the worst passable. At Night we killed a Possum, being Cloy'd with Turkey, made a dish of that, which tasted much between young Pork and Veal; their Fat being as white as any I ever saw.

Our Indian having this Day killed good store of Provision with his Gun, he always shot with a single Ball, missing but two Shoots in about forty; they being curious Artists in managing a Gun to make it carry either Ball or Shot, true. When they have bought a Piece, and find it to shoot any Ways crooked, they take the Barrel out of the Stock, cutting a Notch in a Tree, wherein they set it straight, sometimes shooting away above one hundred Loads of Ammunition, before they bring the Gun to shoot according to their mind. We took up our Quarters by a Fish-pond-side; the Pits in the Woods that stand full of Water naturally breed Fish in them, in Great Quantities. We cooked our Supper, but having neither Bread or Salt, our fat Turkeys began to be loathsome to us, although we were never wanting of a good Appetite, yet a Continuance of one Diet made us weary.

The next morning Santee Jack told us we should reach the Indian Settlement betimes that Day. About Noon we passed by several fair Savannas, very rich and dry; seeing great Copses of many Acres that bore nothing but Bushes, about the Bigness of Box-trees, which (in the Season) afford great Quantities of small, Black-berries, very pleasant Fruit, and much like to our Blues, or Huckleberries, that grow on Heaths in England. Hard by the Savannas we found the Town, where we halted; there was not above one Man left with the Women, the rest being gone a Hunting for the Feast. The Women were very busily engaged in Gaming. The name or Grounds of it I could not learn, though I looked on above two Hours. Their Arithmetick was kept with a Heap of Indian Grain. When their Play was ended, the King, or Chaffetta's Wife, invited us into her Cabin. The Indian Kings always entertaining Travelers, either English or Indian; taking it as a great Affront, if they pass by their Cabins and take up their Quarters at any other Indian's House. The Queen set Victuals before us, which good compliment they use generally as soon as you come under their Roof.

The Town consists not of above a dozen Houses, they having other straggling Plantations up and down the Country, and are seated upon a small Branch of Santee-River. Their Place hath curious dry Marshes and Savannas adjoining to it, and would prove an exceeding thriving Range for Cattle, and Hogs, provided the English were seated thereon. Besides, the Land is good for Plantations.

These Indians are small People, having lost much of their former Numbers, by intestine Broils, but most by the Small-pox, which hath often visited them, sweeping away whole Towns, occasioned by the immoderate Government of themselves in their Sickness, as I have mentioned before, treating of the Sewees. Neither do I know any Savages that have traded with the English but what have been great Losers by this Distemper.

We found here good Store of Chinkapin-Nuts, which they gather in Winter great Quantities of, drying them, so keep these Nuts in great Baskets for their Use; likewise Hickerie-Nuts, which they beat betwixt two great Stones, then sift them, so thicken their Venison-Broth therewith, the small Shells precipitating to the Bottom of the Pot, whilst the Kernel, in form of Flower, mixes it with the Liquor. Both these Nuts made into Meal makes a curious Soop, either with clear Water, or in any Meat-Broth.

From the Nation of Indians, until such Time as you come to the

Turkeiruros in North Carolina, you will see no long Moss upon the Trees, which Space of Ground contains above five hundred Miles. This seeming Miracle in Nature is occasioned by the Highness of the Land, it being dry and healthful; for though this most bears a Seed in a Sort of a small Cod, yet it is generated in or near low swampy Grounds.

The Congerees are kind and affable to the English, the Queen being very kind, giving us what Rarities her Cabin afforded, as loblolly made with Indian Corn, and dried Peaches. These Congerees have abundance of Storks and Cranes in their Savannas. They take them before they can fly, and breed them as tame and familiar as a Dung-hill-Fowl. They had a tame Crane at one of these Cabins, that was scarecely less than six foot in Heighth, his Head being round, with a shining, natural Crimson Hue, which they all have. These are a very Comely Sort of Indians, there being a strange Difference in the Proportions and Beauty of these Heathens. Although their Tribes or Nations border one upon another, yet you may discern as great an Alteration in their Features and Dispositions, as you can in their Speech, which generally proves quite different from each other, though their Nations be not above ten or twenty Miles in Distance. The Women here being as handsome as most I have met withal, being several fine fingered Brounettos amongst them. These Lasses stick not upon Hand long, for they marry when very young, as at twelve or fourteen Years of Age. The English Traders are seldom without an Indian Female for his Bed-fellow, alleging these Reasons as sufficient to allow of such Familiarty. First, They being remote from any white People, that it preserves their Friendship with the Heathens, they esteeming a white Man's Child much above one of their getting, the Indian Misses ever securing her white Friend Provisions whilst he stays Amongst them. And lastly, This Correspondence makes them learn the Indian Tongue much the sooner, they being of the Frenchman's Opinion, how that an English Wife teaches her Husband more English in one Night than a School-master can in a Week.

We saw at the Caffetta's Cabin the strangest Spectacle of Antiquity I ever knew, it being an old Indian Squah, that had I been to have guessed at her Age, by her Aspect, old Parr's Head (the Welch Methusalem) was a Face in Swadling-clouts to hers. Her Skin hung in Reaves like a Bag of Tripe. By a fair Computation, one might have justly thought it would have contained three such Carcasses as hers then was. She had one of her Hands contracted by some Accident in the Fire, they sleeping always by it, and often fall into sad Disasters, especially in their drunken Moods. I made the strictest Enquiry that was possible, and by what I could gather, she was considerably above one hundred Years old, nothwithstanding she smoked Tobacco and eat her Victuals, to all Appearances, as heartily as one of eighteen. One of our Company spoke some of their Language, and having not quite forgotten his former Intrigues with the Indian Lasses, would have been dealing with some of the young Female Fry; but they refused him, he having nothing that these Girls esteemed. At night we were laid in the King's Cabin, where the Queen and the old Squah piged with us. The former was very much disfigured with tetters, and very reserved, which disappointed our Fellow-Traveler in his Intrigues.

The Women smoke much Tobacco, (as most Indians do.) They have Pipes whose Heads are cut out of Stone, and will hold an Ounce of Tobacco, and some much less. They have large wooden Spoons, as big as small Ladles, which they make little Use of, lading the Meat out of the Bowles with their Fingers.

In the Morning we rose before Day, having hired a Guide over Night to conduct us on our Way; but it was too soon for him to stir out, the Indians never setting forward till the Sun is an Hour or two high and hath exhaled the Dew from the Earth. The Queen got us a good Breakfast before we left her; she had a young Child, which was much afflicted with the Cholic; for which distemper she infused a Root in Water, which was held in a Gourd; this she took into her Mouth and spurted it into the Infant's, which gave it ease. After we had eaten, we set out with our new Guide, for the Wateree

Indians. We went over a great deal of indifferent Land this Day. Here begins to appear very good Marble, which continues more and less for the Space of five hundred Miles. We lay all Night by a Run of Water, as we always do if possible, for the Convenience of it. The Weather was very cold. We went this Day about thirty miles from the Congerees.

In the Morning we made no Stay to get our Breakfast, but hastened on our Voyage, the Land increasing in Marble and Richness of Soil. At Noon we halted, getting our Dinner upon a Marble-Stone, that rose itself half a Foot above the Surface of the Earth, and might contain the Compass of a Quarter an Acre of Land, being very even, there growing upon it in some Places a small red Berry, like a Salmon-Spawn, there boiling out of the main Rock curious Springs of as delicious Water as ever I drank in any Parts I ever traveled in.

These Parts likewise affords good free Stone, fit for Building, and of several Sorts. The Land here is pleasantly seated, with pretty little Hills and Valleys, the rising Sun at once showing his glorious reflecting Rays on a great many of these little Mountains. We went this Day about twenty Miles, our Guide walking like a Horse, till we had saddled him with a good heavy Pack of some Part of our Cloaths and Bedding, by which Means we kept Pace with him.

This Night we lay by a Run-side, where I found a fine yellow Earth, the same with Bruxel's-Sand, which Goldsmiths use to cast withal, giving a good Price in England and other Parts. Here is likewise the true Blood-Stone and considerable Quantities of Fuller's-Earth, which I took a Proof of by scouring great Spots out of Woolen, and it proved very good.

As we were on our Road this Morning our Indian shot a Tyger that crossed the Way, he being a great Distance from us. I believe he did him no Harm, because he sat on his Breech afterwards, and looked upon us. I suppose he expected to have had a Spaniel Bitch that I had with me, for his Breakfast, who ran towards him, but in the Midway stopped her Career, and came sneaking back to us with her tail betwixt her legs.

We saw in the Path a great many Trees blown up by the Roots, at the Bottom thereof stuck great Quantities of fine red Bole: I belive nothing inferior to that of Venice or Lemma. We found some Holes in the Earth which were full of a Water as black as Ink. I thought that Tincture might proceed from some Mineral, but had not Time to make a farther Discovery. About Noon we passed over a pleasant stony Brook, whose Water was of a bluish Cast, as it is for several hundreds of Miles towards the Heads of the Rivers, I suppose occasioned by the vast Quantities of Marble lying in the Bowels of the Earth. The Springs that feed these Rivulets, lick up some Portion of the Stones in the Brooks; which Dissolution gives this Tincture, as appears in all, or most of the Rivers and Brooks in this Country, whose rapid Streams are like those in Yorkshire and other Northern Counties of England. The Indians talk of many Sorts of Fish which they afford, but we had not Time to discover their Species.

I saw here had been some Indian Plantations formerly, there being several pleasant Fields of cleared Ground and excellent Soil, now well spread with fine bladed Grass, and Strawberry-Vines.

The Mould here is excessive rich, and a Country very pleasing to the Eye, had it the Convenience of a navigable River, as all new Colonies, (of Necessity) require, it would make a delightful Settlement.

We went eight Miles farther and came to the Wateree Chickanee Indians. The Land holds good, there being not a Spot of bad Land to be seen in several Day's going.

The people of this Nation are likely tall Persons and great Pilferers, stealing from us any Thing they could lay their Hands on, though very respectful in giving us what Victuals we wanted. We lay in their Cabins all Night, being dark smoky Holes as ever I saw any Indians dwell in. This Nation is much more populous than the Congerees and their Neighbors, yet understand not one another's speech. They are very poor in English Effects, several of them having no Guns, making Use of Bows and Arrows, being a lazy, idle People, a Quality incident to most Indians, but none to that Degree as these, as I ever met withal.

Their Country is wholy free from Swamps and Quagmires, being high dry Land, and consequently healthful, producing large Corn-Stalks, and fair Grain.

Next Morning we took off our Beards with a Razor, the Indians looking on with a great deal of Admiration. They told us they had never seen the like before, and that our Knives cut far better than those that came amongst the Indians. They would fain have borrowed our Razors as they had our Knives, Scissors and Tobacco-Tongs the day before, being as ingenious at picking of pockets as any, I believe, the World affords; for they will steal with their feet. Yesterday, one of our Company, not walking so fast as the rest, was left behind. He being out of Sight before we missed him, and not coming up to us, though we staid a considerable time on the Road for him, we stuck up Sticks in the Ground, and left other Tokens to direct him which way we were gone; but he came not to us that Night, which gave us Occasion to fear some of the Heathen had killed him for his Cloaths, or the savage Beasts had devoured him in the Wilderness, he having nothing about him to strike Fire withal. As we were debating which way we should send to know what was become of him, he overtook us, having a Waxsaw Indian for his Guide. He told us he had missed the Path and got to another Nation of Indians but three Miles off, who at that time held great feasting. They had entertained him very respectfully, and sent that Indian to invite us amongst them, wondering that we would not take up our Quarters with them, but make our Abode with such a poor Sort of Indians, that were not capable of entertaining us according to our Deserts. We received the Messenger with a great many Ceremonies acceptable to those sort of Creatures. Bidding our Wateree King adieu, we set forth towards the Waxsaws, going along cleared Ground all the Way. Upon our Arrival, we were led into a very large and lightsome Cabin, the like I have not met withal. They laid Furs and Deer-Skins upon Cane

Benches for us to sit or lie upon, bringing (immediately), stewed Peaches and green Corn, that is preserved in their Cabins before it is ripe, and sodden and boiled when they use it, which is a pretty sort of Food, and a great Increaser of the Blood.

These Indians are of an extraordinary Stature, and called by their Neighbors flat Heads, which seems a very suitable Name for them. In their Infancy, their Nurses lay the Back-part of their Children's Heads on a Bag of Sand, (such as Engravers use to rest their Plates upon.) They use a Roll which is placed upon the Babe's Forehead, it being laid with its Back on a flat Board, and swaddled hard down thereon, from one End of this Engine to the other. This Method makes the Child's Body and Limbs as straight as an Arrow, There being some young Indians that are perhaps crokkedly inclined, at their first coming into the World, who are made perfectly straight by this Method. I never saw an Indian of mature Age that was any ways crooked, except by Accident, and that way seldom; for they cure and prevent Deformities of the Limbs and Body very exactly. The Instrument I spoke of before being a sort of a Press, that is let out and in, more or less, according to the Discretion of the Nurse, in which they make the Child's Head flat: it makes the Eyes stand a prodigious Way asunder, and the Hair hang over the Forehead like the Eves of a House, which seems very frightful. They being asked the Reason why they practiced this Method, replied, the Indian's Sight was much strengthened and quicker thereby to discern the Game in hunting at larger Distance, and so never missed of becoming expert Hunters, the Perfection of which they all aim at, as we do to become experienced Soldiers, learned School-Men, or Artists in Mechanics. He that is a good Hunter never misses of being a Favorite amongst the Women; the prettiest Girls being always bestowed upon the chiefest Sports-Men, and those of a grosser Mould upon the useless Lubbers. Thus they have a Graduation amongst them, as well as other nations. As for the Solemnity of Marriages amongst them, kept with so much ceremony as divers Authors affirm, it never appeared amongst those many Nations I have been withal, any otherwise than in the Manner I have mentioned hereafter.

The Girls, at twelve or thirteen Years of Age, as soon as Nature prompts them, freely bestow their Maidenheads on some Youth about the same Age, continuing her Favors on whom she most affects, changing her Mate very often, few or none of them being constant to one, till a greater Number of Years has made her capable of managing domestic Affairs, and she hath tried the Vigor of most of the Nation she belongs to. Multiplicity of Gallants never being a Stain to a Female's Reputation, or the least Hinderance of her Advancement; but the more Whorrish, the more Honorable, and they of all most coveted by those of the first Rank to make a Wife of. The Flos Virginis, so much coveted by the Europeans, is never valued by these Savages. When a Man and Woman have gone through their Degrees, (there being a certain Graduation amongst them,) and are allowed to be House-Keepers, which is not till they arrive at such an Age, and have passed the Ceremonies practiced by their Nation, almost all Kingdoms differing in the Progress thereof, then it is that the Man makes his Addresses to some one of these thoroughpaced Girls or other, whom he likes best. When she is won the Parents of both Parties (with Advice of the King) agree about the Matter, making a Promise of their Daughter to the Man that requires her, it often happening that they converse and travel together for several Moons before the Marriage is published openly. After this, at the least Dislike, the Man may turn her away, and take another; or if she disapproves of his Company, a Price is set upon her, and if the Man that seeks to get her, will pay the fine to her Husband, she becomes free from him; Likewise, some of their War Captains, and great Men, very often will retain three or four Girls at a time for their own Use, when at the same time he is so impotent and old, as to be incapable of making Use of one of them, so that he seldom misses of wearing greater Horns than the Game he kills. The Husband is never so enraged as to put his Adulteress to Death; if she is caught in the Fact, the Rival becomes

Debtor to the cornuted Husband, in a certain Quantity of Trifles, valuable amongst them, which he pays as soon as discharged, and then all Animosity is laid aside betwixt the Husband and his Wife's Gallant. The Man proves often so goodhumored as to please his Neighbor and gratify his Wife's Inclinations, by letting her out for a Night or two, to the Embraces of some other, which perhaps she has a greater Liking to, though this is not commonly practiced.

They set apart the youngest and prettiest Faces for trading Girls; these are remarkable by their Hair, having a particular Tonsure by which they are known and distinguished from those engaged to Husbands. They are mercenary, and whoever makes Use of them, first hires them, the greatest Share of the Gain going to the King's Purse, who is the chief Bawd, exercising his Prerogative over all the Stews of his Nation, and his own Cabin (very often,) being the chiefest Brothel-House. As they grow in Years, the hot Assaults of Love grow cooler; and then they commonly are so staid, as to engage themselves with more Constancy to each other. I have seen several Couples amongst them that have been so reserved, as to live together for many Years, faithful to each other, admitting none to their Beds but such as they owned for their Wife or Husband, so continuing to their Life's end.

At our Waxsaw's Landlord's Cabin, was a Womon employed in no other Business than Cookery, it being a House of great resort. The Fire was surrounded with Roast-meat, or Barbecues, and the Pots continually boiling full of Meat, from Morning till Night. This She-Cook was the cleanliest I ever saw amongst the Heathens of America, washing her Hands before she undertook to do any Cookery; and repeated this unusual Decency very often in a day. She made us as White-Bread as any English could have done, and was full as neat and expeditious in her Affairs. It happened to be one of their great Feasts, when we were there. The first day that we came amongst them, arrived an Ambassador from the King of Sapona, to treat with these Indians about some important Affairs. He was painted with Vermilion all over his Face, having a very large

Cutlass stuck in his Girdle, and a Fusee in his Hand. At Night the Revels began, where this Foreign Indian was admitted; the King and War-Captain inviting us to see their Masquerade. This Feast was held in Commemoration of the plentiful Harvest of Corn they had reaped the Summer before, with an united Supplication for the like plentiful Produce the Year ensuing. These Revels are carried on in a House made for that purpose, it being done round with white Benches of fine Canes, joining along the Wall; and a place for the Door being left, which is so low that a Man must stoop very much to enter therein. This Edifice resembles a large Hay-Rick, its Top being Pyramidal, and much bigger than their other Dwellings, and at the Building whereof, every one assists till it is finished. All their Dwelling-Houses are covered with Bark, but this differs very much; for it is very artificially thatched with Sedge and Rushes. As soon as finished, they place some one of their chiefest Men to dwell therein, charging him with the diligent Preservation thereof, as a Prince commits the Charge and Government of a Fort or Castle, to some Subject he thinks worthy of that Trust. In these State-Houses is transacted all Public and Private Business relating to the Affairs of the Government, as the Audience of Foreign Ambassadors from other Indian Rulers, Consultation of waging and making War, Proposals of their Trade with neighboring Indians, or the English who happen to come amongst them. In this Theatre, the most Aged and Wisest meet, determining what to Act, and what may be most convenient to Omit. Old Age being held in as great Veneration amongst these Heathens, as amongst any People you shall meet withal in any Part of the World.

Whensoever an Aged Man is speaking, none ever interrupts him, (the contrary Practice the English and other Europeans too much use,) the Company yielding a great deal of Attention to his Tale with a continued Silence and an exact Demeanor, during the Oration. Indeed, the Indians are a People that never interrupt one another in their Discourse; no Man so much as offering to open his Mouth till the Speaker has uttered his intent: When an English-

man comes amongst them, perhaps every one is acquainted with him, yet, first, the King bids him Welcome, after him the War Captain, so on gradually from High to Low; not one of all these speaking to the White Guest, till his Superior has ended his Salutation. Amongst Women, it seems impossible to find a Scold: if they are provoked or affronted, by their Husbands, or some other they resent the Indignity offered them in silent tears, or by refusing their Meat. Would some of our European Daughters of Thunder set these Indians for a Pattern, there might be more quiet Families found amongst them, occasioned by that unruly Member, the Tongue.

Festination proceeds from the Devil, (says a Learned Doctor,) a Passion the Indians seem wholly free from; they determining no Business of Moment without a great deal of Deliberation and Wariness. None of their Affairs appear to be attended with Impetuosity or Haste, being more content with the common Accidents incident to human Nature, (as losses, contrary Winds, bad Weather, and Poverty,) than those of more civilized Countries.

Now, to return to our State-House, whither we were invited by the Grandees. As soon as we came into it, they placed our English men near the King, it being my Fortune to sit next him, having his great General or War-Captain on my other Hand. The House is as dark as a Dungeon, and as hot as one of the Dutch-Stoves in Holland. They had made a circular Fire of split Canes in the middle of the House. It was one Man's Employment to add more split Reeds to the one end as it consumed at the other, there being a small Vacancy left to supply it with Fewel. They brought in great store of Loblolly and other Medleys, made of Indian Grain, stewed Peaches, Bear-Venison, &c., every one bringing some Offering to enlarge the Banquet, according to his Degree and Quality. When all the Viands were brought in, the first Figure began with kicking out the Dogs, which are seemingly Wolves, made tame with starving and beating, they being the worst Dog-Masters in the World; so that it is an infallible Cure for Sore-Eyes, ever to see an

Indian's Dog fat. They are of a quite contrary Disposition to Horses, some of their Kings having gotten by great chance, a Jade, stolen by some neighboring Indian, and transported farther into the Country and sold, or bought sometimes of a Christian that trades amongst them. These Creatures they continually cram and feed with Maiz, and what thè Horse will eat, till he is as fat as a Hog; never making any farther use of him than to fetch a Deer home, that is killed somewhere near the Indian's Plantation.

After the Dogs had fled the Room, the Company was summoned by Beat of Drum; the Music being made of a dressed Deer's-Skin, tied hard upon an Earthen Porridge-Pot. Presently in came fine Men dressed up with Feathers, their Faces being covered with Vizards made of Gourds; round their Ancles and Knees were hung Bells of several sorts; having Wooden Falchions in their Hands, (such as Stage-Fencers commonly use); in this Dress they danced about an Hour, showing many strange Gestures, and brandishing their Wooden Weapons as if they were going to fight each other; oftentimes walking very nimbly round the Room, without making the least Noise with their Bells, (a thing I much admired at); again turning their Bodies, Arms and Legs, into such frightful Postures, that you would have guessed they had been quite raving mad: At last, they cut two or three high Capers and left the Room. In their stead came in a parcel of Women and Girls, to the number of Thirty odd, every one taking place according to her Degree of Stature, the tallest leading the Dance, and the least of all being placed last; with these they made a circular Dance, like a Ring, representing the Shape of the Fire they danced about. Many of these had great Horse Bells about their Legs and small Hawk Bells about their Necks. They had Musicians, who were two Old Men, one of whom beat a Drum, while the other rattled with a Gourd that had Corn in it to make a Noise withal. To these Instruments they both sung a mournful Ditty; the Burthen of their Song was, in Remembrance of their former Greatness, and Numbers of their Nation, the famous Exploits of their Renowned Ancestors, and all

Actions of Moment that had, (in former Days,) been performed by their Forefathers. At these Festivals it is, that they give a Traditional Relation of what hath passed amongst them, to the younger Fry. These verbal Deliveries being always published in their most Public Assemblies, serve instead of our Traditional Notes by the use of Letters. Some Indians, that I have met withal, have given me a very curious Description of the great Deluge, the Immortality of the Soul, with a pithy Account of the Reward of good and wicked Deeds in the Life to come; having found amongst some of them, great Observers of Moral Rules, and the Law of Nature; indeed, a worthy Foundation to build Christianity upon, were a true Method found out and practiced for the Performance thereof.

Their way of Dancing is nothing but a sort of stamping Motion, much like the treading upon Founder's Bellows. This Female-Gang held their Dance for above six Hours, being all of them of a white Lather, like a Running Horse, that has just come in from his Race. My Landlady was the Ringleader of the Amazons, who, when in her own House, behaved herself very discreetly, and Warily in her Domestic Affairs; yet, Custom had so infatuated her, as to almost break her Heart with Dancing amongst such a confused Rabble. During this Dancing, the Spectators do not neglect their Business in working the Loblolly-Pots, and the other Meat that was brought thither; more or less of them being continually Eating, whilst the others were Dancing. When the Dancing was ended, every Youth that was so disposed, catched hold of the Girl he liked best, and took her that Night for his Bed-Fellow, making as short Courtship and expeditious Weddings, as the Foot-Guards used to do with the Trulls in Salisbury-Court.

Next we shall treat of the Land hereabouts, which is a Marl as red as Blood, and will lather like Soap. The Town stands on this Land, which holds considerably farther in the Country, and is, in my Opinion, so durable that no Labor of Man in one or two Ages, could make it poor. I have formerly seen the like in Leicestershire, bordering upon Rutland. Here are Corn-Stalks in their Fields as thick as the Small of a Man's Leg, and they are ordinarily to be seen.

We lay with these Indians one Night, there being by my Bedside one of the largest Iron Pots I had ever seen in America, which I much wondered at, because I thought there might be no navigable Stream near that Place. I asked them where they got that Pot. They laughed at my Demand and would give me no Answer, which makes me guess it came from some Wreck, and that we were nearer the Ocean or some great River than I thought.

The next day, about Noon, we accidentally met with a Southward-Indian amongst those that used to trade backwards and forwards, and spoke a little English, whom we hired to go with us to the Esaw Indians, a very large Nation, containing many thousand People. In the Afternoon we set forward, taking our Leaves of the Wisack Indians, and leaving them some Trifles. On our Way we met with several Towns of Indians, each Town having its Theatre, or State-House; such Houses being found all along the Road till you come to Sapona, and then no more of those Buildings, it being about one hundred and seventy Miles. We reached ten Miles this day, lying at another Town of the Wisacks. The Man of the House offered us Skins to sell, but they were two heavy Burdens for our long Voyage.

Next Morning we set out early, breaking the Ice we met withal in the stony Runs, which were many. We passed by several Cottages, and about 8 of the Clock came to a pretty big Town, where we took up our Quarters in one of their State-Houses, the Men being all out hunting in the Woods, and none but Women at home. Our Fellow Traveler, of whom I spoke before at the Congerees, having a great Mind for an Indian Lass for his Bed-Fellow that Night, spoke to our Guide, who soon got a Couple, reserving one for himself. That which fell to our Companion's Share was a pretty young Girl. Though they could not understand one Word of what each other spoke, yet the Female Indian, being no Novice at her Game, but understanding what she came thither for, acted her Part dexterously enough with her Cully, to make him sensible of what she wanted, which was to pay the Hire before he rode the Hackney. He showed her all the Treasure he was possessed of, as Beads, Red Cadis, &c., which she liked very well, and permitted him to put them into his Pocket again, endearing him with all the Charms which one of a better Education than Dame Nature had bestowed upon her, could have made use of to render her Consort a surer Captive. After they had used this Sort of Courtship a small time, the Match was confirmed by both Parties, with the Approbation of as many Indian Women as came to the House to celebrate our Winchester-Wedding. Every one of the Bride-Maids were as great Whores as Mrs. Bride, though not quite so handsome. Our happy Couple went to Bed together before us all, and with as little Blushing as if they had been Man and Wife for seven Years. The rest of the Company, being weary with traveling, had more Mind to take their Rest, than add more Weddings to that hopeful one already consummated; so that, though the other virgins offered their Service to us, we gave them their Answer and went to sleep. About an Hour before day, I awaked and saw somebody walking up and down the Room, in a seemingly deep Melancholy. I called out to know who it was, and it proved to be Mr. Bridegroom, who in less than twelve Hours, was Batchelor, Husband, and Widower, his dear Spouse having picked his Pocket of the Beads, Cadis, and what else should have gratified the Indians for the Victuals we received of them: however, that did not serve her turn, but she had also got his Shooes away, which he had made the Night before, of a dressed Buck-Skin. Thus early did our Spark already repent his new Bargain, walking barefoot in his Penitentials, like some poor Pilgrim to Loretto.

After the Indians had laughed their Sides sore at the Figure Mr. Bridegroom made, with much ado, we mustered up another Pair of Shooes or Moggisons, and set forward on our intended Voyage, the Company (all the way) lifting up their Prayers for the new married Couple, whose Wedding had made away with that which should have purchased our Food.

Relying wholly on Providence, we marched on, now and then paying our Respects to the new-married Man. The Land held rich and good; in many Places there were great Quantities of Marble. The Water was still of wheyish Color. About ten of the Clock we waded through a River about the bigness of Derwent, in Yorkshire, which I took to be one of the Branches of Winjaw River. We saw several Flocks of Pigeons, Field-Fares and Thrushes, much like those of Europe. The Indians of these Parts use Sweating very much. If any Pain seize their Limbs or Body, immediately they take Reeds or small Wands and bend them Umbrella-Fashion, covering them with Skins and Matchcoats. They have a large Fire not far off, wherein they heat Stones, or (where they are wanting), Bark; putting it into this Stove, which casts an extraordinary Heat. There is a Pot of Water in the Bagnio, in which is put a Bunch of an Herb, bearing a Silver Tassel, not much unlike the *Aurea Virga*. With this Vegetable they rub the Head, Temples and other Parts, which is reckoned a Preserver of the Sight and Strengthener of the Brain. We went this day about twelve Miles, one of our Company being lame of his Knee. We passed over an exceeding rich Tract of Land, affording Plenty of great free Stones, marble Rocks and abounding in many pleasant and delightful Rivulets. At noon we stayed and refreshed ourselves at a Cabin, where we met with one of their War-Captains, a Man of great Esteem among them. At his Departure from the Cabin, the Man of the House scratched this War-Captain on the Shoulder, which is looked upon as a very great Compliment among them. The Captain went two or three Miles on our way with us, to direct us in our Path. One of our Company gave him a Belt, which he took very kindly, bidding us call at his House, (which was in our Road,) and stay till the lame Traveler was well, and speaking to the Indian to order his Servant to make us welcome. Thus we parted, he being on his Journey to the Congerees and Savannas, a famous, warlike, friendly Nation of

Indians, living to the South-End of Ashley River. He had a Man-Slave with him who was loaded with European Goods, his Wife and Daughter being in Company. He told us, at his Departure, that James had sent Knots to all the Indians thereabouts, for every Town to send in ten Skins, meaning Captain Moor, then Governor of South Carolina. The Towns being very thick hereabouts, at Night we took up our Quarters at one of the chief Men's Houses, which was one of the Theatres I spoke of before. There ran, hard by this Town, a pleasant River, not very large, but, as the Indians told us, well stored with Fish. We being now among the powerful Nation of Esaws, our Landlord entertained us very courteously, showing us, that Night, a pair of Leather-Gloves which he had made; and comparing them with ours, they proved to be very ingeniously done, considering it was the first Tryal.

In the Morning, he desired to see the lame Man's affected Part, to the end he might do something which (he believed) would give him ease. After he had viewed it accordingly, he pulled out an Instrument, somewhat like a Comb, which was made of a split Reed, with fifteen Teeth of Rattle-Snakes, set at much the same distance as in a large Horn-Comb. With these he scratched the place where the Lameness chiefly lay till the Blood came, bathing it both before and after Incision, with warm Water, spurted out of his Mouth. This done, he ran into his Plantation and got some Sassafras Root, (which grows here in great plenty), dried it in the Embers, scraped off the outward Rind, and having beat it betwixt two Stones, applied it to the Part afflicted, binding it up well. Thus, in a day or two, the Patient became sound. This day we passed through a great many Towns and Settlements that belong to the Sugeree Indians, no barren Land being found amongst them, but great plenty of Free-Stone and good Timber. About three in the Afternoon we reached the Kadapau King's House, where we met with one John Stewart, a Scot, then an Inhabitant of James-River, in Virginia, who had traded there for many Years. Being alone, and hearing that the Sinnagers (Indians from Canada) were abroad in that Country, he durst not venture homewards till he saw us, having heard that we were coming above twenty days before. It is very odd that News should fly so swiftly among these People. Mr. Stewart had left Virginia ever since the October before, and had lost a day of the Week, of which we informed him. He had brought seven Horses along with him, loaded with English Goods for the Indians, and having sold most of his Cargo, told us if we would stay two Nights he would go along with us. Company being very acceptable, we accepted the Proposal.

The next day we were preparing for our Voyage and baked some Bread to take along with us. Our Landlord was King of the Kadapau Indians, and always kept two or three trading Girls in his Cabin. Offering one of these to some of our Company, who refused his Kindness, his Majesty flew into a violent Passion, to be thus slighted, telling the Englishmen that they were good for nothing. Our old Gamester, particularly, hung his Ears at the Proposal, having too lately been a loser by that sort of Merchandise. It was observable that we did not see one Partridge from the Waterees to this place, though my Spaniel-Bitch, which I had with me in this Voyage, had put up a great many before.

On Saturday Morning we all set out for Sapona, killing in these Creeks, several Ducks of a strange Kind, having a red Circle about their Eyes, like some Pigeons that I have seen, a Top-knot reaching from the Crown of their Heads almost to the middle of their Backs, and abundance of Feathers of pretty Shades and Colors. They proved excellent Meat. Likewise here is good store of Woodcocks, not so big as those in England, the Feathers of the Breast being of a Carnation-Colour, exceeding ours for Delicacy of Food. The Marble here is of different Colours, some or other of the Rocks representing most Mixtures, but chiefly the white having black and blue Veins in it, and some that are red. This day we met with seven heaps of Stones, being the Monuments of seven Indians that were slain in that place by the Sinnagers or Troquois. Our Indian Guide added a Stone to each heap. We took up our Lodgings near a Brook-side, where the Virginia Man's Horses got away and went back to the Kadapaus.

This day one of our Company, with a Sapona Indian, who attended Stewart, went back for the Horses. In the mean time, we went to shoot Pigeons, which were so numerous in these Parts that you might see many Millions in a Flock; they sometimes split off the Limbs of stout Oaks and other Trees upon which they roost o' Nights. You may find several Indian Towns of not above seventeen Houses, that have more than one hundred gallons of Pigeon's Oil or Fat; they using it with Pulse or Bread, as we do Butter, and making the Ground as white as a Sheet with their Dung. The Indians take a Light and go among them in the Night, and bring away some thousands, killing them with long Poles, as they roost in the Trees. At this time of the Year, the Flocks, as they pass by, in great measure, obstruct the Light of the day.

On Monday we went about twenty-five Miles, traveling through a pleasant, dry Country, and took up our Lodgings by a Hill-side that was one entire Rock, out of which gushed out pleasant Fountains of well-tasted Water.

The next day, still passing along such Land as we had done for many days before, which was Hills and Vallies, about ten a'Clock we reached the Top of one of these Mountains, which yielded us a fine Prospect of a very level Country, holding so, on all sides, farther than we could discern. When we came to travel through it, we found it very stiff and rich, being a sort of Marl. This Valley afforded as large Timber as any I ever met withal, especially of Chesnut-Oaks, which render it an excellent Country for raising great Herds of Swine. Indeed, were it cultivated, we might have good hopes of as pleasant and fertile a Valley, as any our English in America afford. At Night we lay by a swift Current, where we saw plenty of Turkies, but perched upon such lofty Oaks that our Guns would not kill them, though we shot very often, and our Guns were very good. Some of our Company shot several times at one Turkey before he would fly away, the Pieces being loaded with large Goose-shot.

Next Morning we got our Breakfast, roasted Acorns being one of the Dishes. The Indians beat them into Meal and thicken their Venison-Broth with them, and oftentimes make a palatable Soop. They are used instead of Bread, boiling them till the Oil swims on top of the Water, which they preserve for use, eating the Acorns with Flesh-meat. We traveled this day about twenty-five Miles over pleasant Savanna Ground, high and dry, having very few Trees upon it, and those standing at a great distance. The Land was very good and free from Grubs and Underwood. A man near Sapona may more easily clear ten Acres of Ground, than in some places he can one; there being much loose Stone upon the Land, lying very convenient for making of dry Walls or any other durable Fence. This Country abounds likewise with curious, bold Creeks, (navigable for small Craft,) disgorging themselves into the main Rivers, that vent themselves into the Ocean. These Creeks are well stored with sundry sorts of Fish and Fowl, and are very convenient for the Transportation of what Commodities this Place may produce. This Night we had a great deal of Rain with Thunder and Lightning.

Next Morning, it proving delicate Weather, three of us separated ourselves from the Horses, and the rest of the Company, and went directly for Sapona town. That day, we passed through a delicious Country, (none that I ever saw exceeds it.) We saw fine bladed grass six foot high, along the Banks of these pleasant Rivulets. We passed by the Sepulchres of several slain Indians. Coming that day about thirty Miles, we reached the fertile and pleasant Banks of Sapona River, whereon stands the Indian Town and Fort. Nor could all Europe afford a pleasanter Stream, were it inhabited by Christians, and cultivated by ingenious Hands. These Indians live in a clear Field about a Mile square, which they would have sold me; because I talked sometimes of coming into those Parts to live. This most pleasant River may be something broader than the Thames at Kingston, keeping a continual pleasant warbling Noise, with its reverberating on the bright Marble Rocks. It is beautified with a numerous Train of Swans, and other sorts of Water-Fowl, not common, though extraordinary pleasing to the Eye. The forward Spring welcomed us with her innumerable Train of small Choristers, which inhabit those fair Banks; the Hills redoubling and adding Sweetness to their melodious Tunes by their shrill Echoes. One side of the River is hemmed in with mountainy Ground, the other side proving as rich as Soil to the Eye of a knowing Person with us, as any this Western World can afford. We took up our Quarters at the King's Cabin, who was a good Friend to the English, and had lost one of his Eyes, in their Vindication. Being upon his march towards the Appalatche Mountains, amongst a Nation of Indians in their Way, there happened a Difference, while they were measuring of Gun-powder, and the Powder by accident taking fire, blew out one of this King's Eyes, and did a great deal more mischief upon the spot. Yet this Sapona King stood firmly to the Englishman's Interest, with whom he was in Company, still siding with him against the Indians. They were intended for the South Sea, but were too much fatigued by the vast Ridge of Mountains, though they hit the right Passage; it being no less than five day's Journey through a Ledge of Rocky Hills and sandy Desarts. And which is yet worse, there is no Water, nor scarce a Bird to be seen, during your Passage over these barren Crags and Valleys.[1] The Sapona River proves to be the West Branch of Cape-Fair, or Clarendon River, whose Inlet, with other Advantages, makes it appear as noble a River to plant a Colony in, as any I have met withal.

The Saponas had (about ten days before we came thither) taken Five Prisoners of the Sinnagers or Jennitos, a Sort of People that range several thousands of Miles, making all Prey they lay their Hands on. These are feared by all the savage Nations I ever was among, the Westward Indians dreading their Approach. They are all sorted in, and keep continual Spies and Out-Guards for their better Security. Those Captives they did intend to burn, few Prisoners of War escaping that Punishment. The Fire of Pitch-Pine being got ready, and a Feast appointed, which is solemnly kept at the time of their acting this Tragedy, the Sufferer has his Body stuck thick with Light-Wood-Splinters, which are lighted like so many Candles, the tortured Person dancing round a great Fire, till his Strength fails, and disables him from making them any farther Pastime. Most commonly, these Wretches behave themselves, (in the Midst of their Tortures) with a great deal of Bravery and Resolution, esteeming it Satisfaction enough to be assured that the same Fate will befall some of their Tormentors, whensoever they fall into the Hands of their Nation. More of this you will have in the other Sheets.

The Toteros, a neighboring Nation, came down from the Westward Mountains to the Sapona's, desiring them to give them those prisoners into their Hands, to the Intent they might send them back into their own Nation, being bound in Gratitude to be serviceable to the Sinnagers, since not long ago, those Northern Indians had taken some of the Toteros Prisoners and done them no Harm, but treated them civilly whilst among them, sending them, with Safety, back to their own People, and affirming that it would be the best Method to preserve Peace on all Sides. At that time these Toteros, Saponas, and the Keyauwees, three small Nations, were going to live together, by which they thought they should strengthen themselves and become formidable to their Enemies. The Reasons offered by the Toteros being heard, the Sapona King, with the Consent of his Counsellors, delivered the Sinnagers up to the Toteros to conduct them home.

Friday Morning the old King having showed us two of his Horses, that were as fat as if they had belonged to the Dutch Troopers, left us, and went to look after his Beaver-Traps, there being abundance of those amphibious Animals in this River, and the Creeks adjoining. Taken with the Pleasantness of the Place, we walked along the River-side, where we found a very delightful Island made by the River and a Branch; there being several such Plots of Ground environed with this Silver-Stream, which are fit

Pastures for Sheep, and free from any offensive Vermin. Nor can any thing be desired by a contented Mind, as to a pleasant Situation, but what may here be found; Every Step presenting some new Object, which still adds Invitation to the Traveler in these Parts. Our Indian King and his Wife entertained us very respectfully.

On Saturday the Indians brought in some Swans and Geese, which we had our Share of. One of their Doctors took me to his Cabin, and showed me a great Quantity of medicinal Drugs, the Produce of those Parts; Relating their Qualities as to the Emunctories they worked by, and what great Maladies he had healed by them. This Evening came to us the Horses with the Remainder of our Company, their Indian Guide (who was a Youth of this Nation) having killed, in their Way, a very fat Doe, Part of which they brought to us.   ,

This day the King sent out all his able Hunters, to kill Game for a great Feast, that was to be kept at their Departure from the Town, which they offered to sell me for a small matter. That Piece of Ground, with a little Trouble, would make an Englishman a most curious Settlement, containing above a Mile square of rich Land. This Evening came down some Toteros, tall, likely Men, having great Plenty of Buffaloes, Elks, and Bears, with other sort of Deer amongst them, which strong Food makes large, robust Bodies. Enquiring of them if they never got any of the Bezoar Stone, and giving them a Description how it was found, the Indians told me, they had great plenty of it, and asked me, What use I could make of it? I answered them, That the white Men used it in Physic, and that I would buy some of them, if they would get it against I came that way again. Thereupon, one of them pulled out a Leather-Pouch, wherein was some of it in Powder; he was a notable Hunter, and affirmed to me, That that Powder blown into the Eyes, strengthened the Sight and Brain exceedingly, that being the most common Use they made of it. I bought, for two or three Flints, a large Peach-Loaf, made up with a pleasant sort of Seed; and this did us a singular Kindness in our Journey. Near the Town, within their cleared Land, are several Bagnios, or Sweating-Houses, made of Stone, in Shape like a large Oven. These they make much Use of; especially for any Pains in the Joints, got by Cold or Traveling. At Night, as we lay in our Beds, there arose the most violent N. W. Wind I ever knew. The first Puff blew down all the Palisadoes that fortified the Town; and I thought it would have blown us all into the River, together with the Houses. Our one-eyed King, who pretends much to the Art of Conjuration, ran out in the most violent Hurry, and in the Middle of the Town, fell to his Necromantik Practice; though I thought he would have been blown away or killed, before the Devil and he could have exchanged half a dozen Words: but in two Minutes, the Wind was ceased, and it became as great a Calm as ever I knew in my Life. As I much admired at that sudden Alteration, the old Man told me the Devil was very angry, and had done thus because they had not put the Sinnagers to Death.

On Monday Morning our whole Company, with the Horses, set out from the Sapona-Indian Town, after having seen some of the Locust, which is gotten thereabouts, the same Sort that bears Honey. Going over several Creeks, very convenient for Water-Mills, about eight Miles from the Town we passed over a very pretty River, called Rocky River, a fit Name, having a Ridge of high Mountains running from its Banks to the Eastward, and disgorging itself into Sapona-River, so that there is a most pleasant and convenient Neck of Land betwixt both Rivers, lying upon a Point where many thousand Acres may be fenced in, without much Cost or Labor. You can scarce go a Mile without meeting with one of these small, swift Currents, here being no Swamps to be found, but pleasant, dry Roads all over the Country. The Way that we went this day was as full of Stones as any which Craven, in the West of Yorkshire, could afford; and having nothing but Moggisons on my Feet, I was so lamed by this stony Way that I thought I must have taken up some Stay in these Parts. We went this day not above fifteen or twenty Miles. After we had supped, and all lay down to sleep, there came a Wolf close to the Fire-side where we lay. My Spaniel soon discovered him, at which, one of our Company fired a Gun at the Beast; but, I believe, there was a Mistake in the loading of it, for it did him no Harm. The Wolf stayed till he had almost loaded again, but the Bitch making a great Noise, at last left us and went aside. We had no sooner laid down, but he approached us again, yet was more shy, so that we could not get a Shot at him.

Next day we had fifteen Miles farther to the Keyauwees. The Land is more mountainous, but extremely pleasant, and an excellent Place for the breeding Sheep, Goats, and Horses, or Mules, if the English were once brought to the Experience of the Usefulness of those Creatures. The Valleys are here very rich. At Noon we passed over such another stony River, as that eight Miles from Sapona. This is called Heighwaree, and affords as good blue Stone for Mill-Stones as that from Cologn, good Rags, some Hones and large Pebbles in great abundance, besides Free-Stone of several Sorts; all very useful. I knew one of these Hones made use of by an acquaintance of mine, and it proved rather better than any from Old Spain or elsewhere. The Veins of Marble are very large and curious on this River and the Banks thereof.

Five Miles from this River, to the N. W., stands the Keyauwees town. They are fortified in with wooden Puncheons, like Sapona, being a People much of the same Number. Nature has so fortified this Town with Mountains, that were it a Seat of War, it might easily be made impregnable; having large Corn-Fields joining to their Cabins, and a Savanna near the Town at the Foot of these Mountains, that is capable of keeping some hundred Heads of Cattle. And all this environed round with very high Mountains, so that no hard Wind ever troubles these Inhabitants. Those high Clifts have no Grass growing on them, and very few Trees, which are very short, and stand at a great Distance one from another. The Earth is of a Red Colour and seems to me to be wholly designed by

Nature for the Production of Minerals, being of too hot a Quality to suffer any Verdure upon its Surface. These Indians make use of Lead-Ore, to paint their Faces withal, which they get in the neighboring Mountains. As for the refining of Metals, the Indians are wholly ignorant of it, being content with the Realgar. But if it be my Chance once more to visit these Hilly Parts, I shall make a longer Stay amongst them: For were a good Vein of Lead found out, and worked by an ingenious Hand, it might be of no small Advantage to the Undertaker, there being great Convenience for smelting, either by Bellows or Reverberation, and the Working of these Mines might discover some that are much richer.

At the Top of one of these Mountains is a Cave that one hundred Men may sit very conveniently to dine in, whether natural or artificial I could not learn. There is a fine Bole between this Place and the Saps. These Valleys, thus hemmed in with Mountains, would, doubtless, prove a good place for propagating some sort of Fruits, that our Easterly Winds commonly blast. The Vine could not miss of thriving well here; but we of the Northern Climate are neither Artists, nor curious in propagating that pleasant and profitable Vegetable. Near the Town is such another Current as Heighwaree.

We being six in Company, divided ourselves into Two Parties; and it was my Lot to be at the House of Keyauwees Jack, who is King of that People. He is a Congeree-Indian, and ran away when he was a Boy. He got this Government by Marriage with the Queen; the Female Issue carrying the Heritage, for fear of Imposters; the Savages well knowing how much Frailty possesses the Indian Women, betwixt the Garters and the Girdle.

The next day, having some occasion to write, the Indian King who saw me, believed that he could write as well as I. Whereupon I wrote a Word, and gave it to him to copy, which he did with more Exactness than any European could have done that was illiterate. It was so well that he who could read mine, might have done the same by his. Afterwards he took great Delight in making Fish-hooks of his own Invention, which would have been a good Piece for an Antiquary to have puzzled his Brains withal, in tracing out the Characters of all the Oriental Tongues. He sent for several Indians to his Cabin to look at his Handy-work, and both he and they thought I could read his Writing as well as I could my own. I had a Manual in my Pocket that had King David's Picture in it, in one of his private Retirements. The Indian asked me, Who that Figure represented. I told him, It was the Picture of a good King, that lived, according to the Rules of Morality, doing to all as he would be done by, ordering all his Life to the Service of the Creator of all things; and being now above us all in Heaven, with God Almighty, who had rewarded him with all the delightful Pleasures imaginable in the other World, for his Obedience to him in this. I concluded with telling them, that we received nothing here below, as Food, Raiment, &c., but what came from that Omnipotent Being. They listened to my Discourse with a profound Silence, assuring me that they believed what I said to be true. No Man living will ever be able to make these heathens sensible of the Happiness of a future State, except he now and then mentions some lively carnal Representation, which may quicken their Apprehensions and make them thirst after such a gainful Exchange; for, were the best Lecture that ever was preached by Man, given to an ignorant sort of People in a more learned Style than their mean Capacities are able to understand, the Intent would prove ineffectual, and the Hearers would be left in a greater Labyrinth than their Teacher found them in. But dispense the Precepts of our Faith according to the Pupil's Capacity, and there is nothing in our Religion but what an indifferent Reason is, in some measure, able to comprehend; though a New-England Minister blames the French Jesuits for this way of Proceeding, as being quite contrary to a true Christian Practice, and affirms it to be no ready or true Method to establish a lively Representation of our Christian Belief amongst these Infidels.

All the Indians hereabouts carefully preserve the Bones of the Flesh they eat and burn them, as being of Opinion that if they omitted that Custom the Game would leave their Country, and they should not be able to maintain themselves by their Hunting. Most of these Indians Wear Mustachoes or Whiskers, which is rare; by reason the Indians are a People that commonly pull the Hair of their Faces and other Parts, up by the Roots and suffer none to grow. Here is plenty of Chesnuts which are rarely found in Carolina, and never near the Sea or Salt-Water, though they are frequently in such Places in Virginia.

As the other House where our Fellow Travelers lay, they had provided a Dish in great Fashion amongst the Indians, which was Two young Fawns taken out of the Does' Bellies, and boiled in the same slimy Bags Nature had placed them in, and one of the Country-Hares, stewed with the Guts in her Belly, and her Skin with the Hair on. This new fashioned Cookery wrought Abstinence in our Fellow-Travelers, which I somewhat wondered at, because one of them made nothing of eating Allegators as heartily as if it had been Pork and Turneps. The Indians dress most things after the Woodcock Fashion, never taking the Guts out. At the House we lay at, there was very good Entertainment of Venison, Turkies and Bears; and which is customary amongst the Indians, the Queen had a Daughter by a former Husband, who was the beautifulest Indian I ever saw, and had an Air of Majesty with her quite contrary to the general Carriage of the Indians. She was very kind to the English during our Abode, as well as her Father and Mother.

This Morning most of our Company having some Inclination to go straight away for Virginia, when they left this Place, I and one more took our leaves of them, resolving (with God's Leave) to see North-Carolina, one of the Indians setting us in our way. The rest being indifferent which way they went, desired us, by all means, to leave a Letter for them at the Achonechy Town. The Indian that put us in our Path, had been a Prisoner amongst the Sinnagers, but had outrun them, although they had cut his Toes and half his Feet away, which is a Practice common amongst them. They first raise the Skin, then cut away half the Feet, and so wrap the Skin over the Stumps and make a present Cure of the Wounds. This commonly disables them from making their Escape, they being not so good Travelers as before, and the Impression of their Half-Feet making it easy to trace them. However, this fellow was got clear of them, but had little Heart to go far from home, and carried always a Case of Pistols in his Girdle, besides a Cutlass and a Fuzee. Leaving the rest of our Company at the Indian-Town, we traveled that day about twenty Miles, in very cold, frosty Weather; and passed over two pretty Rivers, something bigger than Heighwaree, but not quite so stony. We took these two Rivers to make one of the Northward Branches of Cape-Fair River, but afterwards found our Mistake.

The next day we traveled over very good Land, but full of Free-Stone and Marble, which pinched our Feet severely. We took up our Quarters in a sort of Savanna-Ground that had very few Trees in it. The Land was good and had several Quarries of Stone, but not loose as the others used to be.

Next Morning we got our Breakfast of Parched Corn, having nothing but that to subsist on for above one hundred Miles. All the Pine-Trees were vanished, for we had seen none for two days. We passed through a delicate rich Soil this day; no great Hills, but pretty Risings and Levels, which made a beautiful Country. We likewise passed over three Rivers this day, the first about the bigness of Rocky River, the other not much differing in Size. Then we made not the least Question, but we had passed over the North West Branch of Cape Fair, traveling that day above thirty Miles. We were much taken with the Fertility and Pleasantness of the Neck of Land between these two Branches, and no less pleased that we had passed the River which used to frighten Passengers from fording it. At last determining to rest on the other side of a Hill which we saw before us; when we were on the Top thereof, there appeared to us such another delicious, rapid Stream as that of Sapona, having large Stones, about the bigness of an ordinary House, lying up and down the River. As the Wind blew very cold at N. W.

and we were very weary and hungry, the Swiftness of the Current gave us some cause to fear; but, at Last, we concluded to venture over that Night. Accordingly we stripped, and with great Difficulty, (by God's Assistance) got safe to the North-side of the famous Hau-River, by some called Reatkin; the Indians differing in the Names of Places according to their several Nations. It is called Hau-River from the Sissipahau Indians, who dwell upon this Stream, which is one of the main Branches of Cape Fair, there being rich Land enough to contain some Thousands of Families; for which Reason I hope, in a short time, it will be planted. This River is much such another as Sapona, both seeming to run a vast way up the Country. Here is plenty of good Timber, and especially of a Scaly-barked-Oak. And as there is Stone enough in both Rivers, and the Land is extraordinary Rich, no Man that will be content within the Bounds of Reason, can have any grounds to dislike it. And they that are otherwise are the best Neighbors when farthest off.

As soon as it was day we set out for the Achonechy-Town, it being, by Estimation, twenty Miles off, which I believe is pretty exact. We were got about half way, (meeting great Gangs of Turkies), when we saw at a Distance, thirty loaded Horses, coming on the Road, with four or five Men on other Jades driving them. We charged our Pieces and went up to them Enquiring whence they came from? They told us from Virginia. The leading Man's Name was Massey, who was born about Leeds in Yorkshire. He asked from whence we came? We told him. Then he asked again, Whether we wanted anything that he had? telling us we should be welcome to it. We accepted of Two Wheaten Biskets, and a little Ammunition. He advised us by all means, to strike down the Country for Ronoack, and not think of Virginia, because of the Sinnagers, of whom they were afraid, though so well armed and numerous. They persuaded us also to call upon one Enoe Will, as we went to Adshusheer, for that he would conduct us safe among the English, giving him the Character of a very faithful Indian, which we afterwards found true by Experience. The Virginia-Men asking our opinion of the Country we were then in. We told them it was a very pleasant one. They were all of the same Opinion, and affirmed, That they had never seen twenty Miles of such extraordinary rich Land lying all together like that betwixt Hau-River and the Achonechy Town. Having taken our Leaves of each other, we set forward; and the Country through which we passed, was so delightful that it gave us a great deal of Satisfaction. About Three a Clock we reached the Town, and the Indians presently brought us good fat Bear, and Venison, which was very acceptable at that time. Their Cabins were hung with a good sort of Tapestry, as fat Bear, and barbacued or dried Venison; no Indians having greater Plenty of Provisions than these. The Savages do indeed, still possess the Flower of Carolina, the English enjoying only the Fag-end of that fine Country. We had not been in the Town two Hours when Enoe Will came into the King's Cabin, which was our Quarters. We asked him if he would conduct us to the English, and what he would have for his Pains; he answered he would go along with us, and for what he was to have he left that to our Discretion.

The next Morning we set out with Enoe Will towards Adshusheer, leaving the Virginia Path, and striking more to the Eastward for Ronoak. Several Indians were in our Company belonging to Will's Nation, who are the Shoccories, mixed with the Eno-Indians, and those of the Nation of Adshusheer. Enoe Will is their chief Man, and rules as far as the Banks of Reatkin. It was a sad, stony Way to Adshusheer. We went over a small River by Achonechy, and in this fourteen Miles, through several other Streams which empty themselves into the Branches of Cape Fair. The stony Way made me quite lame, so that I was an Hour or two behind the rest; but honest Will would not leave me, but bid me welcome when we came to his House, feasting us with hot Bread and Bear's-Oil, which is wholesome Food for Travelers. There runs a pretty Rivulet by this Town. Near the Plantation, I saw a prodigious overgrown Pine-Tree, having not seen any of that Sort of Timber for above one hundred and twenty-five Miles. They brought us two Cocks and pulled their larger Feathers off, never plucking the lesser, but singeing them off. I took one of these Fowls in my Hand to make it cleaner than the Indian had, pulling out his Guts and Liver, which I laid in a Bason; notwithstanding which he kept such a Struggling for a considerable time that I had much a do to hold him in my Hands. The Indians laughed at me, and told me that Enoe Will had taken a Cock of an Indian that was not at home, and the Fowl was designed for another Use. I conjectured that he was designed for an Offering to their God, who, they say, hurts them, (which is the Devil.) In this Struggling he bled afresh, and there issued out of his Body more Blood than commonly such Creatures afford. Notwithstanding all this, we cooked him and eat him; and if he was designed for him, cheated the Devil. The Indians keep many Cocks, but seldom above one Hen, using, very often, such wicked Sacrifices, as I mistrusted this Fowl was designed for. Our Guide and Landlord, Enoe Will, was one of the best and most agreeable Temper that ever I met with in an Indian, being always ready to serve the English, not out of Gain, but real Affection; which makes him apprehensive of being poisoned by some wicked Indians, and was therefore very earnest with me, to promise him to avenge his Death, if it should so happen. He brought some of his chief Men into his Cabin, and two of them having a Drum, and a Rattle, sung by us as we lay in Bed, and struck up their Music to serenade and welcome us to their Town. And though at last, we fell asleep, yet they continued their Concert till Morning. These Indians are fortified in as the former, and are much addicted to a Sport they call Chenco, which is carried on with a Staff and a Bowl made of Stone, which they trundle upon a smooth Place like a Bowling-Green, made for that Purpose, as I have mentioned before.

Next Morning we set out with our Guide and several other Indians who intended to go to the English and buy Rum. We designed for a Nation about forty Miles from Adshusheer, called the Lower-Quarter: The first Night we lay in a rich Pocoson, or low ground, that was hard by a Creek, and good dry Land.

The next day we went over several Tracts of rich Land, but mixed with Pines and other indifferent Soil. In our way there stood a great Stone about the Size of a large Oven, and hollow; this the Indians took great Notice of, putting some Tobacco into the Concavity, and spitting after it. I asked them the Reason of their so doing, but they made me no Answer. In the Evening we passed over a pleasant Rivulet, with a fine gravelly Bottom, having come over such another that Morning. On the other side of this River we found the Indian Town, which was a Parcel of nasty, smoky Holes, much like the Waterrees; their Town having a great Swamp running directly through the Middle thereof. The Land here begins to abate of its Height, and has some few Swamps. Most of these Indians have but one Eye; but what Mischance or Quarrel has bereaved them of the other I could not learn. They were not so free to us as most of the other Indians had been; Victuals being somewhat scarce among them. However, we got enough to satisfy our Appetites. I saw, among these Men, very long Arrows, headed with Pieces of Glass, which they had broken from Bottles. They had shaped them neatly, like the Head of a Dart, but which way they did it I can't tell. We had not been at this Town above an Hour when two of our Company, that had bought a Mare of John Stewart, came up to us, having received a Letter by one of Will's Indians, who was very cautious, and asked a great many Questions to certify him of the Person ere he would deliver the Letter. They had left the Trader and one that came from South-Carolina with us, to go to Virginia, these Two being resolved to go to Carolina with us.

This Day fell much Rain, so we staid at the Indian Town.

This Morning we set out early, being four Englishmen, besides several Indians. We went ten Miles, and then stopped by the Freshes of Enoe-River, which had raised it so high that we could not pass over till it was fallen. I enquired of my Guide, Where this River disgorged itself? He said, It was Enoe-River, and run into a Place called Enoe-Bay, near his Country, which he left when he was a Boy; by which I perceived he was one of the Cores by Birth, this being a Branch of Neus-River.

This Day our Fellow-Traveler's Mare ran away from him, wherefore, Will went back as far as the lower Quarter, and brought her back.

The next Day, early, came two Tuskeruro Indians to the other side of the River, but could not get over. They talked much to us, but we understood them not. In the Afternoon Will came with the Mare, and had some Discourse with them; they told him The English to whom he was going were very wicked People; and, That they threatened the Indians for Hunting near their Plantations. These Two Fellows were going among the Shoccores and Achonechy Indians to sell their Wooden Bowls and Ladles for Raw Skins, which they make great Advantage of, hating that any of these Westward Indians should have any Commerce with the English which would prove a Hinderance to their Gains. Their Stories deterred an Old Indian and his Son from going any farther; but Will told us Nothing they had said should frighten him, he believing them to be a couple of Hog-stealers; and that the English only sought Restitution of their Losses by them, and that this was the only ground for their Report. Will had a Slave, a Sissipahau Indian by Nation, who killed us several Turkies and other game, on which we feasted.

This River is near as large as Reatkin; the South-side having curious Tracts of good Land, the Banks high, and Stone-Quarries. The Tuskeruros being come to us, we ventured over the River, which we found to be a strong Current, and the Water about Breast-high. However, we all got safe to the North-Shore, which is but poor, white, sandy Land, and bears no Timber but small, shrubby Oaks. We went about ten Miles and sat down at the Falls of a large Creek, where lay mighty Rocks, the Water making a strange Noise, as if a great many Water-Mills were going at once. I take this to be the Falls of Neus-Creek, called by the Indians, Wee quo Whom. We lay here all Night. My Guide, Will, desiring to see the Book that I had about me, I lent it him; and as he soon found the Picture of King David, he asked me several Questions concerning the Book and Picture, which I resolved him and invited him to became a Christian. He made me a very sharp Reply, assuring me, That he loved the English extraordinary well, and did believe their Ways to be very good for those that had already practiced them, and had been brought up therein; But as for himself, he was too much in Years to think of a Change, esteeming it not proper for Old People to admit of such an Alteration. However, he told me, If I would take his Son, Jack, who was then about fourteen Years of Age, and teach him to talk in that Book, and make Paper speak, which they call our Way of Writing, he would wholly resign him to my Tuition; telling me he was of Opinion I was very well affected to the Indians.

The next Morning we set out early, and I perceived that these Indians were in some fear of Enemies; for they had an Old Man with them who was very cunning and circumspect, wheresoever he saw any Marks of Footing, or of any Fire that had been made; going out of his Way very often to look for these Marks. We went, this day, above thirty Miles, over a very level Country, and most Pine Land, yet intermixed with some Quantities of Marble; a good Range for Cattle, though very indifferent for Swine. We had now lost our rapid Streams, and were come to slow, dead Waters, of a brown Colour, proceeding from the Swamps, much like the Sluices in Holland, where the Track-Scoots go along. In the Afternoon, we met two Tuskeruros, who told us, That there was a Company of Hunters not far off, and if we walked stoutly we might reach them that Night. But Will, and He that owned the Mare, being gone before, and the Old Indian tired, we rested that Night in the Woods, making a good, light Fire, wood being very plentiful in these Parts.

Next Day about 10 a Clock, we struck out of the Way by the Advice of our Old Indian. We had not gone past two Miles ere we met with about five hundred Tuskeruros in one Hunting-Quarter. They had made themselves Streets of Houses built with Pine-Bark, not with round Tops, as they commonly use, but Ridge-Fashion, after the manner of most other Indians. We got nothing amongst them but Corn, Flesh being not plentiful, by reason of the great Number of their People. For though they are expert Hunters, yet they are too populous for one Range, which makes Venison very scarce to what it is amongst other Indians, that are fewer; no Savages living so well for Plenty as those near the Sea. I saw amongst these a Hump-backed Indian, which was the only crooked one I ever met withal. About two a Clock we reached one of their Towns, in which there was no body left but an Old Woman or two, the rest being gone to their Hunting-Quarters. We could find no Provision at that Place. We had a Tuskeruro that came in company with us from the lower Quarter, who took us to his Cabin and gave us what it afforded, which was Corn-meat.

This Day we passed through several Swamps, and going not above a dozen Miles came to a Cabin, the Master whereof used to trade amongst the English. He told us, If we would stay Two Nights, he would conduct us safe to them, himself designing, at that time, to go and fetch some Rum; so we resolved to tarry for his Company. During our Stay, there happened to be a Young Woman troubled with Fits. The Doctor who was sent for to assist her, laid her on her Belly and made a small Incision with Rattle-Snake-Teeth; then laying his Mouth to the Place, he sucked out near a Quart of black conglutinated Blood, and Serum. Our Land-lord gave us the Tail of a Bever, which was a choice Food. There happened also to be a Burial of one of their Dead, which Ceremony is much the same with that of the Santees, who make a great Feast at the Interment of their Corpse. The small Runs of Water here-about afford great Plenty of Craw-Fish, full as large as those in England, and nothing inferior in Goodness.

Saturday Morning, our Patron, with Enoe Will and his Servant, set out with us for the English. In the Afternoon we ferried over a River, (in a Canoe), called by the Indians Chattookau, which is the N. W. Branch of Neus River. We lay in the Swamp, where some Indians invited us to go to their Quarters, which some of our Company accepted, but got nothing extraordinary, except a dozen Miles' March out of their Way. The Country here is very thick of Indian Towns and Plantations.

We were forced to march this day for Want of Provisions. About ten a Clock we met an Indian that had got a parcel of Shad-Fish ready barbakued. We bought twenty-four of them for a dressed Doe-Skin, and so went on through many Swamps, finding this day the long ragged Moss on the Trees, which we had not seen for above six hundred Miles. In the Afternoon we came upon the Banks of Pampticough, about twenty Miles above the English Plantations by Water, though not so far by Land. The Indian found a Canoe which he had hidden, in which we all got over, and went about six Miles farther. We lay that Night under two or three Pieces of Bark, at the Foot of a large Oak. There fell abundance of Snow and Rain in the Night, with much Thunder and Lightning.

Next Day it cleared up, and it being about twelve Miles to the English, about half way we passed over a deep Creek, and came safe to Mr. Richard Smith's of Pampticough River, in North Carolina; where, being well received by the Inhabitants and pleased with the Goodness of the Country, we all resolved to continue.

FINIS

A Description of North Carolina

THE Province of Carolina is separated from Virginia by a due West-Line, which begins at Currituck Inlet, in 36 Degrees 30 Minutes of Northern-Latitude, and extends indefinitely to the Westward, and thence to the Southward, as far as 29 Degrees; which is a vast Tract of Sea-Coast. But having already treated, as far as is necessary, concerning South Carolina, I shall confine myself in the ensuing Sheets, to give my Reader a description of that Part of the Country only, which lies betwixt Currituck and Cape Fair, and is almost 34 Degrees North, And this is commonly called North Carolina.

This Part of Carolina is faced with a Chain of Sand-Banks, which defends it from the Violence and Insults of the Atlantic Ocean; by which Barrier a vast Sound is hemmed in, which fronts the Mouths of the Navigable and Pleasant Rivers of this Fertile Country, and into which they disgorge themselves. Through the same are Inlets of several Depths of Water. Some of their Channels admit only of Sloops, Brigantines, and small Barks and Ketches; and such are Currituck, Ronoak, and up the Sound above Hatteras; Whilst others can receive Ships of Burden, as Ocacock, Topsail-Inlet, and Cape-Fair, as appears by my Chart.

The first Discovery and Settlement of this Country was by the Procurement of Sir Walter Raleigh, in Conjunction with some public spirited Gentlemen of that Age, under the Protection of Queen Elizabeth; for which Reason it was then named Virginia, being begun on that Part called Ronoak-Island, where the Ruins of a Fort are to be seen at this day, as well as some old English Coins which have been lately found; and a Brass-Gun, a Powder-Horn, and one small Quarter-deck-Gun, made of Iron Staves, and hooped with the same Metal; which Method of making Guns might very probably be made use of in those Days for the Convenience of Infant-Colonies.

A farther Confirmation of this we have from the Hatteras Indians, who either then lived on Ronoack-Island or much frequented it. These tell us that several of their Ancestors were white People and could talk in a Book as we do; the Truth of which is confirmed by gray Eyes being found frequently amongst these Indians and no others. They value themselves extremely for their Affinity to the English, and are ready to do them all friendly Offices. It is probable that this Settlement miscarried for want of timely Supplies from England; or through the Treachery of the Natives, for we may reasonably suppose that the English were forced to cohabit with them for Relief and Conversation; and that in process of Time, they conformed themselves to the Manners of their Indian Relations; And thus we see how apt Human Nature is to degenerate.

I cannot forbear inserting here a pleasant Story that passes for an uncontested Truth amongst the Inhabitants of this Place; which is, that the Ship which brought the first Colonies does often appear amongst them, under Sail, in a gallant Posture, which they call Sir Walter Raleigh's Ship. And the truth of this has been affirmed to me by Men of the Best Credit in the Country.

A second Settlement of this Country was made about fifty Years ago, in that part we now call Albemarl-County, and chiefly in Chuwon Precinct, by several substantial Planters from Virginia, and other Plantations; Who finding mild Winters and a fertile Soil beyond Expectation, producing everything that was planted to a prodigious Increase; their Cattle, Horses, Sheep, and Swine, breeding very fast, and passing the Winter without any assistance from the Planter; so that everything seemed to come by Nature, the Husbandman living almost void of Care, and free from those Fatigues which are absolutely requisite in Winter Countries, for providing Fodder and other Necessaries; these Encouragements induced them to stand their Ground, although but a handful of People, seated at great Distances one from another, and amidst a vast number of Indians of different Nations, who were then in Carolina. Nevertheless, I say, the Fame of this new discovered

Summer-Country spread through the neighboring Colonies, and in a few Years drew a considerable Number of Families thereto, who all found Land enough to settle themselves in, (had they been many Thousands more) and that which was very good and commodiously seated both for Profit and Pleasure. And, indeed, most of the Plantations in Carolina naturally enjoy a noble Prospect of large and spacious Rivers, pleasant Savannas and fine Meadows, with their green Liveries interwoven with beautiful Flowers of most glorious Colours, which the several Seasons afford; hedged in with pleasant Groves of the ever famous Tulip-tree, the stately Laurels and Bays, equalizing the Oak in Bigness and Growth, Myrtles, Jessamines, Woodbines, Honeysuckles, and several other fragrant Vines and Evergreens, whose aspiring Branches shadow and interweave themselves with the loftiest Timbers, yielding a pleasant Prospect, Shade and Smell, proper Habitations for the Sweet-singing Birds, that melodiously entertain such as travel through the Woods of Carolina.

The Planters possessing all these Blessings, and the Produce of great Quantities of Wheat and Indian-Corn, in which this Country is very fruitful, as likewise in Beef, Pork, Tallow, Hides, Deer-Skins, and Furs; for these Commodities the New-England-Men and Bermudians visited Carolina in their Barks and Sloops, and carried out what they made, bringing them in Exchange, Rum, Sugar, Salt, Molasses, and some wearing Apparel, though the last at very extravagant Prices.

As the Land is very fruitful, so are the Planters kind and hospitable to all that come to visit them; there being very few House-keepers but what live very nobly, and give away more Provisions to Coasters and Guests who come to see them than they expend amongst their own Families.

OF THE INLETS AND HAVENS OF THIS COUNTRY.

The Bar of Currituck being the Northernmost of this Country, presents itself first to be treated of. It lies in 36 Deg. 30 Min.

and the Course over is S. W. by W., having not above seven or eight Foot on the Bar, though a good Harbour when you are over where you may ride safe, and deep enough; but this Part of the Sound is so full of Shoals as not to suffer any thing to trade through it that draws above three Foot Water, which renders it very incommodious. However, this affects but some part of the Country, and may be easily remedied by carrying their Produce, in small Craft down to the Vessels which ride near the Inlet.

Ronoak Inlet has Ten Foot Water, the Course over the Bar is almost W., which leads on through the best of the Channel. This Bar, as well as Currituck, often shifts by the Violence of the N.E. Storms, both lying exposed to those Winds. Notwithstanding which, a considerable Trade might be carried on, provided there was a Pilot to bring them in; for it lies convenient for a large Part of this Colony whose Product would very easily allow of that Charge, Lat. 35 deg. 50 min.

The Inlet of Hatteras lies to the Westward of the Cape, round which is an excellent Harbour. When the Wind blows hard at N. or N.E., if you keep a small League from the Cape-Point, you will have three, four and five Fathom, the outermost Shoals lying about seven or eight Leagues from Shoar. As you come into the Inlet keep close to the South Breakers, till you are over the Bar, where you will have two Fathom at Low-Water. You may come to an Anchor in two Fathom and a Half when you are over, then steer over close aboard the North-Shoar, where is four Fathom close to a Point of Marsh; then stir up the Sound a long League, till you bring the North-Cape of the Inlet to bear S. S. E. half E. then steer W. N. W., the East-point of Bluff-Land at Hatteras bearing E. N. E. the Southernmost large Hammock towards Ocacock, bearing S. S. W. half S. then you are in the Sound, over the Bar of Sand, whereon is but six Foot Water; then your Course to Pampticough is almost West. It flows on these three bars S. E. by E. one-fourth E. about Eight of the Clock, unless there is a hard Gale of Wind at N. E. which will make it flow two hours longer; but as soon as the

Wind is down, the Tides will have their natural Course. A hard Gale at N. or N. W. will make the Water ebb, sometimes twenty-four hours, but still the Tide will ebb and flow though not seen by the turning thereof, but may be seen by the Rising of the Water, and Falling of the same, Lat. 35° 20'.

Ocacock is the best Inlet and Harbour yet in this Country; and has thirteen Foot at Low-water upon the Bar. There are two Channels, one is but narrow and lies close aboard the South-Cape; the other in the Middle, viz: between the Middle Ground and the South Shoar, and is above half a Mile wide. The Bar itself is but half a Cable's Length over, and then you are in seven or eight Fathom Water; a good Harbour. The Course into the Sound is N. N. W. At High-water, and Neap-tides here is eighteen Foot Water; it lies S. W. from Hatteras Inlet, Lat. 35° 8'.

Topsaid Inlet is above two Leagues to the Westward of Cape Look-out. You have a fair Channel over the Bar, and two Fathom thereon, and a good Harbour in five or six Fathom to come to an Anchor. Your Course over this Bar is almost N. W., Lat. 34° 44'.

As for the Inlet and River of Cape Fair, I cannot give you a better Information thereof, than has been already delivered by the Gentlemen who were sent on purpose from Barbados, to make a Discovery of that River, in the Year 1663, which is thus:

From Tuesday, the 29th of September, to Friday the 2nd of October, we ranged along the Shoar from Lat. 32 deg. 20 min. to lat. 33 deg. 11 min., but could discern no Entrance for our Ship, after we had passed to the Northward of 32 deg. 40 min. On Saturday, October 3, a violent Storm overtook us, the Wind between North and East; which Easterly Winds and Foul Weather continued till Mondy the 12th, by reason of which Storms and Foul Weather, we were forced to get off to Sea, to secure Ourselves and Ship, and were driven by the Rapidity of a strong Current to Cape Hatteras, in Lat. 35° 30'. On Monday, the 12th aforesaid, we came to an Anchor in seven Fathom at Cape Fair Road, and took the Meridian Altitude of the Sun, and were in Latitude 33 deg.

43 Min., the Wind continuing still easterly, and Foul Weather, till Thursday, the 15th; and on Friday the 16th, the Wind being at N. W., we weighed and sailed up Cape-Fair-River, some four or five Leagues, and came to an Anchor in six or seven Fathom, at which Time several Indians came on board, and brought us great Store of fresh Fish, large Mullets, young Bass, Shads, and several other sorts of very good, well tasted Fish. On Saturday, the 17th, we went down to the Cape, to see the English Cattle, but could not find them, though we rounded the Cape. And having an Indian Guide with us, here we rode till Oct. 24. The Wind being against us, we could not go up the River with our Ship; but went on Shoar and viewed the Land of those Quarters. On Saturday we weighed and sailed up the River, some four Leagues, or thereabouts. Sunday the 25th, we weighed again and rode up the River, it being calm, and got up some fourteen Leagues from the harbour's Mouth, where we mored our Ship. On Monday, Oct. the 26th, we went down with the Yawl to Necoes, an Indian Plantation, and viewed the Land there. On Tuesday, the 27th, we rowed up the main River with our Long-Boat and twelve Men, some ten Leagues, or thereabouts. On Wednesday, the 28th, we rowed up about eight or ten Leagues more; Thursday the 29th, was Foul Weather, with much Rain and Wind, which forced us to make Huts and lie still. Friday the 30th, we proceeded up the main River, seven or eight Leagues. Saturday the 31st, we got up three of four Leagues more, and came to a Tree that lay cross the River; but because our Provisions were almost spent, we proceeded no farther, but returned downward before Night, and on Monday the 2nd of November, we came aboard our Ship. Tuesday, the 3rd, we lay still to refresh ourselves. On Wednesday, the 4th, we went five or six leagues up the River, to search a Branch that run out of the main River towards the N. W., in which Branch we went up five or six Leagues; but not liking the Land, returned on board that Night about Midnight and called that Place Swampy-Branch. Thursday, November the 5th, we stayed aboard. On Friday, the

6th, we went up Green's River, the Mouth of it being against the Place at which rode our Ship. On Saturday the 7th, we proceeded up the said River, some fourteen or fifteen Leagues in all, and found it ended in several small Branches; The Land, for the most part, being marshy and Swamps, we returned towards our Ship and got aboard it in the Night. Sunday November the 8th, we lay still, and on Monday the 9th, we went again up the main River, being well stocked with Provisions, and all things necessary, and proceeded upwards till Thursday noon, the 12th, at which time we came to a Place, where were two Islands in the Middle of the River; and by reason of the Crookedness of the River at that Place, several Trees lay cross both Branches, which stopped the Passage of each Branch, so that we Could proceed no farther with our Boat; but went up the River side by Land, some three or four Miles, and found the River wider and wider. So we returned, leaving it as far as we could see, up a long Reach, running N. E. we judging ourselves near Fifty Leagues North from the River's Mouth. In our Return, we viewed the Land on both Sides the River, and found as good Tracts of dry, well wooded, pleasant and delightful Ground as we have seen any where in the World, with abundance of long thick Grass on it, the Land being very level, with steep Banks on both Sides the River, and in some Places very high, the Woods stored every where, with great Numbers of Deer and Turkies, we never going on Shoar, but we saw of each Sort; as also great Store of Partridges, Cranes, and Conies, in several Places we likewise heard several Wolves howling in the Woods, and saw where they had torn a Deer in Pieces. Also in the River we saw great Store of Ducks, Teal, Widgeon; and in the Woods great Flocks of Parrakeetos. The Timber that the Woods afford, for the most part, consists of Oaks of four or five Sorts, all differing in Leaves, but each bearing very good Acorns. We measured many of the Oaks in several Places, which we found to be in bigness, some Two, some Three, and others almost four Fathom in Height, before you come to Boughs or Limbs; forty, fifty, sixty Foot and some more; and those Oaks very common in the upper Parts of both Rivers; also a very tall large Tree of great Bigness, which some call Cyprus, the right Name we know not, growing in Swamps; Likewise, Walnut, Birch, Beech, Maple, Ash, Bay, Willow, Alder, and Holly; and in the lowermost Parts innumerable Pines, tall and good for Boards or Masts, growing, for the most part, in barren and sandy, but in some Places up the River, in good Ground, being mixed amongst Oaks and other Timbers. We saw Mulberry-Trees, multitudes of Grape-Vines, and some Grapes which we ate of. We found a very large and good Tract of Land on the N. W. Side of the River, thin of Timber, except here and there a very great Oak, and full of Grass, commonly as high as a Man's Middle, and in many Places to his Shoulders, where we saw many Deer and Turkies; one Deer having very large Horns and great Body, therefore called it Stag-Park. It being a very pleasant and delightful Place, we traveled in it several Miles, but we saw no End thereof. So we returned to our Boat, and proceeded down the River, and came to another Place, some twenty-five Leagues from the River's Mouth, on the same Side, where we found a Place, no less delightful than the former; and far as we could judge both Tracts came into one. This lower Place we called Rocky Point, because we found many Rocks and Stones of several Sizes upon the Land, which is not common. We sent our Boat down the River before us, ourselves traveling by Land many Miles. Indeed, we were so much taken with the Pleasantness of the Country, that we traveled in to Wood too far to recover our Boat and Company that Night. The next day being Sunday, we got to our Boat; and on Monday, the 16th of November, proceeded down to a Place on the East-Side of the River, some twenty-three Leagues from the Harbour's Mouth, which we called Turky-Quarters, because we killed several Turkies thereabouts; we viewed the Land there and found some Tracts of good Ground, and high, facing upon the River about one Mile inward, but backwards some two miles, all Pine Land, but good Pasture Ground. We returned to our Boat and proceeded down some two or three Leagues where we had formerly viewed, and found it a Tract of as good Land as any we have seen, and had as good Timber on it. The Banks on the River being high, therefore we called it High-Land-Point. Having viewed that we proceeded down the River, going on Shoar in several places on both Sides, it being generally large Marshes, and many of them dry, that they may more fitly be called Meadows. The Wood-Land against them is, for the most part, Pine, and in some Places as barren as ever we saw Land, but in other Places good Pasture-Ground. On Tuesday, November the 17th, we got aboard our Ship, riding against the Mouth of Green's River, where our Men were providing Wood and fitting the Ship for the Sea. In the interium, we took a View of the Country on both sides of the River, there finding some good Land and more bad, and the best not comparable to that above. Friday the 20th, was foul Weather; yet in the Afternoon we weighed, went down the River about two Leagues and came to an Anchor against the Mouth of Hilton's River, and took a View of the Land there on both sides, which appeared to us much like that at Green's River. Monday the 23rd, we went, with our Long-Boat well victualed and manned up Hilton's River; and when we came three Leagues, or thereabouts, up the same, we found this and Green's River to come into one, and so continued for four or five Leagues, which makes a great Island betwixt them. We proceeded still up the River till they parted again, keeping up Hilton's River on the Larboard side, and followed the said River five or six Leagues farther, where we found another large Branch of Green's River to come into Hilton's, which makes another great Island. On the Star-board side, going up, we proceeded still up the River some four Leagues and returned, taking a view of the Land on both sides, and then judged ourselves to be from our Ship some 18 Leagues W. and by N. One League below this Place came four Indians in a Canoe to us, and sold us several Baskets of Acorns, which we satisfied them for, and so left them; but one of them followed us on the Shoar some two or three Miles, till he came on the Top of a high Bank facing on the River; and as we rowed underneath it, the Fellow shot an Arrow at us which very narrowly missed one of our Men and stuck in the upper edge of the Boat, but broke in pieces leaving the Head behind. Hereupon we presently made to the Shoar and went all up the Bank (except Four to guide the Boat) to look for the Indian, but could not find him. At last we heard some sing, further in the Woods, which we looked upon as a Challenge to us to come and fight them. We went towards them with all Speed; but before we came in Sight of them, heard two Guns go off from our Boat; whereupon we retreated as fast as we could to secure our Boat and Men. When we came to them we found all well, and demanded the Reason of their firing the Guns. They told us than an Indian came creeping along the Bank, as they supposed, to shoot at them; and therefore they shot at him at a great distance, with small Shot, but thought they did him no Hurt, for they saw him run away. Presently after our Return to the Boat, and while we were thus talking, came two Indians to us with their Bows and Arrows, crying Bonny, Bonny. We took their Bows and Arrows from them, and gave them Beads to their Content; then we led them by the Hand to the Boat, and showed them the Arrowhead sticking in her Side, and related to them the whole Passage, which, when they understood, both of them showed a great Concern, and signified to us, by Signs, that they knew nothing of it; so we let them go, and marked a Tree on the Top of the Bank, calling the Place Mount-Skerry. We looked up the River as far as we could discern, and saw that it widened, and came running directly down the Country. So we returned, viewing the Land on both sides the River, and finding the Banks steep in some places, but very high in others. The Bank-sides are generally Clay, and as some of our Company did affirm, some marl. The Land and Timber up this River is no way inferior to the best in the other, which we call the main River. So far as we could discern, this seemed as fair, if not fairer, than the former, and we think runs farther into the country because a strong Current comes down, and a great deal more

Drift-Wood. But to return to the Business of the Land and Timber. We saw several Plots of Ground cleared by the Indians after their weak manner, compassed round with great Timber Trees, which they are no wise able to fell, and so keep the Sun from Corn-Fields very much; yet nevertheless, we saw as large Corn-stalks, or larger, than we have seen anywhere else. So we proceeded down the River till we found the Canoe the Indian was in, who shot at us. In the Morning we went on Shoar and cut the same in pieces. The Indians perceiving us coming towards them ran away. Going to his Hutt we pulled it down, broke his Pots, Platters, and Spoons, tore the Deer-Skins and Matts in pieces, and took away a Basket of Acorns; and afterwards proceeded down the River two Leagues, or thereabouts, and came to another Place of Indians, bought Acorns and some Corn of them, and went downwards two Leagues more. At last espying an Indian peeping over a high Bank, we held up a Gun at him, and calling to him Skerry, presently several Indians came in Sight of us, and made great Signs of Friendship, saying Bonny, Bonny. Then running before us, they endeavored to persuade us to come on Shoar; but we answered them with stern Countenances, and called out Skerry, taking up our Guns, and threatening to shoot at them, but they still cried, Bonny, Bonny; And when they saw they could not prevail nor persuade us to come on shoar, two of them came off to us in a Canoe, one paddling with a great Cane, the other with his Hand. As soon as they overtook us, they laid hold of our Boat, sweating and blowing, and told us, it was Bonny on shoar, and at last persuaded us to go on shoar with them. As soon as we landed, several Indians, to the Number of near forty lusty Men, came to us, all in a great Sweat, and told us Bonny. We showed them the Arrow-Head in the Boat-Side, and a Piece of the Canoe we had cut in Pieces; Whereupon, the chief Man amongst them made a long Speech, threw Beads into our Boat, which is a Sign of great Love and Friendship, and gave us to understand, that when he head of the Affront which we had received, it caused him to cry, and that he and his

Men were come to make Peace with us, assuring us, by Signs, that they would tye the arms and cut off the Head of the fellow who had done us that Wrong. And for a farther Testimony of their Love and Good-Will towards us, they presented us with two very handsome, proper, young Indian Women, the tallest that ever we saw in this Country, which we supposed to be the King's Daughters, or Persons of Distinction amongst them. Those young Women were so ready to come into our Boat that one of them crowded in, and would hardly be persuaded to go out again. We presented the King with a Hatchet and several Beads, and made Presents of Beads also to the young Women, the chief Men, and the rest of the Indians, as far as our Beads would go. They promised us, in four Days, to come on board our Ship, and so departed from us. When we left the place, which was soon after, we called it Mount Bonny, because we had there concluded a firm Peace. Proceeding down the River two or three Leagues farther, we came to a Place where were nine or ten Canoes, all together. We went ashore there and found several Indians, but most of them were the same which had made Peace with us before. We staid very little at that Place, but went directly down the River, and came to our Ship before day. Thursday the 26th of November, the Wind being at South, we could not go down to the River's Mouth, but on Friday the 27th, we weighed at the Mouth of Hilton's River, and got down a League towards the Harbour's Mouth. On Sunday the 29th, we got down to Crane-Island, which is four Leagues or thereabouts, above the Entrance of the Harbour's Mouth. On Tuesday the 1st of December, we made a Purchase of the River and Land of Cape Fair, of Wat-Coosa, and such other Indians as appeared to us to be the chief of those Parts. They brought us Store of fresh Fish aboard, as Mullets, Shads, and other Sorts very good. This River is all fresh Water, fit to drink. Some eight Leagues within the Mouth, the Tide runs up about thirty-five Leagues, but stops and rises a great deal farther up. It flows at the Harbour's Mouth, S. E. and N. W. six Foot at Neap-Tides, and eight Foot at Spring-Tides. The Channel on the East-side, by the Cape-Shoar is the best, and lies close aboard the Cape-Land, being three Fathoms at high Water, in the shallowest Place in the Channel, just at the Entrance: but as soon as you are past that Place, half a Cable's Length inward, you have six or seven Fathoms, a fair turning Channel into the River, and so continuing five or six Leagues upwards. Afterwards the Channel is more difficult, in some Places six or seven Fathoms, in others four or five, and in others but nine or ten Foot, especially where the River is broad. When the River comes to part, and grows narrow, there it is all Channel from side to side in most Places; though in some you shall have five, six or seven Fathoms, but generally two or three, Sand and Oaze. We viewed the Cape Land and judged it to be little worth, the Woods of it being shrubby and low, and the Land sandy and barren; in some Places Grass and Rushes, in others nothing but clear Sand. A place fitter to starve Cattle, in our Judgment, than to keep them alive; yet the Indians, as we understand, keep the English Cattle down there and suffer them not to go off of the said Cape, (as we suppose) because the Country Indians shall have no Part with them, and, therefore, 'tis likely they have fallen out about them, which shall have the greatest Share. They brought on board our Ship very good and fat Beef several times, which they sold us at a very reasonable Price; also fat and very large Swine, good and cheap, but they may thank their Friends of New-England who brought their Hogs to so fair a Market. Some of the Indians brought very good Salt aboard us, and made Signs, pointing to both sides of the River's Mouth, that there was great Store thereabouts. We saw up the River several good Places for the sitting up of Corn or Saw-Mills. In that time, as our Business called us up and down the River and Branches, we killed of wild Fowl, four Swans, ten Geese, twenty-nine Cranes, ten Turkies, forty Ducks and Mallards, three dozen of Parrakeeto's, and six dozen of other small Fowls, as Curlues and Plover, &c.

Whereas there was a Writing left in a Post at the Point of Cape

Fair River, by those New-England-Men, that left Cattle with the Indians there, the Contents whereof tended not only to the Disparagement of the Land about the said River, but also to the great Discouragement of all such as should hereafter come into those parts to settle. In answer to that scandalous Writing, we, whose Names are underwritten, do affirm, That we have seen, facing both sides the River and Branches of Cape-Fair aforesaid, as good Land, and as well timbered, as any we have seen in any other Part of the World, sufficient to accommodate Thousands of our English Nation, and lying commodiously by the said River's Side.

On Friday the 4th of December, the Wind being fair, we put out to Sea, bound for Barbados; and, on the 6th of February 166¾, came to an Anchor in Carlisle-Bay; it having pleased God, after several apparent Dangers both by Sea and Land, to bring us all in Safety to our long wished for and much desired Port, to render an Account of our Discovery; the Verity of which we do assert.

> ANTHONY LONG.
> WILLIAM HILTON.
> PETER FABIAN.

Thus you have an Account of the Latitude, Soil and Advantages of Cape-Fair, or Clarendon-River, which was settled in the Year 1661, or thereabouts, and had it not been for the irregular Practices of some of that Colony against the Indians, by sending away some of their Children (as I have been told) under Pretence of instructing them in Learning and the Principles of the Christian Religion; which so disgusted the Indians, that, though they had then no Guns, yet they never gave over till they had entirely rid themselves of the English, by their Bows and Arrows; with which they did not only take off themselves but also their Stocks of Cattle; And this was so much the more ruinous to them in that they could have no Assistance from South Carolina, which was not then planted, and the other Plantations were but in their Infancy. Were it not for such ill Practices, I say, it might, in all Probability, have been at this day, the best Settlement in their Lordships' great Province of Carolina.

The Sound of Albermarl, with the Rivers and Creeks of that Country, afford a very rich and durable Soil. The Land, in most Places, lies indifferent low, (except in Chuwon and high up the Rivers) but bears an incredible Burden of Timber; the low-grounds being covered with beech, and the High-Land yielding lofty Oaks, Walnut-Trees, and other useful Timber. The Country, in some Plantations, has yearly produced Indian Corn, or some other Grain, ever since this Country was first seated, without the Trouble of Manuring or Dressing; and yet, (to all appearance), it seems not to be, in the least, impoverished, neither do the Planters ever miss of a good Crop, unless a very unnatural Season visits them, which seldom happens.

A DESCRIPTION OF THE CORN OF CAROLINA.

The Wheat of this Place is very good, seldom yielding less than thirty fold, provided the Land is good where it is sown; Not but that there has been Sixty-six Increase for one measure sown in Piny-Land, which we account the meanest Sort. And I have been informed by People of Credit, that Wheat which was planted in a very rich Piece of Land, brought a hundred and odd Pecks for one. If our Planters, when they found such great Increase, would be so curious as to make nice Observations of the Soil and other remarkable Accidents, they would soon be acquainted with the Nature of the Earth and Climate and be better qualified to manage their Agriculture to more Certainty and greater Advantage, whereby they might arrive to the Crops and Harvests of Babylon, and those other fruitful Countries so much talked of. For I must confess I never saw one Acre of Land managed as it ought to be in Carolina since I knew it; and were they as negligent in their Husbandry in Europe as they are in Carolina, their Land would produce nothing but Weeds and Straw.

They have tried Rye, and it thrives very well; but having such Plenty of Maize, they do not regard it, because it makes black Bread, unless very curiously handled.

Barley has been sowed in small quantities, and does better than can be expected; because that Grain requires the ground to be very well worked with repeated Ploughings, which our general Way of breaking the Earth with Hoes, can, by no means perform, though in several Places we have a light rich, deep, black mould, which is the particular Soil in which Barley best thrives.

The naked Oats thrive extraordinary well; and the other would prove a very bold Grain; but the Plenty of other Grains makes them not much coveted.

The Indian Corn, or Maize, proves the most useful Grain in the World; and had it not been for the Fruitfulness of this Species, it would have proved very difficult to have settled some of the Plantations in America. It is very nourishing, whether in Bread, sodden, or otherwise; and those poor Christian Servants in Virginia, Maryland, and the other northerly Plantations that have been forced to live wholly upon it, do manifestly prove that it is the most nourishing Grain for a Man to subsist on, without any other Victuals. And this Assertion is made good by the Negro-Slaves, who, in many Places eat nothing but this Indian Corn and Salt. Pigs and Poultry fed with this Grain, eat the sweetest of all others. It refuses no Ground, unless the barren Sands, and when planted in good Ground, will repay the Planter, seven or eight hundred fold; besides the Stalks bruised and boiled, make very pleasant Beer, being sweet like the Sugar Cane.

There are several sorts of Rice, some bearded, others not, besides the red and the white, But the white Rice is the best. Yet there is a sort of perfumed Rice in the East Indies, which gives a curious Flavor in the Dressing. And with this sort America is not yet acquainted; neither can I learn that any of it has been brought over to Europe, the Rice of Carolina being esteemed the best that comes to that Quarter of the World. It is of great Increase, yielding from eight hundred to a thousand fold, and thrives best in wild Land that has never been broken up before.

Buck-Wheat is of great Increase in Carolina; but we make no other use of it, than instead of Maiz, to feed Hogs and Poultry; and Guinea Corn, which thrives well here, serves for the same use.

Of the Pulse-kind, we have many sorts. The first is the Bushel-Bean, which is a spontaneous Product. They are so called, because they bring a Bushel of Beans for one that is planted. They are set in the Spring, round Arbors, or at the Feet of Poles, up which they will climb and cover the Wattling, making a very pretty Shade to sit under. They continue flowering, budding and ripening all the Summer long, till the Frost approaches when they forbear their Fruit and die. The Stalks they grow on come to the Thickness of a Man's Thumb; and the Bean is white and mottled, with a purple Figure on each side it, like an Ear. They are very flat, and are eaten as the Windsor-Bean is, being an extraordinary well relished Pulse, either by themselves or with Meat.

We have the Indian Rounceval, or Miraculous Peas, so called from their long Pods, and great Increase. These are later Peas, and require a pretty long Summer to ripen in. They are very good; and so are the Bonavis, Calavancies, Nanticokes, and abundance of other Pulse, too tedious here to name, which we found the Indians possessed of, when first we settled in America, some of which sorts afford us two Crops in one Year; as the Bonavis and Colavancies, besides several others of that kind.

Now I am launched into a Discourse of the Pulse, I must acquaint you that the European Bean planted here, will, in time, degenerate into a dwarfish sort, if not prevented by a yearly Supply of foreign Seed, and an extravagant rich Soil; yet these Pigmy-Beans are the sweetest of that kind I have ever met withal.

As for all the sorts of English Peas that we have yet made tryal of, they thrive very well in Carolina. Particularly the white and gray Rouncival, the common Field-Peas, and Sickle-Peas, yield very well, and are of a good Relish. As for the other sorts, I have not seen made any tryal of as yet, but question not their coming to great Perfection with us.

The Kidney-Beans were here before the English came, being very plentiful in the Indian Corn-Fields.

The Garden-Roots that thrive well in Carolina are, Carrots, Leeks, Parsnips, Turneps, Potatoes of several delicate sorts, Ground Artichokes, Radishes, Horse-Radish, Beet, both sorts, Onions, Shallot, Garlick, Cives, and Wild-Onions.

The Sallads are, the Lettice, Curled, Red Cabbage and Savoy. The Spinage, round and prickley, Fennel, sweet and the common Sort, Samphire, in the Marshes excellent, so is the Dock, or Wild-Rhubarb, Rocket, Sorrell, French and English, Cresses, of several Sorts, Purslain wild, and that of a larger Size which grows in the Gardens; for this Plant is never met withal in the Indian Plantations, and is, therefore, supposed to proceed from Cow-Dung, which Beast they keep not. Parsley, two Sorts, Asparagus thrives to a Miracle, without hot Beds or dunging the Land, White-Cabbage from European, or New England Seed, for the People are negligent and unskilful, and dont care to provide Seed of their own. The Colly-Flower we have not yet had an Opportunity to make tryal of, nor has the Artichoke ever appeared amongst us, that I can learn. Coleworts, plain and curved, Savoys; besides the Water-Melons of several Sorts, very good, which should have gone amongst the Fruits. Of Musk-Melons we have very large and good, and several sorts, as the Golden, Green, Guinea, and Orange. Cucumbers, long, short and prickley, all these from the Natural Ground, and great Increase, without any help of Dung or Reflection; Pompions, yellow and very large, Burmillions, Cashaws, and excellent Fruit boiled; Squashes, Simnals, Horns, and Gourds, besides many other Species of less Value, too tedious to name.

Our Pot herbs and others of use, which we already possess, are Angelica, wild and tame, Balm, Bagloss, Borage, Burnett, Clary, Marigold, Pot-Marjoram, and other Marijorams, Summer and Winter Savory, Columbines, Tansey, Wormwood, Nep, Mallows, several sorts, Drage, red and white, Lambs Quarters, Thyme, Hyssop, of very large Growth, sweet Bazzil, Rosemary, Lavender. The more Physical are Carduns, Benedictus, the Scurvy-grass of America, I never here met any of the European sort; Tobacco of Many sorts, Dill, Carawa, Cummin, Anise, Coriander, all sorts of Plantain of England, and two sorts spontaneous, good Vulneraries, Elecampane, Comfrey, Needle, the Seed from England, none Native; Monks-Rhubarb, Burdock, Asarum, wild in the Woods, reckoned one of the Snake-Roots; Poppies in the Garden, none wild yet discovered; Wormseed, Feverfew, Rue, Ground-Ivey, spontaneous but very small and scarce, Aurea-Virga, four sorts of Snake-Root, besides the common Species, which are great Antidotes against that Serpent's Bite, and are easily raised in the Garden; Mint, James-Town weed, so called from Virginia, the Seed it bears is very like that of an Onion, it is excellent for curing Burns, and assuaging Inflamations, but taken inwardly brings on a sort of drunken Madness. One of our Marsh-Weeds, like a Dock, has the same Effect, and possesses the Party with Fear and Watchings. The Red-Root, whose Leaf is like Spear-Mint, is good for Thrushes and sore Mouths, Camomil, but it must be kept in the Shade, otherwise it will not thrive; Housleek, first from England; Vervin, Night-Shade, several kinds; Harts-Tongue, Yarrow abundance, Mullein the same, both of the Country; Sarsparilla, and abundance more I could name, yet not the hundreth part of what remains, a Catalogue of which is a Work of many Years, and without any other Subject, would swell to a large Volume, and requires the Abilities of a skillful Botanist. Had not the ingenious Mr. Banister (the greatest Virtuoso we ever had on the Continent) been unfortunately taken out of this World, he would have given the best Account of the Plants of America, of any that ever yet made such an Attempt in these parts. Not but we are satisfied, the Species of Vegetable in Carolina are so numerous that it requires more than one Man's Age to bring the chiefest Part of them into regular Classes; the Country being so different in its Situation and Soil, that what one place plentifully affords, another is absolutely a Stranger to; yet we generally observe that the greatest Variety is found in the Low Grounds, and Savannas.

The Flower-Garden in Carolina is as yet arrived but to a very poor and jejune Perfection. We have only two sorts of Roses; the Clov-July-Flowers, Violets, Prince Feather and Tres Colores. There has been nothing more cultivated in the Flower-Garden, which at present occurs to my Memory; but as for the wild spontaneous Flowers of this Country, Nature has been so liberal that I cannot name one tenth part of the valuable ones; And since, to give Specimens would only swell the Volume, and give little Satisfaction to the Reader, I shall therefore proceed to the Present State of Carolina, and refer the Shrubs and other Vegetables of larger growth till hereafter, and then shall deliver them and the other Species in their Order.

THE PRESENT STATE OF CAROLINA.

When we consider the Latitude and convenient Situation of Carolina, had we no farther Confirmation thereof, our Reason would inform us that such a Place lay fairly to be a delicious Country, being placed in that Girdle of the World which affords Wine, Oil, Fruit, Grain and Silk, with other rich Commodities, besides a sweet Air, moderate Climate and fertile Soil; these are the Blessings, (under Heaven's Protection) that spin out the Thread of Life to its utmost Extent, and crown our Days with the Sweets of Health and Plenty, which, when joined with Content, renders the Possessors the Happiest Race of Men upon Earth.

The Inhabitants of Carolina, through the Richness of the Soil, live an easy and pleasant Life. The Land being of several sorts of Compost, some stiff, others light, some marl, others rich, black Mould, here barren of Pine, but affording Pitch, Tar and Masts; there vastly rich, especially on the Freshes of the Rivers, one part bearing great Timbers others being Savannas or natural Meads, where no Trees grow for several Miles, adorned by Nature with a pleasant Verdure, and beautiful Flowers, frequent in no other Places, yielding abundance of Herbage for Cattle, Sheep, and Horses. The Country in general affords pleasant Seats, the Land, (except in some few Places,) being dry and high Banks, parcelled out into most convenient Necks, (by the Creeks,) easy to be fenced in for securing their Stocks to more strict Boundaries, whereby, with a small trouble of fencing, almost every man may enjoy, to himself, an entire Plantation, or rather Park. These, with the other Benefits of Plenty of Fish, Wild-Fowl, Venison, and the other Conveniences which this Summer-Country naturally furnishes, has induced a great many Families to leave the more Northerly Plantations and sit down under one of the mildest Governments in the World; in a Country that, with moderate Industry, will afford all the Necessaries of Life. We have yearly abundance of Strangers come among us, who chiefly strive to go Southerly to settle, because there is a vast Tract of rich Land betwixt the Place we are seated in and Cape Fair, and upon that River, and more Southerly which is inhabited by none but a few Indians, who are at this time well affected to the English, and very desirous of their coming to live among them. The more Southerly the milder Winters, with the Advantages of purchasing the Lords Land at the most easy and moderate Rate of any Lands in America, nay, (allowing all Advantages thereto annexed,) I may say the Universe does not afford such another; Besides, Men have a great Advantage of choosing good and commodious Tracts of Land at the first Seating of a Country or River, whereas the Later Settlers are forced to purchase smaller Dividends of the old Standers, and sometimes at very considerable Rates; as now in Virginia and Maryland where a thousand Acres of good Land cannot be bought under twenty shillings an Acre, besides two Shillings yearly Acknowledgement for every hundred Acres; which Sum, be it more or less, will serve to put the Merchant or Planter here into a good posture of Buildings, Slaves, and other Necessaries, when the Purchase of his Land comes to him on such easy Terms. And as our Grain and

Pulse thrives with us to admiration, no less do our Stocks of Cattle, Horses, Sheep and Swine multiply.

The Beef of Carolina equalizes the best that our neighboring Colonies afford; the Oxen are of a great size when they are suffered to live to a fit Age. I have seen fat and good Beef at all times of the Year, but October and the cool Months are the Seasons we kill our Beeves in, when we intend them for Salting or Exportation; for then they are in their prime of Flesh, all coming from Grass, we never using any other Food for our Cattle. The Heifers bring Calves at eighteen or twenty Months old, which makes such a wonderful Increase, that many of our Planters, from the very mean Beginnings, have raised themselves, and are now Masters of hundreds of fat Beeves and other Cattle.

The Veal is very good and white, so is the Milk very pleasant and rich, there being at present considerable Quantities of Butter and Cheese made that is very good, not only serving our own Necessities, but we send out a great deal among our Neighbors.

The Sheep thrive very well at present, having most commonly two Lambs at one yeaning. As the Country comes to be open, they prove still better, Change of Pasture being agreeable to that useful Creature. Mutton is (generally) exceeding Fat and of a good Relish; their Wool is very fine and proves a good Staple.

The Horses are well shaped and swift; the best of them would sell for ten or twelve Pounds in England. They prove excellent Drudges and will travel incredible Journeys. They are troubled with very few Distempers, neither do the cloudy faced grey Horses go blind here as in Europe. As for Spavins, Splints and Ring-Bones, they are here never met withal, as I can learn. Were we to have our Stallions and choice of Mares from England, or any other of a good Sort, and careful to keep them on the Highlands, we could not fail of a good Breed; but having been supplied with our first Horses from the neighboring Plantations, which were but mean, they do not as yet come up to the Excellency of the English Horses; though we generally find that the Colt exceeds in Beauty and Strength, its Sire and Dam.

The Pork exceeds any in Europe; the great Diversity and goodness of the Acorns and Nuts which the Woods afford, making that Flesh of an excellent Taste and produces great Quantities; so that Carolina, (if not the chief,) is not inferior in this one Commodity to any Colony in the hands of the English.

As for Goats, they have been found to thrive and increase well, but being mischievous to Orchards and other Trees, makes People decline keeping them.

Our Produce for Exportation to Europe and the Islands in America, are Beef, Pork, Tallow, Hides, Deer-Skins, Furs, Pitch, Tar, Wheat, Indian-Corn, Peas, Masts, Staves, Heading, Boards and all sorts of Timber and Lumber for Madera and the West-Indies, Rozin, Turpentine and several sorts of Gums and Tears, with some medicinal Drugs, are here produced; Besides Rice and several other foreign Grains, which thrive very well. Good Bricks and Tiles are made and several sorts of useful Earths, as Bole, Fuller's-Earth, Oaker and Tobacco-pipe-Clay, in great plenty; Earths for the Potter's Trade and fine Sand for the Glass-Makers. In building with Brick, we make our Lime of Oyster-Shells, though we have great Store of Lime-stone towards the Heads of our Rivers, where are Stones of all sorts that are useful, besides vast Quantities of excellent Marble. Iron-Stone we have plenty of, both in the Low-Grounds and on the Hills. Lead and Copper has been found, so has Antimony heretofore; But no Endeavors have been used to discover those Subteraneous Species; otherwise we might in all probability, find out the best Minerals, which are not wanting in Carolina. Hot Baths we have an account of from the Indians that frequent the Hill-Country, where a great likelihood appears of making Salt-peter, because the Earth in many places, is strongly mixed with a nitrous Salt, which is much coveted by the Beasts, who come at some Seasons in great Droves and Herds, and by their much licking of this Earth, make great Holes in those Banks, which sometimes lie at the heads of great precipices, where their Eagerness after this salt hastens their End by falling down the high Banks, so that they are dashed in Pieces. It must be confessed that the most noble and sweetest Part of this Country is not inhabited by any but the Savages; and a great deal of the richest Part thereof, has no Inhabitants but the Beasts of the Wilderness; For, the Indians are not inclinable to settle in the richest Land, because the Timbers are too large for them to cut down, and too much burthened with Wood for their Laborers to make Plantations of; besides, the Healthfulness of those Hills is apparent by the Gigantick Stature and Grey-Heads so common amongst the Savages that dwell near the Mountains. The great Creator of all things having most wisely diffused his Blessings, by parceling out the Vintages of the World into such Lots as his wonderful Foresight saw most proper, requisite and convenient for the Habitations of his Creatures. Towards the Sea we have the Conveniency of Trade Transportation and other Helps the Water affords; but oftentimes those Advantages are attended with indifferent Land, a thick Air, and other Inconveniences; when backwards, near the Mountains, you meet with the richest Soil, a sweet, thin Air, dry Roads, pleasant small murmuring Streams, and several beneficial Productions and Species, which are unknown in the European World. One Part of this Country affords what the other is wholly a Stranger to.

We have Chalybeate Waters of several Tastes and different Qualities, some purge, others work by the other Enunctories. We have amongst the Inhabitants, a Water that is inwardly, a great Apersive, and outwardly, cures Ulcers, Tetters and Sores by washing therewith.

There has been a Coal-Mine lately found near the Mannakin town, above the falls of James River in Virginia, which proves very good, and is used by the Smiths for their Forges; and we need not doubt of the same amongst us, towards the Heads of our Rivers; but the Plenty of Wood, (which is much the better Fuel,) makes us not inquisite after Coal-Mines. Most of the French, who lived at that Town on James River, are removed to Trent-River, in North Carolina, where the rest were expected daily to come to them when I came away, which was in August, 1708. They are much taken with the Pleasantness of that Country, and indeed are a very industrious People. At present they make very good Linnen-Cloath and Thread, and are very well versed in cultivating Hemp and Flax, of both which they raise very considerable Quantities; and design to try an Essay of the Grape for making of Wine.

As for those of our own Country in Carolina, some of the Men are very laborious, and make great Improvements in their Way; but I dare hardly give them that Character in general. The Easy way of living in that plentiful Country makes a great many Planters very negligent, which, were they otherwise, that Colony might now have been in a far better Condition than it is, (as to Trade and other Advantages,) which an universal Industry would have led them into.

The Women are the most industrious Sex in that Place, and, by their good Housewifery, make a great deal of Cloath of their own Cotton, Wool and Flax; some of them keeping their Families, (though large), very decently appareled, both with Linnens and Woollens, so that they have no occasion to run into the Merchants Debt, or lay their money out on Stores for Cloathing.

The Christian Natives of Carolina are a straight, clean-limbed People; the Children being seldom or never troubled with Rickets, or those other Distempers that the Europeans are visited withal. 'Tis next to a Miracle to see one of them deformed in Body. The Vicinity of the Sun makes Impression on the Men who labour out of doors, or use the Water. As for those Women that do not expose themselves to the Weather, they are often very fair, and generally as well featured as you shall see any where, and have very brisk, charming Eyes which sets them off to Advantage. They marry very young; some at Thirteen or Fourteen; and She that stays till Twenty is reckoned a stale Maid, which is a very indifferent Character in that warm Country. The Women are very fruitful, most Houses being full of Little Ones. It has been observed that Women long married and without Children in other Places, have removed to Carolina and become joyful Mothers. They have very easy Travail in their Childbearing, in which they are so happy as seldom to miscarry. Both Sexes are generally spare of Body and not Cholerick, nor easily cast down at Disappointments and losses, seldom immoderately grieving at Misfortunes, unless for the Loss of their nearest Relations and Friends, which seems to make a more than ordinary Impression upon thm. Many of the Women are very handy in Canoes and will manage them with great Dexterity and Skill, which they become accustomed to in this watery Country. They are ready to help their Husbands in any servile Work, as Planting, when the Season of the Weather requires Expedition; Pride seldom banishing good Housewifery. The Girls are not bred up to the Wheel and Sewing only, but the Dairy, and affairs of the House they are very well acquainted withal; so that you shall see them, whilst very young, manage their Business with a great deal of Conduct and Alacrity. The Children of both Sexes are very docile and learn any thing with a great deal of Ease and Method, and those that have the Advantages of Education, write very good Hands, and prove good Accountants, which is most coveted, and indeed, most necessary in these Parts. The young Men are commonly of a bashful, sober Behaviour; few proving Prodigals to consume what the Industry of their Parents has left them, but commonly improve it. The marrying so young, carries a double Advantage with it, and that is that the Parents see their Children provided for in Marriage, and the young married People are taught by their Parents how to get their Living; for their Admonitions make great Impressions on their Children. I had heard (before I knew this new World) that the Natives of America were a short lived People, which, by all the Observations I could ever make, proves quite contrary; for those who are born here, and in other Colonies, live to as great Ages as any of the Europeans, the Climate being free from Consumptions, which Distemper, fatal to England, they are Strangers to. And as the Country becomes more cleared of Wood it still becomes more healthful to the Inhabitants and less addicted to the Ague, which is incident to most new Comers into America from Europe, yet not mortal. A gentle Emetic seldom misses of driving it away; but if it is not too troublesome, tis better to let the Seasoning have its own course, in which case the Party is commonly free from it ever after, and very healthful.

And now, as to the other Advantages the Country affords, we cannot guess at them at present, because, as I said before, the best Part of this Country is not inhabited by the English, from whence probably will hereafter spring Productions that this Age does not dream of, and of much more Advantage to the Inhabitants than any things we are yet acquainted withal; And as for several Productions of other Countries, much in the same Latitude, we may expect with good Management, they will become familiar to us, as Wine, Oil, Fruit, Silk, and other profitable Commodities, such as Drugs, Dyes, &c., And at present, the Curious may have a large Field to satisfy and divert themselves in, as Collections of strange Beasts, Birds, Insects, Reptiles, Shells, Fishes, Minerals, Herbs, Flowers, Plants, Shrubs, Intricate Roots, Gums, Tears, Rozins, Dyes, and Stones, with several other that yield Satisfaction and Profit to those whose inclinations tend that Way. And as for what may be hoped for, towards a happy Life and Being, by such as design to remove thither, I shall add this: that with Prudent Management, I can affirm, by Experience, not by Hearsay, That any Person, with a small Beginning, may live very comfortably, and not only provide for the Necessaries of Life, but likewise for those that are to succeed him. Provisions being very plentiful, and of good Variety to accommodate genteel Housekeeping, and the neighboring Indians are friendly, and in many Cases serviceable to us in making us Wares to catch Fish in, for a small matter, which proves of great Advantage to large Families, because those Engines take great Quantities of many Sorts of Fish that are very good and nourishing. Some of them hunt and fowl for us at reasonable Rates, the Country being as plentifully provided with all Sorts of Game as any Part of America; the poorer Sort of Planters often

get them to plant for them by hiring them for that Season, or for
so much Work, which commonly comes very reasonable. Moreover, it is remarkable, That No Place on the Continent of America
has seated an English Colony so free from Blood-shed as Carolina,
but all the others have been more damaged and disturbed by the
Indians than they have; which is worthy Notice, when we consider how oddly it was first planted with Inhabitants.

The Fishing-Trade in Carolina might be carried on to great Advantage, considering how many Sorts of excellent Fish our Sound
and Rivers afford, which cure very well with Salt, as has been experienced by some small Quantities, which have been sent abroad
and yielded a good Price. As for the Whale-fishing, it is no otherwise regarded than by a few People who live on the Sand-Banks;
and those only work on dead Fish cast on Shoar, none being struck
on our Coast, as they are to the Northward; although we have
plenty of whales there. Great Plenty is generally the Ruin of Industry. Thus our Merchants are not many, nor have those few
there be applied themselves to the European Trade. The Planter
sits contented at home, whilst his Oxen thrive and grow fat, and
his Stocks daily increase: The fatted Porkets and Poultry are easily
raised to his Table, and his Orchard affords him Liquor, so that he
eats and drinks away the Cares of the World, and desires no greater
Happiness than that which he daily enjoys. Whereas, not only the
European, but also the Indian-Trade, might be carried on to a great
Profit, because we lie as fairly for the Body of Indians as any Settlement in English-America; And for the small Trade that has been
carried on in that Way, the Dealers therein have throve as fast as
any Men, and the soonest raised themselves of any People I have
known in Carolina.

Lastly, As to the Climate, it is very healthful; our Summer is
not so hot as in other places to the Eastward in the same Latitude;
neither are we ever visited by Earthquakes, as many places in Italy
and other Summer-Countries are. Our Northerly Winds, in Summer, cool the Air, and free us from pestilential Fevers, which Spain,

Barbary, and the neighboring Countries in Europe, &c., are visited withal. Our Sky is generally serene and clear, and the Air very thin, in comparison of many Parts of Europe, where Consumptions and Catarrhs reign amongst the Inhabitants. The Winter has several Fitts of sharp Weather, especially when the Wind is at N. W. which always clears the Sky, though never so thick before. However, such Weather is very agreeable to European Bodies, and makes them healthy. The N. E. Winds blowing in Winter, bring with them thick Weather, and, in the Spring sometimes, blight the Fruits; but they very seldom endure long, being blown away by Westerly Winds, and then all becomes fair and clear again. Our spring in Carolina is very beautiful, and the most pleasant Weather a Country can enjoy. The Fall is accompanied with cool Mornings, which come in towards the latter end of August, and so continue (most commonly) very moderate Weather till about Christmas; then Winter comes on apace. Though these Seasons are very piercing, yet the Cold is of no continuance. Perhaps you will have cold Weather for three or four days at a time, then pleasant, warm Weather follows such as you have in England, about the latter end of April or beginning of May. In the year 1707, we had the severest Winter in Carolina, that ever was known since the English came to settle there; for our Rivers, that were not above half a Mile wide, and fresh Water, were frozen over, and some of them, in the North-part of this Country, were passable for People to walk over.

One great Advantage of North-Carolina is, that we are not a Frontier, and near the Enemy, which proves very chargeable and troublesome in time of War to those Colonies that are so seated. Another great Advantage comes from its being near Virginia, where we come often to a good Market, at the Return of the Guinea-Ships for Negroes, and the Remnant of their Stores, which is very commodious for the Indian-Trade, besides in War-time, we lie near at hand to go under their Convoy, and to sell our Provisions to the Tobacco-fleets; for the Planting of Tobacco generally in those Colonies, prevents their being supplied with Stores, sufficient for victualing their Ships.

As for the Commodities which are necessary to carry over to this Plantation for Use and Merchandise, and are, therefore, requisite for those to have along with them that intend to transport themselves thither; they are Guns, Powder and Shot, Flints, Linnens of all sorts, but chiefly ordinary Blues, Osnaburgs, Scotch and Irish Linnen, and some fine; Men's and Women's Cloaths, ready made up, some few Broad-Cloaths, Kerseys, and Druggets; to which you must add Haberdasher's-Wares, Hats, about Five or Six Shillings a piece, and a few finer; a few Wiggs, not long and pretty thin of Hair; thin Stuffs for Women; Iron-Works, as Nails, Spades, Axes, broad and narrow Hoes, Frows, Wedges, and Saws of all sorts, with other Tools for Carpenters, Joiners, Coopers, Shoemakers, Shave-locks, &c., all which, and others which are necessary for the Plantations, you may be informed of and buy at very reasonable Rates, of Mr. James Gilbert, Ironmonger in Mitre-Tavern-Yard, near Aldgate. You may also be used very kindly for your Cuttlery-Ware, and other advantageous Merchandises, and your Cargoes well sorted by Capt. Sharp at the Blue-gate in Cannon-street, and for Earthern-Ware, Window-Glass, Grind-Stones, Mill-Stones, Paper, Ink-Powder, Saddles, Bridles, and what other things you are minded to take with you for Pleasure or Ornament.

And now I shall proceed to the rest of the Vegetables that are common in Carolina, in reference to the Place where I left off, which is the Natural History of that Country.

OF THE VEGETABLES OF CAROLINIA.

The spontaneous Shrubs of this Country are the Lark-heel-Tree; three sorts of Honey-Suckle-Tree, the first of which grows in Branches as our Piemento-Tree does, that is, always in low, moist Ground; the other grows in clear, dry Land, the Flower more cut and lacerated; the third, which is the most beautiful, and, I think, the most charming Flower of its Color I ever saw, grows betwixt two and three Foot high, and for the most part, by the side of a swampy Wood, or on the Banks of our Rivers, but never near the

Salt-Water. All the Sorts are white; the last grows in a great Bunch of these small Honey-Suckles set upon one chief Stem, and is commonly the Bigness of a large Turnep. Nothing can appear more beautiful than these Bushes, when in their Splendour, which is in April and May. The next is the Honey-Suckle of the Forest; it grows about a Foot high, bearing its Flowers on small Pedestals, several of them standing on the main Stock, which is the Thickness of a Wheat-Straw. We have also the Woodbind, much the same as in England; Princes-feather, very large and beautiful in the Garden; Tree-Colores, branched Sun-flower, Double Poppies, Lupines of several pretty sorts, spontaneous and the Sensible Plant is said to be near the Mountains which I have not yet seen; Saf-Flower, (and I believe the Saffron of England would thrive here, if planted) the yellow Jessamin is wild in our Woods of a pleasant Smell. Ever-Greens are here plentifully found of a very quick Growth and pleasant Shade; Cypress, or white Cedar, the Pitch Pine, the yellow Pine, the white Pine with long Leaves, and the smaller Almond-Pine, which last bears Kernels in the Apple, tasting much like an Almond, and in some years there falls such plenty as to make the Hogs fat. Horn-Beam, Cedar, two sorts, Holly, two sorts, Bay-Tree, two sorts, one the Dwarf-Bay, about twelve Foot high, the other the Bigness of a middling Pine-Tree, about two Foot and half Diameter; Laurel-Trees, in Height, equalizing the lofty oaks, the Berries and Leaves of this Tree dies a Yellow; the Bay-Berries yield a Wax, which besides its Use in Chirurgery, makes Candles, that in burning, give a fragrant Smell. The Cedar-Berries are infused and made Beer of by the Bermudians, they are Carminative, and much of the Quality of Juniper-Berries; Yew or Box I have never seen or heard of in this Country. There are two sorts of Myrtles, different in Leaf and Berry; the Berry yields Wax that makes Candles, the most lasting of the sweetest smell imaginable. Some mix half Tallow with this Wax, others use it without Mixture; and these are fit for a Lady's Chamber, and incomparable to pass the Line withal, and other hot Countries, because they will stand when others will melt. by the excessive Heat, down in the Binacles. Evergreen Oak, two sorts; Gall-Berry-Tree, bearing a black Berry, with which the Women dye their Cloaths and Yarn black; 'tis a pretty Evergreen and very plentiful, growing always in low swampy Grounds, and amongst Ponds. We have a Prim or Privet, which grows on the dry, barren, sandy Hills by the Sound Side; it bears a smaller sort than that in England, and grows into a round Bush, very beautiful. Last of Bushes, (except Savine, which grows every where wild,) is the famous Yaupon, of which I find two sorts, if not three. I shall speak first of the Nature of this Plant, and afterwards account for the different Sorts. This Yaupon, called by the South Carolina Indians, Cassena, is a Bush that grows chiefly on the Sand-Banks and Islands, bordering on the Sea of Carolina; on this Coast it is plentifully found, and in no other Place that I know of. It grows the most like Box of any Vegetable that I know, being very like it in Leaf, only dented exactly like Tea, but the Leaf somewhat fatter. I cannot say whether it bears any Flower, but a Berry it does, about the Bigness of a grain of Pepper, being first red, then brown, when ripe, which is in December; Some of these Bushes grow to be twelve Foot high, others are three or four. The Wood thereof is brittle as Myrtle, and affords a light ash colored Bark. There is sometimes found of it in Swamps and rich low Grounds, which has the same figured Leaf, only it is larger, and of a deeper Green; This may be occasioned by the Richness that attends the low Grounds thus situated. The third Sort has the same kind of Leaf, but never grows a Foot high, and is found both in rich, low Land and on the Sand-Hills. I don't know that ever I found any Seed or Berries on the dwarfish Sort, yet I find no Difference in Taste, when Infusion is made. Cattle and Sheep delight in this Plant very much, and so do the Deer, all which crop is very short and browze thereon wheresoever they meet with it. I have transplanted the Sand-Bank and dwarfish Yaupon, and find that the first Year the Shrubs stood at a stand, but the second Year they throve as well as in their native Soil. This Plant is the Indian Tea, used and approved by all the Savages on the Coast of Carolina, and from them sent to the Westward Indians and sold at a considerable Price. All which they cure after the same way as they do for themselves, which is thus: They take this Plant (not only the Leaves but the smaller Twigs along with them) and bruise it in a Mortar till it becomes blackish, the Leaf being wholly defaced: Then they take it out, put it into one of their earthern Pots which is over the Fire till it smokes, stirring it all the time till it is cured. Others take it, after it is bruised, and put it into a Bowl to which they put live Coals and cover them with the Yaupon, till they have done smoking, often turning them over. After all, they spread it upon their Mats and dry it in the Sun to keep it for Use. The Spaniards in New Spain have this Plant very plentifully on the Coast of Florida, and hold it in great Esteem. Sometimes they cure it as the Indians do, or else beat it to a Powder, so mix it as Coffee; yet before they drink it, they filter the same. They prefer it above all Liquids to drink with Physic, to carry the same safely and speedily through the Passages for which it is admirable, as I myself have experimented.

In the next Place, I shall speak of the Timber that Carolina affords, which is as follows:

Chesnut-Oak is a very lofty Tree, clear of Boughs and Limbs for fifty or sixty Feet. They bear sometimes four or five foot through all clear Timber; and are the largest Oaks we have, yielding the fairest Plank. They grow chiefly in low Land, that is stiff and rich. I have seen of them so high, that a good Gun could not reach a Turkey, though loaded with Swan-Shot. They are called Chesnut, because of the Largeness and Sweetness of the Acorns.

White, Scaly-Bark Oak: This is used, as the former, in building Sloops and Ships. Though it bears a large Acorn, yet it never grows to the Bulk and Height of the Chesnut-Oak. It is so called, because of a scaly, broken, white Bark, that covers this Tree, growing on dry Land.

We have Red Oak, sometimes, in good Land, very large and

lofty. Tis a porous Wood, and used to rive into Rails for Fences. Tis not very durable, yet some use this, as well as the two former, for Pipe and Barrel-Staves. It makes good Clap-boards.

Spanish Oak is free to rive, bears a whitish, smooth Bark, and rives very well into Clap-boards. It is accounted durable, therefore some use to build Vessels with it for the Sea; it proving well and durable. These all bear good Mast for the Swine.

Bastard-Spanish is an Oak betwixt the Spanish and Red Oak; the chief Use is for Fencing and Clap-boards. It bears good Acorns.

The next is Black-Oak, which is esteemed a durable Wood under Water; but sometimes it is used in House-work. It bears a good Mast for Hogs.

White Iron or Ring-Oak, is so called from the Durability and lasting Quality of this Wood. It chiefly grows on dry, lean Land, and seldom fails of bearing a plentiful Crop of Acorns. This Wood is found to be very durable, and is esteemed the best Oak for Ship-work that we have in Carolina; For though Live-Oak be more lasting, yet it seldom allows Planks of any considerable Length.

Turkey-Oak is so called from a small Acorn it bears, which the wild Turkeys feed on.

Live-Oak chiefly grows on dry sandy Knolls. This is an Evergreen and the most durable Oak all America affords. The shortness of this Wood's Bowl or Trunk, makes it unfit for Plank to build Ships withal. There are some few Trees that would allow a Stock of twelve foot, but the Firmness and great Weight thereof, frightens our Sawyers from the Fatigue that attends the cutting of this Timber. A Nail once driven therein, tis next to an Impossibility to draw it out. The Limbs thereof are so cured that they serve for excellent Timbers, Knees, &c., for Vessels of any sort. The Acorns thereof are as sweet as Chesnuts, and the Indians draw an Oil from them, as sweet as that from the Olive, though of an Amber-Colour. With these Nuts or Acorns, some have counterfeited the Cocoa, whereof they have made Chocolate, not to be distinguished by a good Palate. Window-Frames, Mallets, and Pins for Blocks, are made thereof to an excellent Purpose. I knew two Trees of this Wood among the Indians, which were planted from the Acorn, and grew in the Freshes, and never saw anything more beautiful of that kind. They are of an indifferent, quick Growth, of which there are two sorts. The Acorns make very fine Pork.

Willow-Oak is a sort of Water-Oak. It grows in Ponds and Branches, and is useful for many things. It is so called from the Leaf, which very much resembles a Willow.

The Live-Oak grows in the fresh Water Ponds and Swamps by the River sides, and in low Ground overflown with Water; and is a perennial Green.

Of Ash we have two sorts, agreeing nearly with the English in the Grain. One of our sorts is tough like the English, but differs something in the Leaf, and much more in the Bark. Neither of them bears Keys. The Water-Ash is brittle. The Bark is Food for the Bevers.

There are two sorts of Elm; the first grows on our High-Land and approaches our English; The Indians take the Bark of its Root and beat it, whilst green, to a Pulp, and then dry it in the Chimney, where it becomes of a reddish Colour. This they use as a Sovereign Remedy to heal a Cut or green Wound, or any thing that is not corrupted. It is of a very glutinous Quality. The other Elm grows in low Ground, of whose Bark the English and Indians make Ropes; for as soon as the Sap rises, it strips off with the greatest ease imaginable. It runs in March, or thereabouts.

The Tulip-Trees, which are, by the Planters, called Poplars, as nearest approaching that Wood in Grain grow to a prodigious Bigness, some of them having been found One and twenty foot in Circumference. I have been informed of a Tulip-Tree, that was ten Foot Diameter; and another wherein a lusty Man had his Bed and Household Furniture, and lived in it till his Labour got him a more fashionable Mansion. He afterwards became a noted Man in his Country for Wealth and Conduct. One of these sorts bears a white Tulip, the other a party-coloured, mottled one. The

Wood makes very pretty Wainscot Shingles for Houses, and Planks for several Uses. It is reckoned very lasting, especially under-Ground for Mill-Work. The Buds made into an Ointment, cure Scalds, Inflamations, and Burns. I saw several Bushels thereon. The Cattle are apt to eat of these Buds, which give a very odd Taste to the Milk.

Beech is here frequent, and very large. The Grain seems exactly the same as that in Europe. We make little Use thereof, save for Fire-Wood. 'Tis not a durable Timber. It affords a very sweet Nut, yet the Pork fed thereon (though sweet) is very oily, and ought to be hardened with Indian Corn, before it is killed. Another sort called Buck-Beech is here found.

Horn-Beam grows in some Places very plentifully, yet the Plenty of other Wood makes it unregarded. The Vertues of Sassafras are well known in Europe. This Wood sometimes grows to be above two Foot over, and is very durable and lasting, used for Bowls, Timbers, Post for Houses, and other Things that require standing in the Ground. 'Tis very light. It bears a white Flower, which is very cleansing to the Blood, being eaten in the Spring with other Sallating. The Berry, when ripe, is black; 'tis very oily, Carminative and extremely prevalent in Clysters for the Colick. The Bark of the Root is a Specific to those afflicted with the Gripes. The same in Powder, and a Lotion made thereof, is much used by the Savages to mundify old Ulcers, and for several other Uses, being highly esteemed among them.

Dog-Wood is plentiful on our light Land, inclining to a rich Soil. It flowers the first in the Woods; its white Blossom making the Forest very beautiful. It has a fine Grain, and serves for several Uses within doors, but is not durable. The Bark of this Root infused, is held an infallible Remedy against the Worms.

Laurel, before mentioned; as to its Bigness and Use, I have seen Planks sawn of this Wood, but 'tis not found durable in the Weather, yet pretty enough for many other Uses.

Bay and Laurel generally delight in a low, swampy Ground. I

know no Use they make of them but for Fire-Wood, excepting what I spoke of before, amongst the Ever-Greens.

A famous Ever-Green I must now mention, which was forgotten amongst the rest. It is in Leaf like a Jessamine, but larger and of a harder Nature. This grows up to a large Vine, and twists itself round the Trees it grows near, making a very fine Shade. I never saw any thing of that Nature out-do it, and if it be cut away close to the Ground it will presently spring up again, it being impossible to destroy it when once it has got Root. 'Tis an ornamental Plant and worth the Transplanting. Its Seed is a black Berry.

The Scarlet Trumpet-Vine bears a glorious red Flower like a Bell or Trumpet, and makes a Shade inferiour to none that I ever saw; yet it leaves us when the Winter comes and remains naked till the next Spring. It bears a large Cod that holds its Seed.

The Maycock bears a glorious Flower, and Apple of an agreeable Sweet, mixt with an acid Taste. This is also a Summer-Vine.

The Indico grows plentifully in our Quarters.

The Bay-Tulip-Tree is a fine Ever-green which grows frequently here.

The sweet Gum-Tree, so called Because of the fragrant Gum it yields in the Spring-time upon Incision of the Bark or Wood. It cures the Herpes and Inflamations, being applied to the Morphew and Tettars. 'Tis an extraordinary Balsam, and of great Value to those who know how to use it. No Wood has scarce a better Grain; whereof fine Tables, Drawers, and other Furniture might be made. Some of it is curiously curled. It bears a round Bur, with a sort of Prickle, which is the Seed.

Of the Black Gum, there grows with us two sorts, both fit for Cart-Naves. The one bears a black, well tasted Berry, which the Indians mix with their Pulse and Soups, it giving them a pretty Flavour and scarlet Colour. The Bears crop these Trees for the Berries, which they mightily covet, yet killed in that Season, they eat very unsavory, which must be occasioned by this Fruit, because at other times, when they feed on Mast, Bears-Flesh is a very well tasted Food. The other Gum bears a berry in shape like the others, though bitter and ill tasted. This Tree (the Indians report) is never wounded by Lightning. It has no certain Grain, and it is almost impossible to split or rive it.

The white Gum, bearing a sort of long bunched Flowers, is the most curled and knotted Wood I ever saw, which would make curious Furniture in case it was handled by a good Workman.

The red sort of Cedar is an Ever Green of which Carolina affords plenty. That on the Salts grows generally on the Sand-banks, and that in the Freshes is found in the Swamps. Of this Wood Tables, Wainscot and other Necessaries are made, and esteemed for its sweet smell. It is as durable a Wood as any we have, therefore much used in Posts for Houses and Sills; likewise, to build Sloops, Boats, &c., by reason the Worm will not touch it for several Years. The Vessels built thereof are very durable and good Swimmers. Of this Cedar Ship-loads may be exported. It has been heretofore so plentiful in this Settlement, that they have fenced in Plantations with it, and the Coffins of the Dead are generally made thereof.

White Cedar, so called because it nearly approaches the other Cedar in Smell, Bark and Leaf; only this grows taller, being as straight as an Arrow. It is extraordinary light and free to rive. 'Tis good for Yard, Top-Masts, Booms and Bolt-sprits, being very tough. The best Shingles for Houses are made of this Wood, it being no Strain to the Roof and never rots. Good Pails and other Vessels free from Leakage, are likewise made thereof. The Bark of this and the red Cedar, the Indians use to make their Cabins of, which prove firm and resist all Weathers.

Cypress is not an Ever Green with us, and is therefore called the bald Cypress, because the Leaves, during the Winter-Season turn red, not recovering their Verdure till the Spring. These Trees are the largest for Height and Thickness, that we have in this Part of the World; some of them holding thirty-six foot in Circumference. Upon Incision they yield a sweet-smelling grain, though not in great Quantities; and the Nuts which these Trees bear plentifully, yield a most odoriferous Balsam, that infallibly cures all new and green Wounds which the Inhabitants are well acquainted withal. Of these great Trees the Pereaugers and Canoes are scooped and made, which sort of Vessels are chiefly to pass over the Rivers, Creeks, and Bays, and to transport Goods and Lumber from one River to another. Some are so large as to carry thirty Barrels, though of one entire Piece of Timber. Others that are split down the Bottom and a piece added thereto, will carry eighty or an hundred. Several have gone out of our Inlets on the Ocean to Virginia, laden with Pork and other Produce of the Country. Of these Trees curious Boats for Pleasure may be made, and other necessary Craft. Some years ago a foolish Man in Albemarl and his Son had got one of these Canoes decked. She held, as I take it, sixteen Barrels. He brought her to the Collectors to be cleared for Barbados, but the Officer took him for a Man that had lost his Senses, and argued the Danger and Impossibility of performing such a Voyage in a hollow Tree, but the Fellow would hearken to no Advice of that kind, till the Gentleman told him if he did not value his own Life, he valued his Reputation and Honesty, and so flatly refused clearing him; Upon which the Canoe was sold, and, I think, remains in being still. This Wood is very lasting, and free from the Rot. A Canoe of it will outlast four Boats, and seldom wants Repair. They say that a Chest made of this Wood will suffer no Moth or Vermine to abide therein.

The Locust for its enduring the Weather, is chosen for all sorts of Works that are exposed thereto. It bears a Leaf nearest the Liquoric-Plant. Tis a pretty tall Tree. Of this the Indians make their choicest Bows, it being very tough and flexible. We have little or none of this Wood in Pampticough.

The Honey-Tree bears as great a Resemblance to the Locust, as a Shallot does to an onion. It is of that Species but more prickly. They bear a Cod, one side whereof contains the Seed, the other the Honey. They will bear in five years from the Kernel. They were first brought (by the Indian Traders) and propagated by their

Seed, at the Apamaticks in Virginia. Last Year I planted the Seed, and had them sprung up before I came from thence, which was in August. Of the Honey, very good Metheglin is made, there being Orchards planted in Virginia for that intent.

The Sorrel, or Sowr-Wood-Tree, is so called because the Leaves taste like Sorrell. Some are about a Foot or ten inches Diameter. I am unacquainted with its Vertues at present.

Of Pines, there are in Carolina, at least four sorts. The Pitch-Pine, growing to a great Bigness, most commonly has but a short Leaf. Its Wood (being replete with abundance of Bitumen) is so durable, that it seems to suffer no Decay, though exposed to all Weathers, for many Ages; and is used in several Domestic and Plantation Uses. This Tree affords the four great Necessaries, Pitch, Tar, Rosin and Turpentime; which two last are extracted by tapping and the Heat of the Sun, the other two by the Heat of the Fire.

The white and yellow Pines are sawed into Planks for several Uses. They make Masts, Yards, and a great many other necessaries therewith, the Pine being the most useful Tree in the Woods.

The Almond-Pine serves for Masts very Well. As for the Dwarf-Pine, it is for Shew alone, being an Ever green, as they all are.

The Hiccory is of the Walnut-kind, and bears a Nut as they do, of which there are found three sorts. The first is that which we call the common white hiccory. It is not a durable Wood; for if cut down and exposed to the Weather, it will be quite rotten, and spoiled in three Years, as will likewise the Beech of this Country. Hiccory Nuts have very hard Shells, but excellent, sweet Kernels, with which, in a plentiful Year, the old Hogs, that can crack them, fatten themselves, and make excellent Pork. These Nuts are gotten in great Quantities, by the Savages, and laid up for Stores, of which they make several Dishes and Banquets. One of these I cannot forbear mentioning; it is this: They take these Nuts, and break them very small betwixt two Stones, till the Shells and Kernels are indifferent small; And this Powder you are presented withal in their Cabins, in little wooden Dishes; the Kernel dissolves in your Mouth, and the Shell is spit out. This tastes as well as any Almond. Another Dish is the Soup which they make of these Nuts, beaten, and put into Venison-Broth, which dissolves the Nut and thickens, whilst the Shell precipitates, and remains at the bottom. This Broth tastes very rich. There is another sort, which we call red Hiccory, the Heart thereof being very red, firm and durable; of which Walking-Sticks, Mortars, Pestils, and several other fine Turnery-wares are made; The third is called the Flying-barked Hiccory, from its brittle and scaly Bark. It bears a Nut with a bitter Kernel, and a soft Shell, like a French Walnut. Of this Wood Coggs for Mills are made, &c. The Leaves smell very fragrant.

The Walnut-Tree of America is called Black Walnut. I suppose that Name was, at first, to distinguish it from the Hiccories, it having a blacker Bark. This Tree grows in good Land, to a prodigious Bigness. The Wood is very firm and durable, of which Tables and Chests of Drawers are made, and prove very well. Some of this is very knotty, which would make the best Returns for England, though the Masters of Vessels refuse it, not understanding its Goodness. Tis a very good and durable Wood, to bottom Vessels for the Sea withal; and they say that it is never eaten by the Worm. The Nuts have a large Kernel, which is very oily, except lain by, a long time, to mellow. The Shell is very thick, as all the native Nuts of America are. When it has its yellow outward Coat on, it looks and smells much like a Lemon.

The Maple, of which we have two sorts, is used to make Trenchers, Spinning-wheels, &c., withal.

Chinkapin is a sort of Chesnut, whose Nuts are most commonly very plentiful, insomuch that the Hogs get fat with them. They are rounder and smaller than a Chesnut, but much sweeter. The Wood is much of the Nature of Chesnut, having a Leaf and Grain almost like it. It is used to timber Boats, Shallops, &c., and makes anything that is to endure the Weather. This and the Hiccory are very tough Rods, used to whip Horses withal; yet their Wood in Substance is very brittle. This Tree the Vine much delights to twist about. Its good Fire-Wood but very sparkling, as well as Sassafras.

The Birch grows all on the Banks of our Rivers, very high up. I never saw a Tree on the Salts. It differs something in Bark, from the European Birch. Its Buds in April are eaten by the Parrakeetos, which resort from all Parts at that Season to feed thereon. Where this Wood grows we are not yet seated; and as to the Wine or other Profits it would yield, we are, at present, Strangers to.

The Willow here likewise differs both in Bark and Leaf. It is frequently found on the Banks of fresh Water, as the Birch is.

The Sycamore in these Parts grows in a low, swampy Land, by River-sides. Its Bark is quite different from the English, and the most beautiful I ever saw, being mòttled and clowded with several Colours, as white, blue, &c. It bears no Keys but a Bur like the sweet Gum. Its Uses I am ignorant of.

I never saw any Aspin but in Rapahannock-River, from whence I brought one, (that was presented me there as a great Present) but it died by the way.

Of Holly we have two sorts; one having a large Leaf, the other a smaller. They grow very thick in our low Woods. Many of them are very straight and two Foot Diameter. They make good Trenchers and other Turnery-Ware.

The Red-Bud-Tree bears a purple Lark-Heel, and is the best Sallad of any Flower I ever saw. It is ripe in April and May. They grow in Trees generally small, but some are a Foot Diameter.

Pelletory grows on the Sand-Banks and Islands. It is used to cure the Tooth-ach by putting a Piece of the Bark in the Mouth, which being very hot draws a Rhume from the Mouth, and causes much Spittle. The Indians use it to make their Composition, which they give to their young Men and Boys when they are husquenawed, of which you shall hear farther when I come to treat of the Customs, &c., of that People.

Arrow-Wood growing on the Banks, is used by the Indians for Arrows and Gun-Sticks. It grows as straight as if plained, and is of all Sizes. 'Tis as tough and pliable as the smallest Canes.

The Chesnut-Tree of Carolina grows up towards the hilly Part thereof, is a very large and durable Wood, and fit for House-Frames, Palisado's Sills, and many other Uses. The Nut is smaller than those from Portugal, but sweeter.

This is no Tree but called the Oak-Vine, by reason it bears a sort of Bur as the Oak does, and generally runs up those Trees. It is so porous that you suck Liquors through a Length of two Foot.

Prickly-Ash grows up like a Pole, of which the Indians and English make Poles to set their Canoes along in Shoal-Water. It is very light, and full of Thorns or Prickles, bearing Berries in large Clusters of a purple Colour, not much unlike the Alder. The Root of this Tree is Cathartick and Emetick, used in Cachexies.

The Poison Vine is so called because it colours the Hands of those who handle it. What Effects of it may be, I cannot relate, neither do I believe that any has made an Experiment thereof. The Juice of this will stain Linnen never to wash out. It marks a blackish blue Colour, which is done only by breaking a bit of the Vine off, and writing what you please therewith. I have thought that the East India Natives set their Colours by some such Means, into their finest Calicoes. It runs up any Tree it meets withal, and clasps round about it. The Leaves are like Hemlock, and fall off in Winter.

Of Canes and Reeds we have many sorts. The hollow Reed or Cane, such as Angling-Rods are made of and Weavers use, we have great Plenty of, though none to the Northward of James-River in Virginia. They always grow in Branches and low Ground; Their Leaves endure the Winter, in which Season our Cattle eat them greedily. We have them (towards the Heads of our Rivers) so large that one Joint will hold above a pint of Liquor.

The small Bamboo is next, which is a certain Vine, like the rest of these Species, growing in low Land. They seldom, with us, grow thicker than a Man's little Finger, and are very tough. Their Root is a round Ball which the Indians boil as we do Garden-Roots, and eat them. When these Roots have been sometime out of the Ground they become hard and make good Heads to the Canes, on which several pretty Figures may be cut. There are several others of this kind, not thoroughly discovered.

That Palmeto grows with us which we call the dwarfish sort, but the Palmeto Tree I have not yet met withal in North-Carolina, of which you have a Description elsewhere. We shall next treat of the Spontaneous Fruits of this Country; and then proceed to those that have been transplanted from Europe and other Parts.

Among the natural Fruits, the Vine first takes place, of which I find six sorts, very well known. The first is the black Bunch-Grapes which yield a Crimson Juice. These grow common and bear plentifully. They are of a good Relish, though not large, yet well knit in the Clusters. They have a thickish Skin and large Stones, which makes them not yield much Juice. There is another sort of Black Grapes like the former in all respects, save that their Juice is of a light Flesh-Colour, inclining to a White. I once saw a Spontaneous white Bunch-Grape in Carolina; but the Cattle browzing on the Sprouts thereof in the Spring it died. Of those which we call Fox-Grapes, we have four sorts; two whereof are called Summer-Grapes, because ripe in July; the other two Winter-Fruits, because not ripe till September or October. The Summer Fox-Grapes grow not in Clusters or great Bunches, but are about five or six in a Bunch, about the Bigness of a Damson or larger. The black sort are frequent, the white not so commonly found. They always grow in Swamps and low, moist Lands, running sometimes very high and being shady, and therefore proper for Arbours. They afford the largest Leaf I ever saw to my remembrance, the Back of which is of a white Horse-flesh Colour. This Fruit always ripens in the Shade. I have transplanted them into my Orchard and find they thrive well, if manured. A Neighbor of mine has done the same; mine were by Slips, his from the Roots, which thrive to Admiration, and bear Fruit, though not so juicy as the European Grape, but of a glutinous Nature. However it is pleasant enough to eat.

The other Winter Fox-Grapes are much of the same Bigness. These refuse no Ground, swampy or dry, but grow plentifully on the Sand-Hills along the Sea-Coast and elsewhere, and are great Bearers. I have seen near twelve Bushels upon one Vine of the black sort. Some of these, when thoroughly ripe, have a very pretty vinous Taste and eat very well, yet are glutinous. The white sort are clear and transparant, and indifferent small Stones. Being removed by the Slip or Root, they thrive well in our Gardens, and make pleasant Shades.

Persimmons is a Tree that agrees with all Lands and Soils. Their Fruit, when ripe, is nearest our Medlar; if eaten before, draws your Mouth up like a Purse, being the greatest Astringent I ever met withal, therefore very useful in some Cases. The Fruit if ripe, will presently cleanse a foul Wound but causes Pain. The Fruit is rotten, when ripe, and commonly contains four flat Kernels, called Stones, which is the Seed. 'Tis said the Cortex Peruvianus comes from a Persimmon-Tree that grows in New-Spain. I have tried the Drying of this Bark, to imitate it, which it does tolerably well, and agrees therewith. It is binding enough to work the same Effect. The Tree in extraordinary Land, comes sometimes to two Foot Diameter, though not often. There are two sorts of this Fruit; one ripe in Summer, the other when the Frost visits us.

We have three sorts of Mulberries, besides the different Bigness of some Trees' Fruit. The first is the common red Mulberry, whose Fruit is the earliest we have (except the Strawberries) and very sweet. These Trees make a very fine Shade to sit under in Summertime. They are found wild in great Quantities, wherever the Land is light and rich; yet their Fruits is much better when they stand open. They are used instead of Raisins and Currants, and make several pretty Kickshaws. They yield a transparent Crimson Liquor, which would make good Wine; but few People's Inclinations in this Country tend that way. The others are a smooth leaved Mulberry, fit for the Silk-Worm. One bears a white Fruit, which is common; the other bears a small black Berry, very sweet. They would persuade me there, that the black Mulberry with the Silk-Worm smooth leaf, was a white Mulberry, and changed its Fruit.

The Wood hereof is very durable, and where the Indians cannot get Locust, they make use of this to make their Bows. This Tree grows extraordinary round and pleasant to the eye.

The Hiccory, Walnut, Chinkapin, and Chesnut, with their Fruits, we have mentioned before.

The Hazle-Nut grows plentifully in some places of this Country, especially towards the Mountains; but ours are not so good as the English Nuts, having a much thicker Shell (like all the fruits of America, that I have met withal) which in Hardness exceeds those in Europe.

The Cherries of the Woods grow to be very large Trees. One sort which is rarely found, is red, and not much unlike the Cornel-Berry. But the common Cherry grows high and in Bunches, like English Currants, but much larger. They are of a bitterish, sweet Relish, and are equally valuable with our small Black-Cherries for an Infusion in Spirits. They yield a crimson Liquor and are great Bearers.

Our Rasberries are of a purple Colour, and agreeable Relish, almost like the English; but I reckon them not quite so rich. When once planted, tis hard to root them out. They run wild all over the Country, and will bear the same year you transplant them, as I have found by Experience.

The Hurts, Huckle-Berries, or Blues of this Country, are four sorts, which we are well acquainted withal; but more Species of this sort, and all others, Time and Enquiry must discover. The first sort is the same Blue or Bilberry, that grows plentifully in the North of England, and in other Places, commonly on your Heaths, Commons, and Woods, where Brakes or Fern grows.

The second sort grows on a small Bush in our Savannas and Meads, and in the Woods. They are larger than the common Fruit, and have larger Seed.

The third grows on the single Stem of a Stick that grows in low good Land, and on the Banks of Rivers. They grow three or four Foot high, and are very pleasant, likt the first sort but larger.

The fourth sort grows upon Trees, some ten and twelve Foot high, and the Thickness of a Man's Arm; these are found in the Runs and low Grounds, and are very pleasant and bear wonderfully. The English sometimes dry them in the Sun, and keep them to use in Winter, instead of Currants. The Indians get many Bushels and dry them on Mats, whereof they make Plum-Bread, and many other Eatables. They are good in Tarts, or infused in Liquors.

In the same Ground, commonly grows the Piemento, or All-Spice-Tree, whose Berries differ in shape from those in the West-Indies, being Taper or Conick, yet not inferior to any of that sort. This Tree grows much like the Hurts, and is of the same Bigness. I have known it transplanted to the high Land, where it thrives.

Our Dew-Berries are very good, but the Black-Berries are bitter-ish, and not so palatable, as in England.

The Sugar-Tree ought to have taken place before. It is found in no other parts of Carolina or America, that I ever learned, but in Places that are near the Mountains. It is most like one sort of Maple of any Tree, and may be ranked amongst that kind. This Tree, which I am told, is of very tedious Growth, is found very plenti-fully towards the Heads of some of our Rivers. The Indians tap it and make Gourds to receive the Liquor, which Operation is done at distinct and proper times, when it best yields its Juice, of which when the Indians have gotten enough, they carry it home, and boil it to a just Consistence of Sugar, which grains of itself, and serves for the same Uses, as other Sugar does.

The Papau is not a large Tree. I think I never saw one a Foot through; but has the broadest Leaf of any Tree in the Woods, and bears an Apple about the bigness of a Hen's-Egg, yellow, soft, and as sweet as any thing can well be. They make rare Puddings of this Fruit. The Apple contains a large Stone.

The wild Fig grows in Virginia, up in the Mountains, as I am informed by a Gentleman of my acquaintance, who is a person of Credit, and a great Traveler in America. I shall be glad to have an Opportunity to make Trial what Improvement might be made of this wild Fruit.

The wild Plums of America are of several sorts. Those which I can give account of from my own Knowledge, I will, and leave the others till a farther Discovery. The most frequent is that which we call the common Indian Plum, of which there are two sorts, if not more. One of these is ripe much sooner than the other, and differs in the Bark; one of the Barks being very scaly, like our American Birch. These Trees, when in Blossom, smell as sweet as any Jessamine, and look as white as a Sheet, being something prickly. You may make it grow to what Shape you please; they are very ornamental about a House, and make a wonderful fine Shew at a Distance, in the Spring, because of their white Livery. Their Fruit is red, and very palatable to the sick. They are of a quick Growth, and will bear from the Stone in five Years, on their Stock. The English, large black Plum thrives well, as does the Cherry, being grafted thereon.

The American Damsons are both black and white and about the Bigness of an European Damson. They grow anywhere if planted from the Stone or Slip; bear a white Blossom, and are a good Fruit. They are found on the Sand-Banks all along the Coast of America. I have planted several in my Orchard, that come from the Stone, which thrive well amongst the rest of my Trees. But they never grow to the Bigness of the other Trees now spoken of. These are plentiful Bearers.

There is a third sort of Plum about the Bigness of the Damsons. The Tree is taller, seldom exceeding ten Inches in Thickness. The Plum seems to taste physically, yet I never found any Operation it had, except to make their Lips sore, that eat them. The Wood is something porous, but exceeds any Box, for a beautiful Yellow.

There is a very pretty, bushy Tree, about seven or eight Foot high, very spreading, which bears a Winter-Fruit, that is ripe in October. They call them Currants, but they are nearer a Hurt; I have eaten very pretty Tarts made thereof. They dry them instead of Currants. This Bush is very beautiful.

The Bermudos Currants grow in the Woods on a Bush, much

like the European Currant. Some People eat them very much; but for my part, I can see nothing inviting in them, and reckon them a very indifferent Fruit.

We have another Currant, which grows on the Banks of Rivers, or where only Clay hath been thrown up. This Fruit is red, and gone almost as soon as come. They are a pretty Fruit whilst they last, and the Tree (for tis not a Bush) they grow upon, is a very pleasant Vegetable.

The Haw-thorn grows plentifully in some parts of this Country. The Haws are quite different from those in England, being four times as big, and of a very pleasant agreeable Taste. We make no use of this Plant, nor any other, for Hedges because Timber is so plentiful at present. In my Judgement, the Honey-Locust would be the fittest for Hedges; because it is very apt to shoot forth many Sprouts and Succours from the Roots, besides, it is of a quick Growth, and very prickly.

The Black Haw grows on a slender Tree, about the Height of a Quince-Tree, or something higher and bears the black Haw, which People eat, and the Birds covet also. What Vertues the Fruit or Wood is of, I cannot resolve you at present.

Thus have I given an Account of all the Spontaneous Fruits of Carolina, that have come to my Knowledge, excepting Services, which I have seen in the Indians' Hands and eat of them, but never saw how, nor where they grow. There may very well be expected a great many more Fruits, which are the natural Product of this Country, when we consider the Fruitfulness of the Soil and Climate, and account for the vast Tract of Land, (great part of which is not yet found out) according to the Product of that which is already discovered, which, as I once hinted before, is not yet arrived to our Knowledge, we having very little or no Correspondence amongst the mountainous Parts of this Province, and towards the Country of Missiassippi, all which we have strange Accounts of, and some very large ones, with respect to the different and noble Fruits, and several other Ornaments and Blessings of Nature which Missiasippi possesses; more to be coveted, than any of those we enjoy, to the Eastward of the Mountains. Yet when I came to discourse some of the Idolizers of that Country, I found it to be rather Novelty than Truth and reality, that induced those Persons to allow it such Excellencies above others. It may be a brave and fertile Country, as I believe it is; but I cannot be persuaded that it can be near so advantageous as ours, which is much better situated for Trade, being faced all along with the Ocean, as the English America is; when the other is only a direct River, in the midst of a wild unknown Land, greatest part of whose Product must be fetched, or brought a great way, before it can come to a Market. Moreover, such great Rivers commonly allow of more Princes' Territories than one, and thus nothing but War and Contention accompanies the Inhabitants thereof.

But not to trouble our Readers with any more of this, we will proceed, in the next place, to show, what Exotic Fruits we have, that thrive well in Carolina, and what others it may reasonably be supposed would do there, were they brought thither and planted In pursuance of which I will set down a Catalogue of what Fruits we have; I mean Species. For should I pretend to give a regular Name to every one, it's neither possible for me to do it, nor for any one to understand it when done, if we consider that the chiefest part of our Fruit came from the Kernel, and some others from the Succours, or Sprouts of the Tree. First, we will begin with the Apples, which are the

> Golden Russet,
>
> Pearmain, {Winter,
> {Summer,
>
> Harvey Apple. I cannot tell, whether the same as in
>   England.
> Winter Queening,
> Leather Coat,
> Juniting,
> Codlin,

Redstreak,

Long Stalk,

Lady Finger.

The Golden Russet thrives well.

The Pearmains of both sorts, are apt to speck and rot on the Trees; and the Trees are damaged and cut off by the Worm, which breeds in the Forks and other parts thereof; and often makes a Circumposition, by destroying the Bark round the Branches till it dies.

Harvey-Apple—that which we call so, is esteemed very good to make Cider of.

Winter Queening is a durable Apple, and makes good Cider.

Leather Coat—both Apple and Tree stand well.

The Juniting is early ripe, and soon gone in these warm Countries.

Codlin—no better aand fairer Fruit in the World; yet the Tree suffers the same Distemper as the Pearmains, or rather worse; the Trees always dying before they come to their Growth.

The Redstreak thrives very well.

Long-Stalk is a large Apple with a long Stalk, and makes good Summer Cider.

We beat the first of our Codlin Cider against reaping our Wheat, which is from the tenth of June to the five and twentieth.

Lady-Finger, the long Apple, the same as in England and full as good. We have innumerable sorts; some called Rope-Apples, which are small Apples, hanging like Ropes of Onion; Flattings, Grigsons, Cheese-Apples and a great number of Names, given according to every one's Discretion.

The Warden-Pear here grows a good eating Pear, and is not so long ripening as in England.

Katharine, excellent.

Sugar-Pear.

And several others without Name. The Bergamot we have not, nor either of the Bonne Chrestiennes, though I hear they are all three in Virginia. Those sorts of Pears which we have, are as well relished as ever I eat any where. But that Fruit is of very short Continuance with us, for they are gone almost as soon as ripe.

I am not a Judge of the different sorts of Quinces, which they call Brunswick, Portugal and Barbary; But as to the Fruit in general, I believe no Place has fairer and better relish. They are very pleasant eaten raw. Of this Fruit, they make a Wine, or Liquor, which they call Quince-Drink, and which I approve of beyond any Drink which that Country affords, though a great deal of Cider and some Perry is there made. The Quince-Drink most commonly purges those that first drink it and cleanses the Body very well. The Arguments of the Physicians, that they bind People is hereby contradicted, unless we allow the Quinces to differ in the two Countries. The least Slip of this Tree stuck in the Ground, comes to bear in three years.

All Peaches with us are standing; neither have we any Wall-Fruit in Carolina, for we have Heat enough, and therefore do not require it. We have a great many sorts of this Fruit, which all thrive to Admiration, Peach-Trees coming to Perfection, (with us), as easily as the Weeds. A Peach falling to the Ground brings a Peach-Tree that shall bear in three years, or sometimes sooner. Eating Peaches in our Orchards makes them come up so thick from the Kernel, that we are forced to take a great deal of Care to weed them out, otherwise they make our Land a Wilderness of Peach-Trees. They generally bear so full that they break great part of their Limbs down. We have likewise very fair Nectarines, especially the red, that clings to the Stone; the other yellow Fruit, that leaves the Stone. Of the last, I have a Tree that most Years brings me fifteen or twenty Bushels. I see no Foreign Fruit like this, for thriving in all sorts of Land, and bearing its Fruit to Admiration. I want to be satisfied about one sort of this Fruit, which the Indians claim as their own, and affirm they had it growing amongst them before any Europeans came to America. The Fruit I will describe as exactly as I can. The Tree grows very large, most commonly as big as a handsome Apple-tree; the flowers are of a redish, murrey Colour, the

Fruit is rather more downy than the yellow Peach, and commonly very large and soft, being very full of Juice. They part freely from the Stone, and the Stone is much thicker than all the other Peach Stones we have, which seems to me that it is a Spontaneous Fruit of America; yet in those Parts of America that we inhabit, I never could hear that any Peach-Trees were ever found growing in the Woods; neither have the foreign Indians, that live remote from the English, any other sort. And those living amongst us have a hundred of this sort for one other; they are a hardy Fruit, and are seldom damaged by the North-East Blast, as others are. Of this sort we make Vinegar; wherefore we call them Vinegar Peaches, and sometimes Indian Peaches.

This Tree grows to a vast Bigness, exceeding most Apple-Trees. They bear well, though sometimes an early Spring comes on in February, and perhaps when the Tree is fully blown, the Cloudy, North-East Winds, which attend the end of that Month, or the beginning of March, destroy most of the Fruit. The biggest Apricot-Tree I ever saw, as they told me, was grafted on a Peach-Stock in the Ground. I know of no other sort with us, than the Common. We generally raise this Fruit from the Stone, which never fails to bring the same, Fruit. Likewise our Peach-Stones effect the same, without so much as once missing to produce the same sort that the Stones came from.

Damson, Damazeen, and a large, round black Plum are all I have met withal in Carolina. They thrive well enough; the last to Admiration, and becomes a very large Tree, if in stiff Ground; otherwise they will not do well.

Of Figs we have two sorts. One is the low Bush-Fig, which bears a large Fruit. If the Winter happens to have much Frost, the tops thereof die, and in the Spring sprout again, and bear two or three good Crops.

The Tree-Fig is a lesser Fig, though very sweet. The Tree grows to a large Body and Shade, and generally brings a good Burden; especially if in light Land. This Tree thrives no where better than on the Sand-Banks by the Sea.

We have the common, red and black Cherry, which bear well. I never saw any grafted in this Country, the common excepted, which was grafted on an Indian Plum-Stock, and bore well. This is a good way, because our Common Cherry-Trees are very apt to put Scions all around the Tree for a great Distance, which must needs be prejudicial to the Tree and the Fruit. Not only our Cherries are apt to do so, but our Apples and most other Fruit-Trees, which may chiefly be imputed to the Negligence and Unskillfulness of the Gardener. Our Cherries are ripe a Month sooner than in Virginia.

Gooseberries I have seen of the smaller sort, but find they do not do so well as in England, and to the Northward. Want of Dressing may be some Reason for this.

Currants, White, Red and Black, thrive here, as well as any where.

Rasberries, the red and white, I never saw any Trial made of. But there is no doubt of their thriving to Admiration, since those of the Country do so well.

The Mulberries are spontaneous. We have no others than what I have already mentioned in the Class of Natural Fruits of Carolina.

Barberry red, with Stones, and without Stones, grow here.

Strawberries, not Foreign, but those of the Country, grow here in great Plenty. Last April I planted a Bed of two hundred Foot in Length, which bore the same Year.

Medlars we have none.

All sorts of Walnuts from England, France and Maderas thrive well from the Nut.

No Filberts, but Hazle-Nuts; the Filbert-Nut planted, becomes a good Hazle-Nut, and no better.

As for that noble Vegetable, the Vine, without doubt, it may (in this Country) be improved, and brought to the same Perfection, as it is, at this Day, in the same Latitude in Europe, since the chiefest part of this Country is a deep, rich, black Mould, which is up towards the Freshes and Heads of our Rivers, being very rich and mixed with Flint, Pebbles and other Stones. And this sort of Soil is approved of (by all knowing Gardeners and Vigneroons,) as a proper Earth, in which the Grape chiefly delights; and what seems to give farther Confirmation hereof, is that the largest Vines that were ever discovered to grow wild, are found in those Parts, oftentimes in such Plenty, and are so interwoven with one another, that tis impossible to pass through them. Moreover, in these Freshes, towards the Hills, the Vines are above five times bigger than those generally with us, who are seated in the Front-parts of this Country, adjoining to the Salts. Of the wild Vines, which are most of them great Bearers, some Wine has been made, which I drank of. It was very strong and well relished, but what detains them all from offering at great quantities, they add, that this Grape has a large Stone, and a thick Skin, and consequently yields but a small quantity of Wine. Some Essays of this Nature have been made by that Honorable Knight, Sir Nathaniel Johnson, in South Carolina, who, as I am informed, has rejected all Exotick Vines, and makes his Wine from the natural black Grape of Carolina, by grafting it upon its own Stock. What Improvement this may arrive to I cannot tell; but in other Species, I own Grafting and Imbudding yields speedy Fruit, though I never found that it made them better.

New planted Colonies are generally attended with a Force, and Necessity of Planting the known and approved Staple and Product of the Country, as well as all the Provisions their Families spend. Therefore we can entertain but small hopes of the Improvement of the Vine, till some skillful in dressing Vines shall appear amongst us, and go about it with a Resolution, that Ordering the Vineyard shall be one half of their Employment. If this be begun, and carried on, with that Assiduity and Resolution which it requires, then we may reasonably hope to see this a Wine-Country; for then, when it becomes a general Undertaking; every one will be capable to add something to the common Stock, of that which he has gained by his own Experience. This way would soon make the Burden light, and a great many shorter and exacter Curiosities, and real Truths would be found out in a short time. The trimming of Vines, as they do in France, that is, to a Stump, must either here be not followed, or we are not sensible of the exact time, when they ought to be thus pruned; for Experience has taught us, that the European Grape, suffered to run and expand itself at large, has been found to bear, as well in America as it does in Europe; when at the same time, the same sort of Vine trimmed to a Stump, as before spoken of, has born a poor Crop for one Year or two; and by its spilling, after cutting, emaciated, and in three or four Years died. This Experiment, I believe has never failed; for I have trimmed the natural Vine the French way, which has been attended at last, with the same Fate. Wherefore, it seems most expedient, to leave the Vines more Branches here, than in Europe, or let them run up Trees, as some do, in Lombardy, upon Elms. The Mulberries and Chinkapin are tough, and trimmed to what you please, therefore fit Supporters of the Vines. Gelding and plucking away the Leaves, to hasten the ripening of this Fruit, may not be unnecessary, yet we see the natural wild Grape generally ripens in the Shade. Nature in this, and many others, may prove a sure Guide. The Twisting of the Stems to make the Grapes ripe together, loses no Juice, and may be beneficial, if done in Season. A very ingenious French Gentleman, and another from Switzerland, with whom I frequently converse, exclaim against that strict cutting of Vines, the generally approved Method of France and Germany, and say, that they were both out in their Judgement, till of late, Experience has taught them otherwise. Moreover, the French in North Carolina assure me, that if we should trim our Apple and other Fruit-Trees, as they do in Europe, we should spoil them. As for Apples and Plums, I have found by Experience, what they affirm to be true. The French, from the Mannakin Town or Freshes of James River in Virginia, had, for the most part, removed themselves to Carolina, to live there, before I came away; and the rest were following, as their minister, (Monsieur Philip de Rixbourg) told me, who was at Bath-Town, when I was taking my leave of my Friends. He assured me, that their Intent was to propagate Vines, as far as their present Circumstances would permit; provided they could get any Slips of Vines, that would do. At the same time I had gotten some Grape-Seed, which was of the Jesuits white Grape from Madera. The Seed came up very plentifully, and, I hope, will not degenerate, which if it happens not to do, the Seed may prove the best way to raise a Vineyard, as certainly it is most easy for Transportation. Yet I reckon we should have our Seed from a Country, where the Grape arrives to the utmost Perfection of Ripeness. These French Refuges have had small Encouragement in Virginia, because, at their first coming over, they took their Measures of Living, from Europe; which was all wrong; for the small Quantities of ten, fifteen, and twenty Acres to a Family did not hold out according to their way of Reckoning, by Reason they made very little or no Fodder; and the Winter there being much harder than with us, their Cattle failed; chiefly, because the English took up and surveyed all the Land round about them; so that they were hemmed in on all Hands from providing more Land for themselves or their Children, all which is highly prejudicial in America, where the generality are bred up to Planting. One of these French Men being a Fowling, shot a Fowl in the River, upon which his Dog went down the Bank to bring it to his Master; but the Bank was so high and steep that he could not get up again. Thereupon the French Man went down to help his Dog up, and breaking the Mould away accidentally with his feet, he discovered a very rich Coal-Mine. This Adventure he gave an Account of amongst the Neighborhood, and presently one of the Gentlemen of that Part surveyed the Land, and the poor French Man got nothing by his Discovery. The French are good Neighbors amongst us, and give Examples of Industry, which is much wanted in this Country. They make good Flax, Hemp, Linnen-Cloth and Thread, which they exchange amongst the Neighborhood for other Commodities for which they have occasion.

We have hitherto made no Tryal of foreign Herbage; but doubtless it would thrive well, especially Sanfoin, and those Grasses that endure Heat and dry Grounds. As for our Low-Lands, such as Marshes, Savannas and Pocoson-Ground, which lies low, all of them naturally afford good Land for Pasturage.

We will next treat of the Beasts which you shall have an Account of, as they have been discovered.

THE BEASTS OF CAROLINA ARE THE

Buffelo, or wild beef.
Bear.
Panther.
Catamount.
Wild cat.
Wolf.
Tiger.
Polcat.
Otter.
Bever.
Musk-Rat.
Possum.
Raccoon.
Minx.
Water-Rat.
Rabbet, two sorts.
Elks.
Stags.
Fallow-Deer.
Squirrel, four sorts.
Fox.
Lion and Jackall on the Lake.
Rats, two sorts.
Mice, two sorts.
Moles.
Weasel, Dormouse.
Bearmouse.

The Buffelo is a wild Beast of America, which has a Bunch on his Back as the Cattle of St. Laurence are said to have. He seldom appears amongst the English inhabitants, his chief Haunt being in the Land of Messiasippi, which is, for the most part, a plain Country; yet I have known some killed on the Hilly Part of Cape-Fair-River, they passing the Ledges of vast Mountains from the said Messiasippi, before they can come near us. I have eaten of their Meat, but do not think it so good as our Beef; yet the younger Calves are cried up for excellent Food, as very likely they may be. It is conjectured that these Buffelos, mixt in Breed with our tame Cattle, would much better the Breed for Largeness and Milk, which seems very probable. Of the wild Bull's Skin Buff is made. The Indians cut the Skins into Quarters for the Ease of their Transportation, and make Beds to lie on. They spin the Hair into Garters, Girdles, Sashes, aand the like, it being long and curled, and often of a chesnut or red Colour. These Monsters are found to weigh (as I am informed by a Traveler of Credit) from 1600 to 2400 Weight.

The Bears here are very common, though not so large as in Greenland, and the more Northern Countries of Russia. The Flesh of this Beast is very good and nourishing, and not inferior to the best Pork, in Taste. It stands betwixt Beef and Pork, and the young Cubs are a Dish for the greatest Epicure living. I prefer their Flesh before any Beef, Veal, Pork or Mutton, and they look as well as they eat, their fat being as white as Snow and the sweetest of any Creatures in the World. If a Man drink a Quart thereof, melted, it never will rise in his Stomach. We prefer it above all things to fry Fish and other things in. Those that are Strangers to it may judge otherwise, but I who have eaten a great deal of Bear's Flesh in my Life-time (since my being an Inhabitant in America) do think it equalizes, if not excels any Meat I ever eat in Europe. The Bacon made thereof is extraordinary Meat; but it must be well saved, otherwise it will rust. This Creature feeds upon all sorts of wild Fruits. When Herrings run, which is in March, the Flesh of such of those Bears as eat thereof, is naught all that Season, and eats filthily. Neither is it good when he feeds on Gum-berries as I intimated before. They are great Devourers of Acorns, and oftentimes meet the Swine in the Woods, which they kill and eat, especially when they are hungry and can find no other Food. Now and then they get into Fields of Indian Corn or Maiz, where they make a sad Havock, spoiling ten times as much as they eat. The Potatoes of this Country are so agreeable to them, that they never fail to sweep them all clean if they chance to come in their way. They are seemingly a very clumsy Creature, yet are very nimble in running up Trees and traversing every limb thereof. When they come down they run Tail foremost. At catching of Herrings, they are most expert Fishers. They sit by the Creek-sides, (which are very narrow) where the Fish run in, and there they take them up as fast as it is possible they can dip their Paws into the Water. There is one thing more to be considered of this Creature, which is, that no Man, either Christian or Indian, has ever killed a She-bear with Young.

It is supposed that the She-Bears, after conception, hide themselves in some secret and undiscoverable Place till they bring forth their Young, which, in all Probability, cannot be long; otherwise the Indians, who hunt the Woods like Dogs, would, at some time or other, have found them out. Bear-Hunting is a great Sport in America, both with the English and Indians. Some Years ago there were killed five hundred Bears in two Counties of Virginia in one Winter, and but two She-Bears amongst them all, which were not with Young, as I told you of the rest. The English have a breed of Dogs fit for this sport, about the size of Farmers' Curs, and, by Practice, come to know the Scent of a Bear, which as soon as they have found, they run him by the Nose till they come up with him and then bark and snap at him till he trees, when the Huntsman shoots him out of the Tree, there being, for the most part, two or three with Guns, lest the first should miss or not quite kill him. Though they are not naturally voracious, yet they are very fierce when wounded. The Dogs often bring him to a Bay when wounded, and then the Huntsmen make other Shots, perhaps with the Pistols that are stuck in their Girdles. If a Dog is apt to fasten and run into a Bear, he is not good, for the best Dog in Europe is nothing in their Paws; but if ever they get him in their Clutches, they blow his Skin from his Flesh like a Bladder, and often kill him; or if he recovers it he is never good for anything after. As the Paws of this Creature are held for the best bit about him, so is the Head esteemed the worst, and always thrown away, for what reason I know not. I believe none ever made Trial thereof, to know how it eats. The Oil of the Bear is very Sovereign for Strains, Aches and old Pains. The fine Fur at the bottom of the Belly is used for making Hats, in some places the Fur itself is fit for several Uses, as for making Muffs, facing Caps, &c., but the black Cub-skin is preferable to all sorts of that kind for Muffs. Its Grain is like Hog-Skin.

The Panther is of the Cat kind, about the height of a very large Greyhound of a reddish Colour, the same as a Lion. He climbs Trees with the greatest Agility imaginable, is very strong limbed, catching a piece of Meat from any Creature he strikes at. His Tail is exceeding long; his Eyes look very fierce and lively, are large and of a grayish Colour; his Prey is Swine's-Flesh, Deer, or anything he can take; no Creature is so nice and clean as this in his Food. When he has got his Prey he fills his Belly with the Slaughter and carefully lays up the Remainder, covering it very neatly with Leaves, which if anything touches, he never eats any more of it. He purrs as Cats do; if taken when Young is never to be reclaimed from his wild Nature. He hollows like a Man in the Woods when killed, which is by making him take a Tree, as the least Cur will presently do; then the Huntsmen shoot him; if they do not kill him outright, he is a dangerous Enemy when wounded, especially to the Dogs that approach him. This Beast is the greatest Enemy to the Planter of any Vermine in Carolina. His Flesh looks as well as any Shambles-Meat whatsoever; a great many People eat him as choice Food, but I never tasted of a Panther, so cannot commend the Meat by my own Experience. His Skin is a warm Covering for the Indians in Winter, though not esteemed amongst the choice Furs. This Skin dressed, makes fine Women's Shooes or Men's Gloves.

The Mountain-Cat, so called, because he lives in the Mountainous Parts of America. He is a Beast of Prey, as the Panther is, and nearest to him in Bigness and Nature.

This Cat is quite different from those in Europe; being more nimble and fierce, and larger; his Tail does not exceed four inches. He makes a very odd sort of Cry in the Woods, in the Night. He is spotted as the Leopard is, tho' some of them are not, (which may happen, when their Furs are out of Season) he climbs a Tree very dexterously, and preys as the Panther does. He is a great Destroyer of young Swine. I knew an Island, which was possessed by these Vermine, unknown to the Planter, who put thereon a considerable Stock of Swine; but never took one back, for the wild Cats destroyed them all. He takes most of his Prey by Surprise, getting up the Trees, which they pass by or under, and thence, leaping directly upon them. Thus he takes Deer (which he can not catch by running) and fastens his teeth into their Shoulders and sucks them. They run with him, till they fall down for want of strength, and become a Prey to the Enemy. Hares, Birds, and all he meets, that he can conquor, he destroys. The Fur is approved to wear as a Stomacher, for weak and cold Stomachs. They are likewise used to line Muffs and Coats withal in cold Climates.

The Wolf of Carolina, is the Dog of the Woods. The Indians had no other Curs, before the Christians came amongst them. They are made domestic. When wild they are neither so large nor fierce as the European Wolf. They are not Man-slayers, neither is any Creature in Carolina unless wounded. They go in great Droves in the Night to hunt Deer, which they do as well as the best Pack of Hounds. Nay, one of these will hunt down a Deer. They are often so poor that they can hardly run. When they catch no Prey, they go to a Swamp and fill their Belly full of Mud; if afterwards they chance to get any thing of Flesh, they will disgorge the Mud and eat the other. When they hunt in the Night that there is a great many together, they make the most hideous and frightful Noise that ever was heard. The Fur makes good Muffs. The Skin dressed to a Parchment makes the best Drum-Heads, and if tanned makes the best sort of Shooes for the summer Countries.

Tygers are never met withal in the Settlement, but are more to the Westward, and are not numerous on this Side of the Chain of Mountains. I once saw one that was larger than a Panther, and seemed to be a very bold Creature. The Indians that hunt in those Quarters, say they are seldom met withal. It seems to differ from the Tyger of Asia and Africa.

Polcats or Skunks in America are different from those in Europe. They are thicker and of a great many Colours, not all alike, but each differing from another in the particular Colour. They smell like a Fox but ten times stronger. When a Dog encounters them, they piss upon him, and he will not be sweet again in a Fortnight or more. The Indians love to eat their Flesh which has no manner of ill Smell when the Bladder is out. I know no use their Furs are put to. They are easily brought up tame.

There have been seen some Otters from the Westward of Carolina, which were of a white Colour, a little inclining to a yellow. They live on the same Prey here as in Europe, and are the same in all other Respects, so I shall insist no farther on that Creature, their Furs, if black, are valuable.

Bevers are very numerous in Carolina, there being abundance of their Dams in all Parts of the Country where I have traveled. They are the most industrious and greatest Artificers (in building their Dams and Houses) of any four footed Creatures in the World. Their Food is chiefly the Barks of Trees and Shrubs, viz: Sassafras, Ash, Sweet-Gum and several others. If you take them young they become very tame and domestic, but are very mischievous in spoiling Orchards by breaking the Trees and blocking up your Doors in the Night with the Sticks and Wood they bring thither. If they eat anything that is salt it kills them. Their Flesh is a sweet Food, especially their Tail, which is held very dainty. Their Fore-Feet are open like a Dog's; their Hind-Feet webbed like a Water-Fowl's. The Skins are good Furs for several Uses, which every one knows. The Leather is very thick; I have known Shooes made thereof in Carolina, which lasted well. It makes the best Hedgers Mittens that can be used.

Musk Rats frequent fresh Streams and no other, as the Bever does. He has a Cod of Musk which is valuable, as is likewise his Fur.

The Possum is found no where but in America. He is the Wonder of all the Land-Animals, being the size of a Badger, and near that Colour. The Male's Pizzle is placed in retrograde; and in time of coition, they differ from all other Animals, turning tail to tail as dog and bitch when tied. The Female doubtless breeds her young at her Teats; for I have seen them stick fast thereto when they have been no bigger than a small Rasberry, and seemingly inanimate. She has a Paunch, or false Belly, wherein she carries her Young, after they are from those Teats, till they can shift for themselves. Their Food is Roots, poultry or wild Fruits. They have no Hair on their Tails, but a sort of a scale or hard Crust, as the Bevers have. If a Cat has nine Lives, this Creature surely has nineteen; for if you break every Bone in their Skin, and mash their Skull leaving them for Dead, you may come an hour after, and they will be gone quite away, or perhaps you meet them creeping away. They are a very stupid Creature, utterly neglecting their Safety. They are most like Rats of any thing. I have, for Necessity in the Wilderness, eaten of them. Their Flesh is very white, and well tasted; but their ugly Tails put me out of Conceit with that Fare. They climb Trees as the Raccoons do. Their Fur is not esteemed nor used, save that the Indians spin it into Girdles and Garters.

The Raccoon is of a dark, grey Colour. If taken young, as easily made tame; but is the drunkenest Creature living, if he can get any Liquor that is sweet and strong. They are rather more unlucky than a Monkey. When wild, they are very subtle in catching their Prey. Those that Live in the Salt-Water, feed much on Oysters, which they love. They watch the Oyster when it opens, and nimbly put in their Paw and pluck out the Fish. Sometimes the Oyster shuts and holds fast their Paw till the tide comes in that they are drowned, though they swim very well. The way that this Animal catches Crabs, which he greatly admires, and which are plenty in Carolina, is worthy of Remark. When he intends to make a Prey of these Fish, he goes to a Marsh, where, standing on the Land, he lets his Tail hang in the Water. This the Crab takes for a Bait, and fastens his Claws therein, which as soon as the Raccoon perceives, he of a sudden springs forward a considerable way, on the Land, and brings the Crab along with him. As soon as the Fish finds himself out of his Element, he presently lets go his hold, and then the Raccoon encounters him, by getting him crosswise in his Mouth, and devours him. There is a sort of small, Land-Crab, which we call a Fiddler, that runs into a Hole when any thing pursues him. This Crab the Raccoon takes by putting his Fore-Foot in the hole and pulling him out. With a tame Raccoon, this Sport is very diverting. The Chief of his other Food is all sorts of wild Fruits, green Corn, and such as the Bear delights in. This and the Possum are much of a Bigness. The Fur makes good Hats and Linings. The Skin dressed makes fine Womens' Shooes.

The Minx is an Animal much like the English Fillimart or Polcat. He is long, slender and every way shaped like him. His Haunts are chiefly in the Marshes, by the Sea-side and Salt-Waters, where he lives on Fish, Fowl, Mice, and Insects. They are bold Thieves, and will steal anything from you in the Night, when asleep, as I can tell by Experience; for one Winter by Misfortune, I ran my Vessel aground, and went often to the Banks to kill wild Fowl, which we did a great many. One Night we had a mine to sleep on the Banks (the Weather being fair) and wrapt up the Geese which we had killed and not eaten, very carefully, in the Sail of a Canoe, and folded it several Doubles, and for their better Security, laid them all Night under my Head. In the Morning when I waked, a Minx had eaten through every Fold of the Canoe Sail, and through one of the Geese, most part of which was gone. These are likewise found high up in the Rivers, in whose sides they live, which is known by the abundance of Fresh-Water Muscle-Shells (such as you have in England) that lie at the Mouth of their Holes. This is an Enemy to the Tortis, whose Holes in the Sand, where they hide their Eggs, the Minx finds out, and scratches up and eats. The Raccoons and Crows do the same. The Minx may be made domestick; and were it not for his paying a Visit now and then to the Poultry, they are the greatest destroyers of Rats and Mice that are in the World. Their Skins, if good of that kind, are valuable, provided they are killed in Season.

The Water-Rat is found here the same as in England. The Water-Snakes are often found to have of these Rats in their Bellies.

That which the people of Carolina call a Hare is nothing but a Hedge-Coney. They never borough in the Ground, but much frequent Marshes and Meadow-Land. They hide their Young in some Place secure from the Discovery of the Buck, as the European Rabbets do, and are of the same Colour; but if you start one of them and pursue her, she takes into a hollow Tree, and there runs up as far as she can, in which Case the Hunter makes a Fire, and Smokes the Tree, which brings her down, and smothers her. At one time of the Year great Bots or Maggots breed betwixt the Skin and the Flesh of the Creatures. They eat just as the English ones do; but I never saw one of them fat. We fire the Marshes and then kill abundance.

The English or European Coneys are here found, tho' but in one place that I ever knew of, which was in Trent River, where they boroughed among the Rocks. I cannot believe, these are Natives of the Country, any otherwise than that they might come from aboard some Wreck; the Sea not being far off. I was told of several that were upon Bodies island by Ronoak, which came from that Ship of Bodies; but I never saw any. However the Banks are no proper Abode of Safety, because of the many Minxes, in those Quarters. I carried over some of the tame sort from England to

South Carolina, which bred three times going over, we having a long Passage. I turned them loose in a Plantation, and the young ones, and some of the old ones bred great Maggots in their Testicles. At last the great Gust in September 1700, brought a great deal of Rain, and drowned them all in their Holes. I intend to make a second Tryal of them in North Carolina, and doubt not but to secure them.

The Elk is a Monster of the Venison sort. His Skin is used almost in the same Nature as the Buffelo's. Some take him for the red Deer of America; but he is not: For, if brought out and kept in Company with one of that sort, of the contrary Sex, he will never couple. His Flesh is not so sweet as the lesser Deers. His Horns exceed (in weight) all Creatures which the new World affords. They will often resort and feed with the Buffelo, delighting in the same Range as they do.

The Stags of Carolina are lodged in the Mountains. They are not so large as in Europe, but much larger than any Fallow-Deer. They are always fat, I believe, with some delicate Herbage that grows on the Hills, for we find all Creatures that graze much fatter and better Meat on the Hills, than those in the Valleys: I mean towards and near the Sea. Some Deer on these Mountains afford the occidental Bezoar, not coming from a Goat, as some report. What sort of Beast affords the oriental Bezoar, I know not. The Tallow of the Harts make incomparable Candles. Their Horns and Hides are of the same Value, as others of their kind.

Fallow-Deer in Carolina are taller and longer-legged than in Europe; but neither run so fast nor are so well haunched. Their Singles are much longer, and their Horns stand forward as the others incline backwards; neither do they beam or bear their Antlers as the English Deer do. Towards the Salts they are not generally so fat and good Meat as on the Hills. I have known some killed on the Salts in January that have had abundance of Bots in their Throat, which keep them very poor. As the Summer approaches these Bots come out and turn into the finest Butterfly imaginable, being very large and having black, white and yellow Stripes. Deer Skins are one of the best Commodities Carolina affords to ship off for England, provided they be large.

Of Squirrels we have four Sorts. The first is the Fox-Squirrel, so called because of his large Size, which is the Bigness of a Rabbet of two or three Months old. His Colour is commonly gray; yet I have seen several pied ones, and some reddish and black; his chiefest Haunts are in the Piny Land where the Almond-Pine grows. There he provides his Winter-Store; they being a Nut that never fails of bearing. He may be made tame, and is very good Meat when killed.

The next sort of Squirrel is much of the Nature of the English, only differing in Colour. Their Food is Nuts (of all sorts the Country affords) and Acorns. They eat well, and, like, the Bear, are never found with young.

The Flying-Squirrel.—This Squirrel is gray, as well as the others. He is the least of the Three. His Food is much the same with the small gray Squirrel. He has not Wings, as Birds or Bats have, there being a fine thin-Skin covered with Hair, as the rest of the parts are. This is from the Fore-Feet to the Hinder-Feet, which is extended and holds so much Air, as buoys him up, from one Tree to another, that are greater distances asunder, than other Squirrels can reach by jumping or springing. He is made very tame, is an Enemy to a Corn-field, (as all Squirrels are) and eats only the Germinating Eye of that Grain, which is very sweet.

Ground Squirrels are so called because they never delight in running up Trees, and leaping from Tree to Tree. They are the smallest of all Squirrels. Their Tail is neither so long nor bushy, but flattish. They are of a reddish Colour and striped down each Side with black Rows, which make them very beautiful. They may be kept tame in a little Box with Cotton. They and the Flying-Squirrels seldom stir out in Cold Weather, being tender Animals.

The Fox of Carolina is gray but smells not as the Foxes in Great Britain and elsewhere. They have reddish Hair about their Ears and are generally very fat, yet I never saw any one eat them. When hunted, they make a sorry Chase, because they run up Trees when pursued. They are never to be made familiar and tame as the Raccoon is. Their Furs, if in Season, are used for Muffs and other Ornaments. They live chiefly on Birds and Fowls and such small Prey.

I have been informed by the Indians that on a Lake of Water towards the Head of Neus-River, there haunts a Creature which frightens them all from Hunting thereabouts. They say he is the Colour of a Panther, but cannot run up Trees; and that there abides with him a Creature like an Englishman's Dog, which runs faster than he can, and gets his Prey for him. They add that there is no other of that Kind that ever they met withal; and that they have no other way to avoid him but by running up a Tree. The Certainty of this I can not affirm by my own Knowledge, yet they all agree in this Story. As for Lions, I never saw any in America, neither can I imagine how they should come there.

Of Rats we have two sorts; the House-Rat as in Europe; and the Marsh-Rat which differs very much from the other, being more hairy, and has several other Distinctions too long here to name.

Mice are the same here as those in England, that belong to the House. There is one sort that poisons a Cat as soon as she eats of them, which has sometimes happened. These Mice resort not to Houses.

The Dormouse is the same as in England, and so is the Weasel, which is very scarce.

The Bat or Rearmouse, the same as in England. The Indian Children are much addicted to eat Dirt, and so are some of the Christians. But roast a Bat on a Skewer, then pull the Skin off, and and make the Child that eats Dirt eat the roasted Rearmouse and he will never eat Dirt again. This is held as an infallible Remedy. I have put this amongst the Beasts as partaking of both Natures, of the Bird and the Mouse-Kind.

Having mentioned all the sorts of terrestrial or Land-Animals which Carolina affords and are yet known to us, except the Tame and Domestick Creatures, (of which I shall give an Account here-after when I come to treat of the Ways and Manners of Agriculture in that Province.) I shall now proceed to the known Insects of that Place. Not that I pretend to give an ample Account of the whole Tribe, which is too numerous and contains too great a Diversity of Species, many not yet discovered, and others that have slipt my Memory at present; But those which I can remember, I here present my Readers withal.

INSECTS OF CAROLINIA.

Allegators.
Rattle-Snakes.
Ground Rattle-Snakes.
Horn-Snakes.
Water-Snakes, four sorts.
Swamp-Snakes, three sorts.
Red-bellied Land Snakes.
Red-backed Snake.
Black Truncheon Snake.
Scorpion-Lizard.
Green Lizard.
Frogs, many sorts.
Long black Snake.
King-Snake.
Green Snake.
Corn Snake.
Vipers, black and gray.
Tortois.
Terebin, Land and Water.
Brimstone-Snake.
Egg or Chicken-Snake.
Eel-Snake, or great Loach.
Brown Lizard.
Rotten-Wood Worm, &c.

The Allegator is the same as the Crocodile, and differs only in Name. They frequent the sides of Rivers, in the Banks of which they make their Dwellings a great way under Ground; the hole or Mouth of their Dens lying commonly two Feet under Water, after which it rises till it be considerably above the Surface thereof. Here it is that this amphibious Monster dwells all the Winter, sleeping away his time till the Spring appears, when he comes from his Cave, and daily swims up and down the Streams. He always breeds in some fresh Stream or clear Fountain of Water, yet seeks his Prey in the broad Salt Waters, that are brackish, not on the Sea-side, where I never met with any. He never devours Men in Carolina, but uses all ways to avoid them, yet he kills Swine and Dogs, the former as they come to feed in the Marshes, the others as they swim over the Creeks and Waters. They are very mischievous to the Wares made for taking Fish, into which they come to prey on the Fish that are caught in the Ware, from whence they cannot readily extricate themselves, and so break the Ware in pieces, being a very strong Creature. This Animal, in these Parts sometimes exceeds seventeen Foot long. It is impossible to kill them with a Gun, unless you chance to hit them about the Eyes, which is a much softer Place than the rest of their impenetrable Armour. They roar and make a hideous Noise against bad Weather, and before they come out of their Dens in the Spring. I was pretty much frightened with one of these once, which happened thus: I had built a House about half a Mile from an Indian Town on the Fork of Neus-River, where I dwelt by myself, excepting a young Indian Fellow, and a Bull-Dog, that I had along with me. I had not been so long a Sojourner in America, as to be thoroughly acquainted with this creature. One of them had got his Nest directly under my House, which stood on pretty high Land and by a Creek-side, in whose Banks his Entring-place was, his Den reaching the Ground directly on Which my House stood. I was sitting alone by the Fire-side, (about nine a clock at Night, sometime in March,) the Indian Fellow being gone to the Town to see his Relations, so that there was no body in the House but myself and my Dog; when, all of a sudden, this ill-favored Neighbor of mine set up such a Roaring, that he made the House shake about my Ears, and so continued like a Bittern, (but a hundred times louder if possible,) for four or five times. The Dog stared as if he was frightened out of his Senses; nor indeed could I imagine what it was, having never heard one of them before. Immediately again I had another Lesson; and so a third. Being, at that time, amongst none but Savages, I began to suspect they were working some Piece of Conjuration under my House, to get away my Goods; not but that at another time, I have as little Faith in their, or any others, working Miracles, by diabolical Means, as any Person living. At last, my Man came in, to whom when I had told the Story, he laughed at me, and presently undeceived me, by telling me what it was that made that Noise. These Alligators lay Eggs as the Ducks do, only they are longer shaped, larger, and a thicker Shell than they have. How long they are in hatching I cannot tell; but as the Indians say, it is most part of the Summer. They always lay by a Spring-Side the young living in and about the same as soon as hatched. Their Eggs are laid in Nests made in the Marshes, and contain twenty or thirty Eggs. Some of these Creatures afford a great deal of Musk. Their Tail when cut off looks very fair and white, seemingly like the best of Veal. Some People have eaten thereof, and say it is delicate Meat when they happen not to be musky. Their Flesh is accounted proper for such as are troubled with the lame Distemper, (a sort of Rheumatism,) so is the Fat very prevailing to remove Aches and Pains, by Unction. The Teeth of this Creature, when dead, are taken out to make Chargers for Guns, being of several Sizes, fit for all Loads.—They are white and would make pretty Snuff Boxes, if wrought by an Artist. After the Tail of the Alligator is separated from the Body, it will move very freely for four days.

The Rattle-Snakes are found on all the Main of America, that I ever had any account of; being so called from the Rattle at the end of their Tails, which is a Connexion of jointed Coverings, of an ex-

THE BEASTES OF CAROLINA.

crementitious Matter, betwixt the Substance of a Nail and a Horn, though each Tegmen is very thin. Nature seems to have designed these on purpose to give Warning of such an approaching Danger, as the venomous Bite of these Snakes is. Some of them grow to a very great Bigness, as six Foot in Length, their Middle being the Thickness of the Small of a lusty Man's Leg. We have an Account of much larger Serpents of this Kind; but I never met them yet, although I have seen and killed abundance in my time. They are of an Orange, tawney and blackish Colour on the Back; differing (as all Snakes do) in Colour on the Belly; being of an Ash-Colour inclining to Lead. The Male is easily distinguished from the Female, by a black Velvet-Spot on his Head, and besides, his Head is smaller shaped and long. Their Bite is venomous if not speedily remedied, especially if the Wound be in a Vain, Nerve, Tendon or Sinew, when it is very difficult to cure. The Indians are the best Physicians for the Bite of these and all other venomous Creatures of this Country. There are four sorts of Snake-Roots already discovered, which Knowledge came from the Indians, who have performed several great cures. The Rattle-Snakes are accounted the peaceablest in the World; for they never attack any one or injure them, unless they are trod upon or molested. The most Danger of being bit by these Snakes, is for those that survey Land in Carolina; yet I never heard of any Surveyor that was killed or hurt by them. I have myself gone over several of this Sort and others, yet it pleased God, I never came to any harm. They have the Power or Art, (I know not which to call it,) to charm Squirrels, Hares, Partridges, or any such thing, in such a manner that they run directly into their Mouths. This I have seen by a Squirrel and one of these Rattle-Snakes; and other Snakes have, in some measure, the same Power. The Rattle-Snakes have many small Teeth of which I cannot see they make any use, for they swallow everything whole; but the Teeth which poison are only four, two on each side of their Upper-Jaws. These are bent like a Sickle, and hang loose as if by a Joint. Towards the setting on of these, there is in each Tooth a little Hole, wherein you may just get in the Point of a small Needle. And here it is that the Poison comes out, (which is as green as Grass,) and follows the Wound made by the Point of their Teeth. They are much more venomous in the Months of June and July, than they are in March, April or September. The hotter the Weather the more poisonous. Neither may we suppose, that they can renew their Poison as oft as they will; for we have had a Person bit by one of these who never rightly recovered it and very hardly escaped with Life; a second Person bit in the same Place by the same Snake, and received no more Harm than if bitten with a Rat. They cast their Skins every Year, and commonly abide near the Place where the old Skin lies. These cast Skins are used in Physic, and the Rattles are reckoned good to expedite the Birth. The Gall is made up into Pills with Clay, and kept for Use; being given in Pestilential Fevers and the Small-Pox. It is accounted a noble Remedy, known to few and held as a great Arcanum. This Snake has two Nostrils on each side of his Nose. Their Venom, I have Reason to believe, effects no Harm, any otherwise than when darted into the Wound by the Serpent's Teeth.

The Ground Rattle-Snake, wrong named, because it has nothing like Rattles. It resembles the Rattle-Snake a little in Colour, but is darker, and never grows to any considerable Bigness, not exceeding a Foot, or sixteen Inches. He is reckoned amongst the worst of Snakes; and stays out the longest of any Snake I know before he returns (in the Fall of the Leaf) to his Hole.

Of the Horn-Snakes, I never saw but two that I remember. They are like the Rattle-Snake in Colour, but rather lighter. They hiss exactly like a Goose when anything approaches them. They strike at their Enemy with their Tail, and kill whatsoever they wound with it, which is armed at the End with a horny Substance, like a Cock's Spur. This is their Weapon. I have heard it credibly reported, by those who said they were Eye-Witnesses that a small Locust-Tree, about the Thickness of a Man's Arm, being struck by one c' hese Snakes at Ten a clock in the Morning, then verdant and flourishing, at four in the Afternoon was dead, and the Leaves red and Withered. Doubtless, be it how it will, they are very venomous. I think the Indians do not pretend to cure their Wound.

Of Water-Snakes there are four sorts. The first is the Horn-Snake's Colour, though less. The next is a very long Snake, differing in Colour, and will make nothing to swim over a River a League wide. They hang upon Birches and other Trees by the Water-Side. I had the Fortune once to have one of them leap into my Boat, as I was going up a narrow River; the Boat was full of Mats, which I was glad to take out, to get rid of him. They are reckoned poisonous. A third is much of an English Adder's Colour, but always frequent the Salts, and lies under the Drift Sea-weed, where they are in abundance, and are accounted mischievous when they bite. The last is of a sooty, black Colour, and frequents Ponds and Ditches. What his Qualities are I cannot tell.

Of the Swamp-Snakes there are three sorts, which are very near akin to the Water-Snakes, and may be ranked amongst them. The Belly of the first is of a Carnation or Pink colour; his Back a dirty brown; they are large but have not much Venom in them as ever I learnt. The next is a large Snake, of a brown, Dirt Colour, and alalways abides in the Marshes.

The last is mottled and very poisonous. They dwell in Swamp Sides and Ponds, and have prodigious wide Mouths, and, (though not long) arrive to the Thickness of the Calf of a Man's Leg.

Redbelly Land-Snakes.—These frequent the Land altogether, and are so called because of their red Bellies, which incline to an Orange Colour. Some have been bitten with these sort of Snakes, and not hurt, when others have suffered very much by them. Whether there be two sorts of these Snakes which we make no Difference of, I cannot at present determine.

Red-Back Snakes.—I never saw but one of these, which I stept over, and did not see him till he that brought the Chain after me spied him. He has a red Back as the last has a red Belly. They are a long, slender Snake, and very rare to be met withal. I enquired of

the Indian that was along with me, whether they were very venomous, who made Answer that if he had bitten me, even the Indians
could not have cured it.

The Black Truncheon-Snake.—This sort of Snake might very
well have been ranked with the Water-Snakes. They lie under
Roots of Trees, and on the Banks of Rivers. When anything dis-
turbs them, they dart into the Water (which is Salt) like an Arrow out of a Bow. They are thick, and the shortest Snake I ever saw.
What Good or Harm there is in them, I know not. Some of these
Water-Snakes will swallow a black Land-Snake, half as long again
as themselves.

The Scorpion-Lizard is no more like a Scorpion, than a Hedge
Hog; but they very commonly call him a Scorpion. He is of the
Lizard Kind, but much bigger; his Back is of a dark, Copper Colour;
his Belly an Orange; he is very nimble in running up Trees, or on
the Land, and is accounted very poisonous. He has the most Sets
of Teeth in his Mouth and throat that ever I saw.

Green-Lizards are very harmless and beautiful, having a little
Bladder under their Throat, which they fill with Wind, and evacu-
ate the same at Pleasure. They are of a most glorious Green, and
very tame. They resort to the Walls of Houses in the Summer Season, and stand gazing on a Man, without any Concern or Fear.
There are several other Colours of these Lizards, but none so beautiful as the green ones are.

Of Frogs we have several sorts; the most famous is the Bull-Frog,
so called, because he lows exactly like that Beast, which makes
Strangers wonder (when by the side of a Marsh) what is the matter,
for they hear the frogs low and can see no Cattle; he is very large.
I believe I have seen one with as much Meat on him as a Pullet,
if he had been dressed. The small green Frogs get upon Trees and
make a Noise. There are several other Coloured small Frogs; but the
Common Land-Frog is likest a Toad, only he leaps, and is not
poisonous. He is a great Devourer of Ants, and the Snakes devour
him. These Frogs baked and beat to Powder, and taken with Orrice-
Root cures a Tympany.

The long, black Snake frequents the Land altogether, and is the nimblest Creature living. His Bite has no more Venom than a Prick with a Pin. He is the best Mouser than can be; for he leaves not one of that Vermine alive where he comes. He also kills the Rattle-Snake, wheresoever he meets him, by twisting his Head about the Neck of the Rattle-Snake, and whipping him to death with his Tail. This Whipster haunts the Dairies of careless Housewives, and never misses to skim the Milk clear of the Cream. He is an excellent Egg-Merchant, for he does not suck the Eggs, but swallows them whole, (as all Snakes do.) He will often swallow all the Eggs from under a Hen that sits, and coil himself under the Hen in the Nest, where sometimes the Housewife finds him. This Snake, for all his Agility, is so brittle that when he is pursued, and gets his Head into the Hole of a Tree, if any body gets hold of the other end, he will twist and break himself off in the middle. One of these Snakes, whose Neck is no thicker than a Woman's little Finger, will swallow a Squirrel; so much does that part stretch in all these Creatures.

The King-Snake is the longest of all others, and not common; no Snake, they say, will meddle with them. I think they are not accounted very venomous. The Indians make Girdles and Sashes of their Skins.

Green-Snakes are very small, though pretty (if any Beauty be allowed to Snakes.) Every one makes himself very familiar with them, and puts them in their Bosom, because there is no manner of Harm in them.

The Corn-Snakes are but small ones, they are of a brown Colour, mixed with tawny. There is no more hurt in this, than in the green Snake.

Of those we call Vipers, there are two sorts. People call these Vipers, because they spread a very flat Head at any time when they are vexed. One of these is a grayish, like the Italian Viper, the other black and short; and is reckoned amongst the worst of Snakes for Venom.

Tortois, vulgarly called Turtle, I have ranked these among the

Insects because they lay Eggs, and I did not know well where to put them. Among us there are three sorts. The first is the green Turtle, which is not common, but is sometimes found on our Coast. The next is the Hawks-bill, which is common. These two sorts are extraordinary Meat. The third is Logger-Head, which Kind scarce any one covets, except it be for the Eggs, which of this and all other Turtles are very good Food. None of these sorts of Creatures' Eggs will ever admit the White to be harder than a Jelly; yet the Yolk, with boiling, becomes as hard as any other Egg.

Of Terebins there are divers sorts, all which, to be brief, we will comprehend under the Distinction of Land and Water-Terebins.

The Land-Terebin is of several Sizes, but generally Round-Mouthed and not Hawk-Billed, as some are. The Indians eat them. Most of them are good Meat, except the very large ones, and they are good Food too, provided they not Musky. They are an utter Enemy to the Rattle-Snake, for when the Terebin meets him he catches hold of him a little below his Neck and draws his Head into his Shell, which makes the Snake beat his Tail and twist about with all the Strength and Violence imaginable to get away; but the Terebin soon dispatches him and there leaves him. These they call in Europe the Land Tortois; their Food is Snails, Tadpoles, or young Frogs, Mushrooms, and the Dew and Slime of the Earth and Ponds. Water Terebins are small, containing about as much Meat as a Pullet, and are extraordinary Food especially in May and June. When they lay, their Eggs are very good; but they have so many Enemies that find them out, that the hundredth part never comes to Perfection. The Sun and Sand hatch them, which comes out the Bigness of a small Chesnut and seek their own Living.

We now come again to the Snakes. The Brimstone is so called, I believe, because it is almost of a Brimstone Colour. They might as well have called it a Glass-Snake, for it is as brittle as a Tobacco-Pipe, so that if you give it the least Touch of a small Twigg it immediately breaks into several Pieces. Some affirm that if you let it remain where you broke it, it will come together again. What Harm there is in this brittle Ware I can not tell, but I never knew any body hurt by them.

The Egg or Chicken-Snake is so called because it is frequent about the Hen-Yard and eats Eggs and Chickens, they are of a dusky Soot-Colour, and will roll themselves round and stick eighteen or twenty Foot high by the side of a smoothed bark Pine, where there is no manner of Hold, and there sun themselves, and sleep all the Sunny Part of the Day. There is no great matter of Poison in them.

The Wood-Worms are of a Copper, shining Colour, scarce so thick as your little Finger; are often found in Rotten-Trees. They are accounted venomous in case they bite, though I never knew anything hurt by them. They never exceed four or five Inches in length.

The Reptiles, or smaller Insects are too numerous to relate here, this Country affording innumerable Quantities thereof; as the Flying-Stags, with Horns, Beetles, Butterflies, Grasshoppers, Locust, and several hundreds of uncouth Shapes, which in the Summer-Season are discovered here in Carolina, the Description of which requires a large Volume, which is not my Intent at present. Besides, what the Mountainous Part of this Land may hereafter lay open to our View, time and Industry will discover, for we that have settled but a small Share of this large Province, cannot imagine, but there will be a great number of Discoveries made by those that shall come hereafter into the Back-part of this Land, and make Enquiries therein, when, at least, we consider that the Westward of Carolina is quite different in Soil, Air, Weather, growth of Vegetables, and several Animals too, which we at present are wholly Strangers to, and to seek for. As to a right Knowledge thereof, I say, when another Age is come, the Ingenious then in being may stand upon the Shoulders of those that went before them, adding their own Experiments to what was delivered down to them by their Predecessors, and then there will be something towards a complete Natural History, which, (in these days) would be no easy Undertaking to any Author that writes truly and compendiously as he ought to do. It is sufficient, at present, to write an honest and fair Account of any of the Settlements, in this new World, without wandering out of the Path of Truth, or bespattering any Man's Reputation anywise concerned in the Government of the Colony; he that mixes Invectives with Relations of this Nature rendering himself suspected of Partiality in whatever he writes. For my part, I wish all well, and he that has received any severe Dealings from the Magistrate or his Superiors, had best examine himself well, if he was not first in the Fault; if so, then he can justly blame none but himself for what has happened to him.

Having thus gone through the Insects, as in the Table, except the Eel-Snake, (so called though very improperly, because he is nothing but a Loach, that sucks, and cannot bite as the Snakes do.) He is very large, commonly sixteen Inches or a Foot and a half long; having all the Properties that other Loaches have, and dwells in Pools and Waters as they do. Notwithstanding, we have the same Loach as you have in Bigness.

This is all that at present I shall mention, touching the Insects, and go on to give an Account of the Fowls and Birds that are properly found in Carolina, which are these:

BIRDS OF CAROLINA.

Birds in America more beautiful than in Europe.
Eagle bald.
Eagle gray.
Fishing Hawk.
Turkey Buzzard, or Vulture.
Herring-tailed Hawk.
Goshawk.
Falcon.
Merlin.
Sparrow-hawk.
Hobby.
Jay.

Green Plover.
Plover gray or whistling.
Pigeon.
Turtle Dove.
Parrakeeto.
Thrush.
Wood-Peckers, five sorts.
Mocking-birds, two sorts.
Cat-Bird.
Cuckoo.
Blue-Bird.
Bulfinch.
Nightingale.
Hedge-Sparrow.
Wren.
Sparrows, two sorts.
Lark.
Ring-Tail.
Raven.
Crow.
Black Birds, two sorts.
Bunting, two sorts.
Pheasant.
Woodcock.
Snipe.
Partridge.
Moorhen.
Red Bird.
East India Bat.
Martins, two sorts.
Diveling, or swift.
Swallow.
Humming Bird.
Tom-Tit, Ox-Eye.

Owls, two sorts.
Scritch owl.
Baltimore bird.
Throstle, no Singer.
Whippoo Will.
Reed Sparrow.
Wheet bird.
Rice bird.
Cranes and Storks.
Snow birds.
Yellow wings.

WATER FOWL ARE

Swans, called Trompeters.
Swans, called Hoopers.
Geese, three sorts.
Brant, gray.
Brant, white.
Sea-pies or pied Curlues.
Will Willets.
Great Gray Gulls.
Old Wives.
Sea Cock.
Curlues, three sorts.
Coots.
Kings-fisher.
Loons, two sorts.
Bitterns, three sorts.
Hern, gray.
Hern, white.
Water Pheasant.
Little Gray Gull.
Little Fisher or Dipper.
Gannet.

Shear-water.
Great black pied Gull.
Marsh-hens.
Blue Peters.
Sand-birds.
Runners.
Ducks, as in England.
Ducks black, all summer.
Ducks pied, build on Trees.
Ducks whistling, at Sapona.
Ducks, scarlet-eye, at Esaw.
Blue-wings.
Widgeon.
Teal, two sorts.
Shovelers.
Whifflers.
Black Flusterers or bald Coot.
Turkeys, wild
Fishermen.
Divers.
Raft Fowl.
Bull-necks.
Redheads.
Tropick-birds.
Pellican.
Cormorant.
Tutcocks.
Swaddle-bills.
Men.
Sheldrakes.
Bald Faces.
Water Witch, or Ware Coot.

As the Eagle is reckoned the King of Birds, I have begun with him. The first I shall speak of, is the bald Eagle; so called, because his Head to the middle of his Neck and his Tail, is as white as Snow. These Birds continually breed the Year round; for when the young Eagles are just downed, with a sort of white woolly Feathers, the Hen-Eagle lays again, which Eggs are hatched by the Warmth of the young ones in the Nest, so that the Flight of one Brood makes Room for the next, that are but just hatched.

They prey on any living thing they can catch. They are heavy of Flight and cannot get their Food by Swiftness to help which there is a Fishhawk that catches Fishes and suffers the Eagle to take them from her, although she is long winged and a swift Flyer, and can make far better way in her Flight than the Eagle can. The bald Eagle attends the Gunners in Winter, with all the Obsequiousness imaginable, and when he shoots and kills any Fowl, the Eagle surely comes in for his Bird; and besides those that are wounded and escape the Fowler, fall to the Eagle's share. He is an excellent Artist at stealing young Pigs, which Prey he carries alive to his Nest, at which time the poor Pig makes such a Noise over Head, that Strangers that have heard them cry, and not seen the Bird and his Prey, have thought there were Flying Sows and Pigs in that Country. The Eagles Nest is made of Twigs, Sticks and Rubbish. It is big enough to fill a handsome Cart Body, and commonly so full of nasty Bones and Carcasses that it stinks most offensively. This Eagle is not bald till he is one or two years old.

The gray Eagle is altogether the same sort of Bird as the Eagle in Europe; therefore we shall treat no farther of him.

The Fishing-Hawk is the Eagle's Jackal, which most commonly (though not always) takes his Prey for him. He is a large Bird, being above two thirds as big as the Eagle. He builds his Nest as the Eagles do; that is in a dead Cypress-Tree, either standing in or hard by the Water. The Eagle and this Bird seldom sit on a living Tree. He is of a gray pied Colour, and the most dexterous Fowl in Nature at Catching of Fish, which he wholly lives on, never eating any Flesh.

The Turkey-Buzzard of Carolina is a small Vulture which lives on dead Carcasses. They are about the Bigness of the Fishing-Hawk, and have a nasty Smell with them. They are of the Kites Colour, and are reported to be an Enemy to Snakes by killing all they meet withal of that Kind.

The Herring, or Swallow-tailed Hawk, is about the Bigness of a Falcon, but a much longer Bird. He is of a delicate Aurora-Colour; the Pinions of his Wings, and End of his Tail are black. He is a very beautiful Fowl, and never appears abroad but in the Summer. His Prey is chiefly on Snakes, and will kill the biggest we have with a great deal of Dexterity and Ease.

Goshawks are very plentiful in Carolina. They are not seemingly so large as those from Muscovy; but appear to be a very brisk Bird.

The Falcon is much the same as in Europe, and promises to be a brave Bird, though I never had any of them in my Hand; neither did I ever see any of them in any other Posture than on the Wing, which always happened to be in an Evening, and flying to the Westward; therefore, I believe they have their Abode and Nest among the Mountains, where we may expect to find them, and several other Species that we are at present Strangers to.

The Merlin is a small Bird in Europe, but much smaller here, yet he very nimbly kills the smaller sorts of Birds, and sometimes the Partridge; if caught alive, he would be a great Rarity, because of his Beauty and Smallness.

The Sparrow-Hawk in Carolina is no bigger than a Fieldfare in England. He flies at the Bush and sometimes kills a small Bird, but his chiefest Food is Reptiles, as Beetles, Grasshoppers, and such small things. He is exactly of the same Colour, as the Sparrow-Hawk in England, only has a blackish Hood by his Eyes.

Hobbies are the same here as in England, and are not often met withal.

The Ring-tail is a short-winged Hawk, preying on Mice and such Vermine in the Marshes, as in England.

Ravens, the same as in England, though very few. I have not seen above six in eight Years' time.

Crows are here less than in England. They are as good Meat as a Pigeon, and never feed on any Carrion. They are great Enemies to Corn-Fields, and cry and build almost like Rooks.

Black-Birds.—Of these we have two sorts, which are the worst Vermin in America. They fly sometimes in such Flocks that they destroy every thing before them. They (both sorts) build in hollow Trees as Startlings do. The first sort is near as big as a Dove, and is very white and delicate Food. The other sort is very beautiful and about the Bigness of the Owsel. Part of their Head next to the Bill, and the Pinions of their Wings are of an Orange and glorious Crimson Colour. They are as good Meat as the former, though very few here (where large Fowl are so plenty) ever trouble themselves to kill or dress them.

Of the Bunting-Larks we have two sorts, though the Heel of this Bird is not so long as in Europe. The first of these often accompany the Black-birds, and sing as the Bunting-Larks in England do, differing very little. The first sort has an Orange-Colour on the Tops of their Wings, and are as good Meat as those in Europe. The other sort is something less of a lighter Colour; nothing differing therein from those in England as to Feathers, Bigness, and Meat.

The Pheasant of Carolina differs some small matter from the English Pheasant, being not so big, and having some difference in Feather; yet he is not anywise inferior in Delicacy, but is as good Meat or rather finer. He haunts the back Woods and is seldom found near the Inhabitants.

The Woodcocks live and breed here, though they are not in great plenty as I have seen them in some Parts of England and other Places. They want one third of the English Woodcock in Bigness, but differ not in Shape or Feather, save that their Breast is of a Carnation Colour; and they make a Noise (when they are on the Wing) like the Bells about a Hawk's Legs. They are certainly a dainty Meat as any in the World. Their Abode is in all Parts of this Country, in low, boggy Ground, Springs, Swamps, and Pocosons.

The Snipes here frequent the same Places as they do in England,

and differ nothing from them. They are the only wild Bird that is nothing different from the Species of Europe, and keeps with us all the Year. In some Places there are a great many of these Snipes.

Our Partridges in Carolina very often take upon Trees, and have a sort of Whistle and Call quite different from those in England. They are a very beautiful Bird, and great Destroyers of the Peas in Plantations; wherefore they set Traps and catch many of them. They have the same Feather as in Europe, only the Cock wants the Horse-Shooe, in leiu of which he has a fair Half-Circle over each Eye. These (as well as the Woodcock) are less than the European Bird, but far finer Meat. They might be easily transported to any Place, because they take to eating after caught.

The Moorhens are of the black Game. I am informed that the gray Game haunts the Hills. They never come into the Settlement, but keep in the hilly Parts.

Jays are here common and very mischievous in devouring our Fruit and spoiling more than they eat. They are abundantly more beautiful and finer feathered than those in Europe, and not above half so big.

The Lap-wing or Green-Plover are here very common. They cry pretty much as the English Plovers do, and differ not much in Feather, but want a third of their Bigness.

The gray or whistling Plover are very scarce amongst us. I never saw any but three times that fell and settled on the Ground. They differ very little from those in Europe, as far as I could discern. I have seen several great Flocks of them fly overhead; therefore, believe they inhabit the Valleys near the Mountains.

Our wild Pigeons are like the Wood-Queese or Stock-Doves, only have a longer Tail. They leave us in the Summer. This sort of Pigeon (as I said before) is the most like our Stock-Doves or Wood-Pigeons that we have in England; only these differ in their Tails which are very long, much like a Parrakeeto's. You must understand that these Birds do not breed amongst us, (who are settled at and near the Mouths of the Rivers, as I have intimated to you before) but come down (especially in hard Winters) amongst the Inhabitants in great Flocks, as they were seen to do in the Year 1707, which was the hardest Winter that ever was known since Carolina has been seated by the Christians. And if that Country had such hard Weather, what must be expected of the severe Winters in Pennsylvania, New York, and New England, where Winters are ten times (if possible) colder than with us. Although the Flocks are, in such Extremities, very numerous; yet they are not to be mentioned in Comparison with the great and infinite Numbers of these Fowl that are met withal about a hundred or a hundred and fifty Miles to the Westward of the Places where we at present live; and where these Pigeons come down in quest of a small sort of Acorns, which in those parts are plentifully found. They are the same we call Turkey-Acorns, because the wild Turkies feed very much thereon; And for the same Reason those Trees that bear them are called Turkey-Oaks. I saw such prodigious Flocks of these Pigeons in January or February, 1701-2, (which were in the hilly Country between the great Nation of the Esaw-Indians and the pleasant Stream of Sapona, which is the West-Branch of Clarendon or the Cape Fair River) that they had broke down the Limbs of a great many large Trees all over those Woods whereon they chanced to sit and roost, especially the great Pines, which are a more brittle Wood than our sorts of Oak are. These Pigeons, about Sun-Rise, when we were preparing to march on our Journey would fly by us in such vast Flocks that they would be near a Quarter of an Hour before they were all passed by; and as soon as that Flock was gone another would come, and so successfully one after another for great part of the Morning. It is observable that wherever these Fowl come in such Numbers, as I saw them then, they clear all before them, scarce leaving one Acorn upon the Ground, which would, doubtless, be a great Prejudice to the Planters that should seat there, because their Swine would be thereby deprived of their Mast. When I saw such Flocks of the Pigeons I now speak of, none of our Company had any other sort of Shot than that which is cast in Moulds, and was so very large that we could not put above ten or a dozen of them into our largest Pices; Wherefore we made but an indifferent Hand of shooting them; although we commonly killed a Pigeon for every Shot. They were very fat and as good Pigeons as ever I eat. I enquired of the Indians that dwelled in those Parts, where it was that those Pigeons bred, and they pointed toward the vast Ridge of Mountains and said they bred there. Now, whether they make their Nests in the Holes in the Rocks of those Mountains or build in Trees, I could not learn; but they seem to me to be a Wood-Pigeon that build in Trees, because of their frequent sitting thereon, and their Roosting on Trees always at Night, under which their Dung commonly lies half a Foot thick, and kills everything that grows where it falls.

Turtle-Doves are here very plentiful; they devour the Pease; for which Reason People make Traps and catch them.

The Parrakeetos are of a green Colour, and Orange-Coloured half way their Head. Of these and the Allegators, there is none found to the Northward of this Province. They visit us first when Mulberries are ripe, which Fruit they love extremely. They peck the Apples to eat the Kernels, so that the Fruit rots and perishes. They are mischievous to Orchards. They are often taken alive and will become familiar and tame in two days. They have their Nests in hollow Trees, in low Swampy Ground. They devour the Birch-Buds in April, and lie hidden when the Weather is frosty and hard.

The Thrushes in America are the same as in England, and red under the Wings. They never appear amongst us but in hard Weather, and presently leave us again.

Of Wood-peckers we have four sorts. The first is as big as a Pigeon, being of a dark brown Colour, with a white Cross on his Back, his Eyes circled with white, and on his Head stands a Tuft of beautiful Scarlet Feathers. His Cry is heard a long way, and he flies from one rotten Tree to another to get Grubs, which is the Food he lives on.

The second sort are of an Olive-Colour, striped with yellow. They eat Worms as well as Grubs, and are about the Bigness of those in Europe.

The third is the same Bigness as the last; he is pied with black and white, has a Crimson Head, without a Topping, and is a Plague to the Corn and Fruit; especially the Apples. He opens the Covering of the young Corn, so that the Rain gets in and rots it.

The fourth sort of these Wood-peckers, is a black and white speckled or mottled—the finest I ever saw. The Cock has a red Crown; he is not near so big as the others; his Food is Grubs, Corn, and other creeping Insects. He is not very wild, but will let one come up to him, then shifts on the other side of the Tree from your sight; and so dodges you for a long time together. He is about the size of an English Lark.

The Mocking-Bird is about as big as a Throstle in England, but longer; they are of a white and gray Colour, and are held to be the Choristers of America, as indeed they are. They sing with the greatest Diversity of Notes that is possible for a Bird to change to. They may be bred up, and will sing with us tame in Cages; yet I never take any of their Nests, although they build yearly in my Fruit-Trees, because I have their Company as much as if tame, as to the singing Part. They often sit upon our Chimneys in Summer, there being then no Fire in them, and sing the whole Evening and most part of the Night. They are always attending our Dwellings, and feed upon Mulberries and other Berries and Fruits, especially the Mechoacan-Berry, which grows here very plentifully.

There is another sort called the Ground-Mocking-Bird. She is the same Bigness and of a Cinnamon Colour. This Bird sings excellently well, but is not so common amongst us as the former.

The Cat-Bird, so named because it makes a Noise exactly like young Cats. They have a blackish Head and an Ash-coloured Body, and have no other Note that I know of. They are no biger than a Lark, yet will fight a Crow or any other great Bird.

The Cuckoo of Carolina may not properly be so called, because she never uses that Cry; yet she is of the same Bigness and Feather, and sucks the Small-Birds' Eggs, as the English Cuckoo does.

The Blue-Bird is the exact Bigness of a Robin-red-breast. The Cock has the same Coloured Breast as the Robin has, and his Back all the other Parts of him, are of as fine a Blue, as can possibly be seen in any thing in the World. He has a Cry and a whistle They hide themselves all the Winter.

Bulfinches in America differ something from those in Europe in their Feathers, though not in their Bigness. I never knew any one tame, therefore know not what they might be brought to.

The Nightingales are different in Plumes from those in Europe. They always frequent the low Groves where they sing very prettily all Night.

Hedge-Sparrows are here, though few Hedges. They differ scarce any thing in Plume or Bigness, only I never heard this Whistle as the English one does, especially after Rain.

The Wren is the same as in Europe, yet I never heard any Note she has in Carolina.

Sparrows here differ in Feather from the English. We have several Species of Birds called Sparrows, one of them much resembling the Bird called a Corinthian Sparrow.

The Lark with us resorts to the Savannas, or natural Meads, and green Marshes. He is coloured and heeled as the Lark is, but his Breast is of a glittering fair Lemon Colour, and he is as big as a Field-fare, and very fine Food.

The Red-Birds, (whose Cock is all over of a rich Scarlet Feather, with a tufted Crown on his Head of the same Colour) are the Bigness of a Bunting-Lark, and very hardy, having a strong thick Bill. They will sing very prettily, when taken old and put in a Cage. They are good Birds to turn a Cage with Bells; or if taught as the Bulfinch is, I believe would prove very docible.

East India Bats, or Musqueto Hawks, are the Bigness of a Cuckoo, and much of the same Colour. They are so called because the same sort is found in the East Indies. They appear only in the Summer, and live on Flies, which they catch in the Air, as Gnats, Musquetos, &c.

Martins are here of two sorts. The first is the same as in England; the other as big as a Black-Bird. They have white Throats and Breasts, with black Backs. The Planters put Gourds on standing Poles on purpose for these Fowl to build in, because they are a very Warlike Bird, and beat the Crows from the Plantations.

The Swift, or Diveling, the same as in England.

Swallows, the same as in England.

The Humming-Bird is the Miracle of all our winged Animals. He is feathered as a Bird, and gets his Living as the Bees, by sucking the Honey from each Flower. In some of the larger sort of Flowers, he will bury himself, by diving to suck the bottom of it, so that he is quite covered, and often times Children catch them in those Flowers, and keep them alive five or six days. They are of different Colours, the Cock differing from the Hen. The Cock is of a green red, Aurora, and other Colours mixed. He is much less than a Wren, and very nimble. His Nest is one of the greatest pieces of Workmanship the whole Tribe of winged Animals can show, it commonly hanging on a single Briar, most artificially woven, a small Hole being left to go in and out at. The Eggs are the Bigness of Pease.

The Tom-Tit, or Ox-Eyes, the same as in England.

Of Owls, we have two sorts; the smaller sort are like ours in England; the other sort is as big as a middling Goose, and has a prodigious Head. They make a fearful Hollowing in the Night-time, like a Man, whereby they often make Strangers lose their way in the Woods.

Scritch Owls much the same as in Europe.

The Baltimore-Bird, so called from the Lord Baltimore, Proprietor of all Maryland, in which Province many of them are found. They are the Bigness of a Linnet, with yellow Wings, and beautiful in other Colours.

Throstle, the same Size and Feather as in Europe, but I never could hear any of them sing.

The Weet, so called because he cries always before Rain; he resembles nearest the Fire-tail.

Cranes use the Savannas, low Ground and Frogs; they are above five Foot-high, when extended; are of a Cream Colour, and have a Crimson Spot on the Crown of their Heads. Their Quills are excellent for Pens; their Flesh makes the best Broth, yet is very hard to digest. Among them often frequent Storks, which are here seen, and no where besides in America, that I have yet heard of. The Cranes are easily bred up tame, and are excellent in a Garden to destroy Frogs, Worms, and other Vermine.

The Snow-Birds are most numerous in the North Parts of America, where there are great Snows. They visit us sometimes in Carolina, when the Weather is harder than ordinary. They are like the Stones Smach, or Wheat-Ears, and are delicate Meat.

These Yellow-Wings are a very small Bird, of a Linnets Colour, but Wings as yellow as Gold. They frequent high up in our Rivers and Creeks, and keep themselves in the thick Bushes, very difficult to be seen in the Spring. They sing very prettily.

Whippoo-Will, so named because it makes those Words exactly. They are the Bigness of a Thrush, and call their Note under a Bush, on the Ground hard to be seen, though you hear them never so plain. They are more plentiful in Virginia than with us in Carolina; for I never heard but one that was near the Settlement, and that was hard-by an Indian Town.

Red Sparrow.—This nearest resembles a Sparrow, and is the most common Small-Bird we have, therefore we call them so. They are brown and red, cinnamon Colour, striped.

Of the Swans, we have two sorts; the one we call Trompeters, because of a sort of trompeting Noise they make.

These are the largest sort we have, which come in great Flocks in the Winter, and stay, commonly, in the fresh Rivers till February, that the Spring comes on, when they go to the Lakes to breed. A Cygnet, that is, a last Years' Swan, is accounted a delicate Dish, as indeed it is. They are known by their Head and Feathers, which are not so white as Old ones.

The sort of Swans called Hoopers, are the least. They abide more in the Salt-Water, and are equally valuable for Food, with the former. It is observable that neither of these have a black Piece of horny Flesh down the Head and Bill, as they have in England.

Of Geese, we have three sorts, differing from each other only in size. Ours are not the common Geese that are in the Fens in England, but the other sort, with black Heads and Necks.

The gray Brant or Barnicle, is here very plentiful, as all other Water-Fowl are, in the Winter-Season. They are the same which they call Barnicles in Great Britain, and are a very good Fowl, and eat well.

There is also a white Brant, very plentiful in America. This Bird is all over as white as Snow, except the Tips of his Wings, and those are black. They eat the Roots of Sedge and Grass in the Marshes and Savannas, which they tear up like Hogs. The best way to kill these Fowl is, to burn a Piece of Marsh, or Savanna, and as soon as it is burnt, they will come in great Flocks to get the Roots, where you kill what you please of them. They are as good Meat as the other, only their Feathers are stubbed, and good for little.

The Sea-Pie, or gray Curlue, is about the Bigness of a very large Pigeon, but longer. He has a long Bill as other Curlues have, which is the Colour of an English Owsels, that is, yellow, as are his Legs. He frequents the Sand-beaches on the Sea-side, and when killed, is inferior to no Fowl I ever eat of.

Will Willet, is so called from his Cry, which he very exactly calls, Will Willet, as he flies. His Bill is like a Curlues, or Woodcock's, and has much such a Body as the other, yet not so tall. He is good Meat.

The great gray Gulls are good Meat, and as large as a Pullet. They lay large Eggs, which are found in very great Quantities on the Islands in our Sound, in the Months of June and July. The young Squabs are very good Victuals, and often prove a Relief to Travelers by Water, that have spent their Provisions.

Old Wives are a black and white pied Gull, with extraordinary long Wings, and a golden Coloured Bill and Feet. He makes a dismal Noise as he flies, and ever and anon dips his Bill in the Salt-Water. I never knew him eaten.

The Sea-Cock is a Gull that crows at Break of Day, and in the Morning, exactly like a Dunghill Cock, which Cry seems very pleasant in those uninhabited Places. He is never eaten.

Of Curlues there are three sorts, and vast Numbers of each. They have all long Bills and differ neither in Colour nor Shape, only in Size. The largest is as big as a good Hen; the smaller the Bigness of a Snipe or something bigger.

We have three sorts of Bitterns in Carolina. The first is the same as in England; the second of a deep brown with a great Topping and yellowish white Throat and Breast, and is lesser than the former; the last is no bigger than a Woodcock and near the Colour of the second.

We have the same Herns as in England.

White Herns are here very plentiful. I have seen above thirty sit on one Tree at a time. They are as white as Milk and fly very slowly.

The Water-Pheasant (very improperly called so) are a Water-Fowl of the Duck-Kind, having a Topping of pretty Feathers, which sets them out. They are very good Meat.

The little Gray-Gull is of a curious gray Colour, and abides near the Sea. He is about the Bigness of a Whistling-Plover, and delicate Food.

We have the little Dipper or Fisher that catches Fish so dexterously, the same as you have in the Islands of Scilly.

We have of the same Ducks and Mallards with green Heads, in great Flocks. They are accounted the coarsest sort of our Water-Fowl.

The black Duck is full as large as the other, and good Meat. She stays with us all the Summer and breeds. These are made tame by some, and prove good Domestics.

We have another Duck that stays with us all the Summer. She has a great Topping, is pied and very beautiful. She builds her

Nest in a Woodpeckers Hole, very often sixty or seventy Foot high.

Whistling Duck.—Towards the Mountains in the hilly Country on the West-Branch of Cape Fair Inlet, we saw great Flocks of pretty pied Ducks that whistled as they flew, or as they fed. I did not kill any of them.

Scarlet-Eyed Duck.—We killed a curious sort of Ducks in the Country of the Esaw-Indians, which were of many beautiful Colours. Their Eyes were red, having a red Circle of Flesh for their Eyelids, and were very good to eat.

The Blue-Wings are less than a Duck, but fine Meat. These are the first Fowls that appear to us in the Fall of the Leaf, coming then in great Flocks, as we suppose, from Canada, and the Lakes that lie behind us.

Widgeons, the same as in Europe, are here in great Plenty.

We have the same Teal as in England, and another sort that frequents the Fresh-Water, and are always nodding their Heads. They are smaller than the common Teal, and dainty Meat.

Shovellers (a sort of Duck) are gray, with a black Head. They are a very good Fowl.

These are called Whistlers, from the whistling Noise they make as they fly.

Black Flusterers; some call these Old Wives. They are as black as Ink. The Cocks have white Faces. They always remain in the midst of Rivers, and feed upon drift Grass, Carmels or Sea-Nettles. They are the fattest Fowl I ever saw, and sometimes so heavy with Flesh that they cannot rise out of the Water. They make an odd sort of Noise when they fly. What Meat they are I could never learn. Some call these the great bald Coot.

The wild Turkies I should have spoken of when I treated of the Land-Fowl. There are great Flocks of these in Carolina. I have seen about five hundred in a Flock; some of them are very large. I never weighed any myself, but have been informed of one that weighed near sixty Pound Weight. I have seen half a Turkey feed eight hungry Men two Meals. Sometimes the wild breed with the tame ones, which they reckon makes them very hardy, as I believe it must. I see no manner of Difference betwixt the wild Turkies and the tame ones; only the wild are ever of one Colour, viz: a dark gray or brown, and are excellent Food. They feed on Acorns, Huckle-Berries, and many other sorts of Berries that Carolina affords. The Eggs taken from the Nest and hatched under a Hen will yet retain a wild Nature, and commonly leave you and run wild at last, and will never be got into a House to roost but always perch on some high Tree hard by the House, and separate themselves from the tame sort, although, at the same time, they tread and breed together. I have been informed that if you take these wild Eggs when just on the point of being hatched, and dip them (for some small time) in a Bowl of Milk-warm Water, it will take off their wild Nature and make them as tame and domestic as the others. Some Indians have brought these wild Breed, hatched at home, to be a Decoy to bring others to roost near their Cabins, which they have shot. But to return to the Water-Fowl.

Fishermen are like a Duck, but have a narrow Bill, with Setts of Teeth. They live on very small Fish which they catch as they swim along. They taste Fishy. The best way to order them, is upon oc-casion, to pull the Oil-Box from the Rump and then bury them five or six Hours under the Ground. Then they become tolerable.

Of Divers there are two sorts; the one pied, the other gray; both good Meat.

Raft-Fowl includes all the sorts of small Ducks and Teal that go in Rafts along the Shoar, and are of several sorts that we know no Name for.

Bull-Necks.—These are a whitish Fowl about the Bigness of a Brandt; they come to us after Christmas in very great Flocks, in all our Rivers. They are a very good Meat but hard to kill, because hard to come near. They will dive and endure a great deal of Shot.

Red-Heads, a lesser Fowl than Bull-Necks, are very sweet Food, and plentiful in our Rivers and Creeks.

Tropick-Birds are a white Mew, with a forked Tail. They are so called because they are plentifully met withal under the Tropicks and thereabouts.

The Pellican of the Wilderness cannot be the same as ours; this being a Water-Fowl with a great natural Wen or Pouch under his Throat, in which he keeps his Prey of Fish, which is what he lives on. He is Web-footed like a Goose and shaped like a Duck, but is a very large Fowl, bigger than a Goose. He is never eaten as Food. They make Tobacco-pouches of his Maw.

Cormorants are very well known in some Parts of England; we have great Flocks of them with us, especially against the Herrings run, which is in March and April; then they sit upon Logs of dry Wood in the Water and catch the Fish.

The Gannet is a large white Fowl, having one Part of his Wings black; he lives on Fish as the Pellican. His Fat or Grease is as yellow as Saffron, and the best thing known to preserve Fire-Arms from Rust.

Shear-Waters are a longer Fowl than a Duck; some of them lie on the Coast, whilst others range the Seas all over. Sometimes they are met five hundred Leagues from Land. They live without drinking any fresh Water.

We have a great pied Gull, black and white, which seems to have a black Hood on his Head; these lay very fair Eggs which are good; as are the young ones in the Season.

Marsh-Hen, much the same as in Europe, only she makes another sort of Noise and much thriller.

Blue-Peters.—The same as you call Water-Hens in England, are here very numerous, and not regarded for eating.

The Sand-Birds are about the Bigness of a Lark, and frequent our Sand-Beaches; they are a dainty Food, if you will bestow Time and Ammunition to kill them.

Runners.—These are called Runners, because if you run after them they will run along the Sands and not offer to get up; so that you may often drive them together to shoot as you please. They are a pleasant small Bird.

Tutcocks.—A sort of Snipe, but sucks not his Food; they are almost the same as in England.

Swaddle-Bills are a sort of an ash Coloured Duck which have an extraordinary broad Bill, and are good Meat; they are not common as the others are.

Mew.—The same Mew as in England, being a white, slender Bird, with red Feet.

Shel-Drakes,—the same as in England.

Bald-Faces.—The bald or White Faces are a good Fowl. They cannot dive and are easily shotten.

Water-Witch, or Ware-Coots, are a Fowl with Down and no Feathers; they dive incomparably, so that no Fowler can hit them. They can neither fly nor go; but get into the Fish-wares and cannot fly over the Rods, and so are taken.

Thus have we given an Account of what Fowl has come to our Knowledge, since our Abode in Carolina, expect some that, perhaps, have slipt our Memory, and so are left out of our Catalogue. Proceed we now to treat of the Inhabitants of the Watry Element, which though we can as yet do but very imperfectly; yet we are willing to oblige the Curious with the best Account that is in our Power to present them withal.

THE FISH IN THE SALT, AND FRESH WATERS OF CAROLINA ARE,

Whales, several sorts.
Thrashers.
Divel-Fish.
Sword-Fish.
Crampois.
Bottle-Noses.
Porpoises.
Sharks, two sorts.
Dog-Fish.
Spanish Mackarel.
Cavallies.

Bonetos.
Blue-Fish.
Drum red.
Drum-Fish, black.
Angel-Fish.
Bass or Rock-Fish.
Sheeps-Heads.
Plaice.
Flounder.
Soles.
Mullets.
Shad.
Fat Backs.
Guard white.
Guard green.
Scate or Stingray.
Thornback.
Congar-Eels.
Lamprey-Eels.
Eels.
Sun-Fish.
Toad-Fish.
Sea-Tench.
Trouts of the Salt Water.
Crocus.
Herring.
Smelts.
Shads.
Breams.
Taylors.

FRESH WATER FISH ARE

Sturgeon.
Pike.
Trouts.

Gudgeon.
Pearch, English.
Pearch, white.
Pearch, brown, or
Welchmen.
Pearch, flat, and
Mottled or Irishmen.
Pearch, small and flat, with red Spots called round
   Robins.
Carp.
Roach.
Dace.
Loaches.
Sucking-Fish.
Cat-Fish.
Grindals.
Old-Wives.
Fountain-Fish.
White-Fish.

THE SHELL FISH ARE,

Large crabs, called Stone-Crabs.
Smaller flat Crabs.
Oysters, great and small.
Cockles.
Clams.
Muscles.
Conks.
Skellop.
Man of Noses.
Perriwinkles, or Wilks.
Sea-Snail-Horns.
Fidlars.
Runners.

Spanish, or Pearl-Oysters.

Flattings.

Tortois and Terebin, accounted for among the Insects.

Finger-Fish.

Shrimps.

FRESH WATER.

Craw-Fish.

Muscles.

Whales are very numerous on the Coast of North Carolina, from which they make Oil, Bone, &c., to the great Advantage of those inhabiting the Sand-Banks, along the Ocean, where these Whales come ashore, none being struck or killed with a Harpoon in this Place, as they are to the Northward and elsewhere; all those Fish being found dead on the Shoar, most commonly by those that inhabit the Banks and Sea-Side, where they dwell for that Intent, and for the Benefit of Wrecks which sometimes fall in upon that Shoar.

Of these Monsters there are four sorts; the first, which is most choice and rich, is the Sperma Cœti Whale, from which the Sperma cœti is taken. These are rich Prizes; but I never heard but of one found on this Coast, which was near Currituck Inlet.

The other sorts are of a prodigious Bigness. Of these the Bone and Oil is made, the Oil being the Blubber, or oily Flesh, or Fat of that Fish boiled. These differ not only in Colour, some being pied, others not, but very much in shape, one being called a Bottle-Nosed-Whale, the other a Shovel-Nose, which is as different as a Salmon from a Sturgeon. These Fish seldom come ashoar with their Tongues in their Heads, the Thrasher (which is the Whales mortal Enemy, wheresoever he meets him) eating that out of his Head, as soon as he and the Sword-Fish have killed him. For when the Whale catchers (in other Parts) kill any of these Fish, they eat the Tongue, and esteem it an excellent Dish.

There is another sort of these Whales, or great Fish, though not common. I never knew of above one of that sort, found on the Coast of North Carolina, and he was contrary, in Shape, to all others ever found before him; being sixty Foot in length, and not above three or four Foot Diameter. Some Indians in America will go out to Sea, and get upon a Whale's Back, and peg or plug up his Spouts, and so kill him.

The Thrashers are large Fish, and mortal Enemies to the Whale, as I said before. They make good Oil, but are seldom found.

The Divil-Fish lies at some of our Inlets, and as near as I can describe him, is shaped like a Scate, or Stingray; only he has on his Head a Pair of very thick strong Horns, and is of a monstrous Size, and Strength; for this Fish has been known to weigh a Sloop's Anchor, and run with the Vessel a League or two, and bring her back, against Tide, to almost the same Place. Doubtless, they may afford good Oil; but I have no Experience of any Profits which arise from them.

The Sword-Fish is the other of the Whales Enemies, and joins with the Thrasher to destroy that Monster. After they have overcome him, they eat his Tongue, as I said before, and the Whale drives ashoar.

Crampois is a large Fish, and by some accounted a young Whale; but it is not so; neither is it more than twenty-five or thirty Foot long. They spout as the Whale does, and when taken, yield good Oil.

Bottle-Noses are between the Crampois and porpois, and lie near the Soundings. They are never seen to swim leisurely, as sometimes all other Fish do, but are continually running after their Prey in Great Shoals, like wild Horses, leaping now and then above the Water. The French esteem them good Food, and eat them both fresh and salt.

Porpoises are frequent all over the Ocean and Rivers that are salt; nay, we have a Fresh-Water Lake in the great Sound of North Carolina that has Porpoises in it and several sorts of other unknown Fish, as the Indians say, that we are wholly Strangers to. As to the

Porpoises, they make good Oil; they prey upon other Fish, as Drums, yet never are known to take a Bait so as to be catched with a Hook.

Sharks.—Of these there are two sorts; one called Paracooda-Noses, the other Shovel-Noses; they cannot take their Prey before they turn themselves on their Backs; wherefore some Negroes and others that can swim and dive well, go naked into the Water with a Knife in their Hand, and fight the Shark and very commonly kill him or wound him, so that he turns Tail and runs away. Their Livors make good Oil to dress Leather withal; the Bones found in their Head are said to hasten the Birth and ease the Stone by bringing it away. Their Meat is eaten in scarce times; but I never could away with it, though a great Lover of Fish. Their Back-Bone is of one entire Thickness. Of the Bones or Joints, I have known Buttons made, which serve well enough in scarce Times and remote Places.

The Dog-Fish are a small sort of the Shark Kind, and are caught with Hook and Line, fishing for Drums. They say they are good Meat; but we have so many other sorts of delicate Fish that I shall hardly ever make Tryal what they are.

Spanish Mackarel are, in Colour and Shape, like the common Mackarel, only much thicker. They are caught with Hook and Line at the Inlets, and sometimes out a little way at Sea. They are a very fine hard Fish, and of good Taste. They are about two Foot long or better.

Cavallies are taken in the same Places. They are of a brownish Colour, have exceeding small Scales and a very thick Skin; they are as firm a Fish as ever I saw; therefore will keep sweet, (in the hot Weather) two days when others will stink in half a day, unless salted. They ought to be scaled as soon as taken; otherwise you must pull off the Skin and Scales when boiled, the Skin being the choicest of the Fish. The Meat which is white and large, is dressed with this Fish.

Bonetos are a very palatable Fish, and near a Yard long. They haunt the Inlets and Water near the Ocean, and are killed with the Harpoon and Fishgig.

The Blue Fish is one of our best Fishes, and always very fat. They are as long as a Salmon, and indeed, I think, full as good Meat. These Fish come (in the Fall of the Year,) generally after there has been one black Frost, when there appear great Shoals of them. The Hatteras Indians and others run into the Sands of the Sea, and strike them, though some of these Fish have caused Sickness and violent Burnings after eating of them, which is found to proceed from the Gall that is broken in some of them and is hurtful. Sometimes many Cart-loads of these are thrown and left dry on the Sea side, which comes by their eager Pursuit of the small Fish in which they run themselves ashoar, and the Tide leaving them, they cannot recover the Water again. They are called Blue-Fish, because they are of that Colour and have a forked Tail and are shaped like a Dolphin.

The Red Drum is a large Fish much bigger than the Blue-Fish. The Body of this is good firm Meat, but the Head is beyond all the Fish I ever met withal for an excellent Dish. We have greater Numbers of these Fish than any other sort. People go down and catch as many Barrels full as they please with Hook and Line, especially every young Flood when they bite. These are salted up and transported to other Colonies, that are bare of Provisions.

Black Drums are a thicker-made Fish than the Red Drum, being shaped like a fat Pig; they are a very good Fish, but not so common with us as to the Northward.

The Angel-Fish is shaped like an English Bream. He is so called from his golden Colour, which shines all about his Head and Belly. This is accounted a very good Fish as are most in these Parts. The Bermudians have the same sort of Fish, and esteem them very much.

Bass or Rock is both in Salt and Fresh-Water; when young he much resembles a Grayling, but grows to the size of the large Cod-Fish. They are a very good firm Fish. Their Heads are souced, and make a noble Dish, if large.

Sheeps-Head has the general Vogue of being the choicest Fish in this Place. Indeed, it is a very delicate Fish and well relished; yet I think there are several others full as good as the Sheep-Head. He is much of the Bigness of the Angel-Fish, and flat as he is; they sometimes weigh two or three Pound Weight. This Fish hath Teeth like a Sheep, and is therefore so called.

Plaice are here very large and plentiful, being the same as in England.

Flounders should have gone amongst the Fresh-Water Fish, because they are caught there in great Plenty.

Soles are a Fish we have but lately discovered: they are as good as in any other Part.

Mullets the same as in England, and great Plenty in all Places where the Water is salt or brackish.

Shads are a sweet Fish, but very bony; they are very plentiful at some Seasons.

Fat-Backs are a small Fish like Mullets, but the fattest ever known. They put nothing into the Pan to fry these. They are excellent sweet Food.

The white Guard-Fish is shaped almost like a Pike, but slenderer; his Mouth has a long small Bill set with Teeth, in which he catches small Fish; his Scales are knit together like Armour. When they dress him they strip him, taking off Scales and Skin together. His Meat is very white, and rather looks like Flesh than Fish. The English account them no good Fish, but the Indians do. The Gall of this Fish is green, and a violet Cathartic, if taken inwardly.

The green Guard is shaped, in all respects, like the other, save that his Scales are very small and fine. He is indifferent good Meat; his Bones, when boiled or fried, remain as green as Grass. The same sort of Fish come before the Mackarel in England.

Scate or Stingray, the same as in England, and very common; but the great Plenty of other Fish makes these not regarded, for few or none eat them in Carolina, though they are almost at every one's Door.

Thornbacks are the same as in England. They are not so common as the Scate and Whip-Rays.

Congar-Eels always remain in the Salt-Water; they are much more known in the Northward Parts of America than with us.

Lampreys are not common; I never saw but one, which was large, and caught by the Indians in a Ware. They would not eat him but gave him to me.

Eels are no where in the World better, or more plentiful than in Carolina.

Sun-Fish are flat and rounder than a Bream, and are reckoned a fine-tasted Fish, and not without Reason. They are much the size of Angel-Fish.

Toad-Fish are nothing but a Skin full of Prickles, and a few Bones; they are as ugly as a Toad, and preserved to look upon and good for nothing else.

Sea-Tench.—They are taken by a Bait near the Inlet, or out at Sea a little way. They are blackish and exactly like a Tench, except in the Back-fins, which have Prickles like a Pearch. They are as good if not better than any Tench.

Trouts of the Salt-Water are exactly shaped like the Trouts in Europe, having blackish, not red Spots. They are in the Salts and are not red within but white, yet a very good Fish. They are so tender that if they are in or near fresh Water, and a sudden Frost come, they are benummed, and float on the Surface of the Water as if dead; and then they take up Canoe-Loads of them. If you put them into warm Water they presently recover.

The Crocus is a Fish in Shape like a Pearch, and in Taste like a Whiting. They croke and make a Noise in your Hand when taken with a Hook or Net. They are very good.

The Herrings in Carolina are not so large as in Europe. They spawn there in March and April, running up the fresh Rivers and small fresh Runs of Water in great Shoals where they are taken. They become red if salted; and drest with Vinegar and Oil, resemble an Anchovy very much; for they are far beyond an English Herring when pickled.

Smelts, the same as in England; they lie down a great way in the

Sound towards the Ocean, where, (at some certain Seasons), are a great many very fine ones.

Breams.—The fresh Water affords no such Bream as in England that I have as yet discovered; yet there is a Sea-Bream which is a flat and thin Fish, as the European Breams are.

The Taylor is a Fish about the Bigness of a Trout, but of a bluish and green Colour with a forked Tail, as a Mackarel has. They are a delicate Fish and plentiful in our Salt-Waters. Infinite numbers of Species will be hereafter discovered as yet unknown to us; although I have seen and eaten of several other sorts of Fish which are not here mentioned, because, as yet, they have no certain Names assigned them. Therefore I shall treat no farther of our Salt-Water-Fish, but proceed to the Fresh.

The first of these is the Sturgeon, of which we have Plenty, all the fresh Parts of our Rivers being well stored therewith. The Indians upon and towards the Heads and Falls of our Rivers strike a great many of these and eat them; yet the Indians near the Salt-Water will not eat them. I have seen an Indian strike one of these Fish seven Foot long, and leave him on the Sands to be eaten by the Gulls. In May they run up towards the Heads of the Rivers, where you see several hundreds of them in one day. The Indians have another way to take them which is by Nets at the end of a Pole. The Bones of these Fish make good Nutmeg-Graters.

The Jack, Pike or Pickerel is exactly the same in Carolina as they are in England. Indeed, I never saw this Fish so big and large in America as I have in Europe, these with us being seldom above two Foot long, as far as I have yet seen. They are very plentiful with us in Carolina, all our Creeks and Ponds being full of them. I once took out of a Ware above three hundred of these Fish at a time.

Trouts, the same in England as in Carolina; but ours are a great way up the Rivers and Brooks, that are fresh, having swift Currents and stony and gravelly Bottoms.

The same Gudgeons as in Europe are found in America.

The same sort of Pearch as are in England we have likewise in

Carolina, though, I think, ours never rise to be so large as in England.

We have a white Pearch, so called because he is of a Silver Colour, otherwise like the English Pearch. These we have in great Plenty, and they are preferable to the red ones.

The brown Pearch, which some call Welch-men, are the largest sort of Pearches that we have, and very firm, white and sweet Fish. These grow to be larger than any Carp, and are very frequent in every Creek and Pond.

The flat or mottled Pearch are shaped almost like a Bream. They are called Irish-men, being freckled or mottled with black and blue Spots. They are never taken anywhere but in the fresh Water. They are good Fish, but I do not approve of them no more than the other sorts of Pearch.

We have another sort of Pearch which is the least sort of all, but as good Meat as any. These are distinguished from the other sorts by the Name of Round-Robins, being flat and very round shaped; they are spotted with red Spots very beautiful and are easily caught with an Angle, as all the other sort of Pearches are.

We have the same Carp as you have in England.

And the same Roach, only scarce so large.

Dace are the same as yours too; but neither are these so large nor plentiful, as with you.

Loach, the same as in England.

Sucking-Fish are the nearest in Taste and Shape to a Barbel, only they have no Barbs.

Cat-Fish are a round blackish Fish, with a great flat Head, a wide Mouth and no Scales; they sometimes resemble Eels in Taste. Both this sort, and another that frequents the Salt Water, are very plentiful.

Grindals are a long scaled Fish with small Eyes, and frequent Ponds, Lakes, and slow running Creeks and Swamps. They are a soft, sorry Fish, and good for nothing; though some eat them for good Fish.

Old-Wives.—These are a bright scaly Fish, which frequents the Swamps and fresh Runs; they seem to be between an English Roach and a Bream, and eat much like the latter. The Indians kill abundance of these, and barbakue them till they are a crisp, then transport them in wooden Hurdles, to their Towns and Quarters.

The Fountain-Fish are a white sort which breed in the clear Running Springs and Fountains of Water, where the Clearness thereof makes them very difficult to be taken. I cannot say how good they are, because I have not as yet tasted of them.

The White-Fish are very large; some being two Foot and a half long and more. They are found a great way up in the Freshes of the Rivers; and are firm Meat, an extraordinary well-relished Fish.

Barbouts and Millers-Thumbs, are the very same here in all respects, as they are in England. What more are in the fresh Waters we have not discovered, but are satisfied, that we are not acquainted with one-third part thereof; for we are told by the Indians, of a great many strange and uncouth shapes and sorts of Fish, which they have found in the Lakes laid down in my Chart. However as we can give no farther Account of these than by Hear-say, I proceed to treat of the Shell-Fish, that are found in the Salt-Water, so far as they have already come to our Knowledge.

The large Crabs, which we all call Stone-Crabs, are the same sort as in England, having black Tips at the end of their Claws. These are plentifully met withal, down in Core Sound, and the South Parts of North Carolina.

The smaller flat Crabs I look upon to be the sweetest of all the Species. They are the Breadth of a lusty Man's Hand, or rather larger. These are innumerable, lying in most prodigious quantities, all over the Salts of Carolina. They are taken not only to eat, but are the best Bait for all sorts of Fish, that live in the Salt-Water. These Fish are mischievous to Night-Hooks, because they get away all the Bait from the Hooks.

Oysters, great and small, are found almost in every Creek and Gut of Salt-Water, and are very good and well relished. The large Oysters are excellent pickled.

One Cockle in Carolina is as big as five or six in England. They are often thrown upon the Sands on the Sound-Side, where the Gulls are always ready to open and eat them.

Clams are a sort of Cockles, only differing in Shell, which is thicker and not streaked, or ribbed. These are found throughout all the Sound and Salt-Water-Ponds. The Meat is the same for Look and Taste as the Cockle. These make an excellent strong Broth, and eat well, either roasted or pickled.

The Muscles in Carolina have a very large Shell, striped with Dents. They grow by the side of Ponds and Creeks, in Salt-Water, wherein you may get as many of them as you please. I do not like them so well as the English Muscle, which is no good Shell-Fish.

Conks.—Some of the Shells of these fish are as large as a Man's Hand, but the lesser sort are the best Meat, and those not extraordinary. They are shaped like the end of a Horses Yard. Of their Shells, the Peak, or Wampum is made, which is the richest Commodity amongst the Indians. They breed like a long Thing shaped like a Snake, but containing a sort of Joints, in the Hollowness whereof are thousands of small Coaks, no bigger than small Grains of Pepper.

The Skellops, if well dressed, are a pretty Shell-Fish; but to eat them only roasted, without any other Addition, in my Judgment, are too luscious.

Man of Noses are a Shell-Fish commonly found amongst us. They are valued for increasing Vigor in Men and making barren Women fruitful; but I think they have no need of that Fish, for the Women in Carolina are fruitful enough without their Helps.

Wilkes, or Perriwinkles, are not so large here as in the Islands of Scilly, and in other parts of Europe, though very sweet.

The Sea-Snail-Horn is large, and very good Meat. They are exactly shaped as other Snail-Horns are.

Fidlars are a sort of small Crabs, that lie in Holes in the Marshes. The Raccoons eat them very much. I never knew any one try whether they were good Meat or no.

Runners live chiefly on the Sands, but sometimes run into the Sea. They have Holes in the Sand-Beaches and are a whitish sort of a Crab. Though small, they run as fast as a Man, and are good for nothing but to look at.

Spanish Oysters have a very thin Shell, and rough on the outside. They are very good Shell-Fish, and so large, that half a dozen are enow to satisfy an hungry Stomach.

The Flattings are inclosed in a broad, thin Shell, the whole Fish being flat. They are inferior to no Shell-Fish this Country affords.

Finger-Fish are very plentiful in this Country; they are of the Length of a Man's Finger, and lie in the Bottom of the Water about one or two Foot deep. They are very good.

Shrimps are very plentiful and good, and are to be taken with a Small-Bow-Net in great Quantities.

The small Cockles are about the Bigness of the largest English Cockles, and differ nothing from them, unless in the Shells, which are striped cross-wise, as well as long-wise.

The Fresh-Water Shell-Fish are,

Muscles, which are eaten by the Indians, after five or six hours Boiling to make them tender, and then are good for nothing.

Craw-Fish in the Brooks and small Rivers of Water amongst the Tuskeruro Indians and up higher, are found very plentiful, and as good as any in the World.

And thus I have gone through the several Species of Fish, so far as they have come to my Knowledge, in the eight Years that I have lived in Carolina. I should have made a larger Discovery when traveling so far toward the Mountains and amongst the Hills, had it not been in the Winter-Season, which was improper to make any Enquiry into any of the Species before recited. Therefore, as my Intent was, I proceed to what remains of the Present State of Carolina, having already accounted for the Animals and Vegetables as far as this Volume would allow of, whereby the Remainder, though not exactly known, may yet be guessed at if we consider what Latitude Carolina lies in, which reaches from 29 to 36 deg. 30 min.

Northern Latitude as I have before observed. Which Latitude is as fertile and pleasant as any in the World, as well for the Produce of Minerals, Fruits, Grain and Wine, as other rich Commodities. And, indeed, all the Experiments that have been made in Carolina, of the Fertility and natural Advantages of the Country, have exceeded all Expectations as affording some Commodities which other Places, in the same Latitude, do not. As for Minerals as they are subterraneous Products, so in all new Countries, they are the Species that are last discovered; and especially in Carolina, where the Indians never look for any thing lower than the Superficies of the Earth, being a Race of Men the least addicted to delving of any People that inhabit so fine a Country as Carolina is. As good if not better Mines than those the Spaniards possess in America, lie full West from us; and I am certain we have as Mountainous Land and as great Probability of having rich Minerals in Carolina as any of those Parts that are already found to be so rich therein. But waving this Subject till some other Opportunity, I shall now give you some Observations in general, concerning Carolina; which are, first, that it lies as convenient for Trade as any of the Plantations in America; that we have Plenty of Pitch, Tar, Skins of Deer, and Beeves, Furs, Rice, Wheat, Rie, Indian Grain, sundry sorts of Pulse, Turpentine, Rosin, Masts, Yards, Planks and Boards, Staves and Lumber. Timber of many common sorts, fit for any Uses; Hemp, Flax, Barley, Oats, Buck-Wheat, Beef, Pork, Tallow, Hides, Whale-Bone and Oil, Wax, Cheese, Butter, &c., besides Drugs, Dyes, Fruit, Silk, Cotton, Indico, Oil and Wine that we need not doubt of as soon as we make a regular Essay, the Country being adorned with Pleasant Meadows, Rivers, Mountains, Valleys, Hills, and rich Pastures, and blessed with wholesome, pure Air; especially a little backwards from the Sea, where the wild Beasts inhabit, none of which are voracious. The Men are active, the Women fruitful to Admiration, every House being full of Children, and several Women that have come hither barren, having presently proved fruitful. There cannot be a richer Soil, no Place abounding more in Flesh and Fowl, both wild and tame, besides, Fish, Fruit, Grain, Cider, and many other pleasant Liquors, together with several other Necessaries for Life and Trade, that are daily found out, as new Discoveries are made. The Stone and Gout seldom trouble us; the Consumption we are wholly Strangers to, no Place affording a better Remedy for that Distemper than Carolina. For Trade we lie so near to Virginia that we have the Advantage of their Convoys; as also Letters from thence in two or three Days at most, in some Places in as few Hours. Add to this the great Number of Ships which come within those Capes, for Virginia and Maryland take off our Provisions and give us Bills of Exchange for England, which is Sterling Money. The Planters in Virginia and Maryland are forced to do the same, the great Quantities of Tobacco that are planted there, Making Provisions scarce; and Tobacco is a Commodity oftentimes so low as to bring nothing, whereas Provisions and Naval Stores never fail of a Market. Besides, where these are raised in such Plenty as in Carolina, there always appears good Housekeeping, and Plenty of all manner of delicate Eatables. For Instance, the Pork of Carolina is very good, the younger Hogs fed on Peaches, Maiz, and such other natural Produce; being some of the sweetest Meat that the World affords, as is acknowledged by all Strangers that have been there. And as for the Beef in Pamticough and the Southward Parts, it proves extraordinary. We have not only Provisions plentiful, but Cloaths of our own Manufactures, which are made and daily increase; Cotton, Wool, Hemp, and Flax being of our own Growth; and the Women to be highly commended for their Industry in Spinning and ordering their Housewifery to so great Advantage as they generally do, which is much more easy by reason this happy Climate, visited with so mild Winters, is much warmer than the Northern Plantations, which saves abundance of Cloaths, fewer serving our Necessities and those of our Servants. But this is not all, for we can go out with our Commodities to any other Part of the West Indies, or elsewhere, in the Depth of Winter; whereas, those in New England, New York, Pennsylvania, and the Colonies to the Northward of us cannot stir for Ice, but are fast locked into their Harbours. Besides we can trade with South Carolina, and pay no Duties or Customs no more than their own Vessels both North and South being under the Same Lords Proprietors. We have, as I observed before, another great Advantage, in not being a Frontier, and so continually alarmed by the Enemy; and what has been accounted a Detriment to us, proves one of the greatest Advantages any People could wish, which is, our Country's being faced with a Sound near ten Leagues over in some Places, through which, although there be Water enough for as large Ships to come in at, as in any part hitherto seated in both Carolinas; yet the Difficulty of that Sound to Strangers, hinders them from attempting any Hostilities against us; and at the same time, if we consider the Advantages thereof, nothing can appear to be a better Situation, than to be fronted with such a Bulwark, which secures us from our Enemies. Furthermore, our Distance from the Sea rids us of two Curses, which attend most other Parts of America, viz: Muskeetos and the Worm-biting, which eat Ships Bottoms out; whereas at Bath-Town, there is no such thing known; and as for Muskeetos, they hinder us of as little Rest as they do you in England. Add to this, the unaccountable Quantities of Fish this great Water or Sound, supplies us withal, whenever we take the Pains to fish for them; Advantages I have no where met withal in America, except here. As for the Climate, we enjoy a very wholesome and serene Sky, and a pure and thin Air, the Sun seldom missing to give us his daily Blessing, unless now and then on a Winter's Day, which is not often; and when cloudy, the first Appearance of a North-West-Wind clears the Horizon, and restores the Light of the Sun. The Weather, in summer, is very pleasant. The hotter Months being refreshed with continual Breezes of cool reviving Air; and the Spring being as pleasant and beautiful, as in any Place I ever was in. The Winter, most commonly, is so mild, that it looks like an Autum, being now and then attended with clear and thin North-West Winds, that are sharp enough to regulate English Constitutions, and free them from a great many dangerous

Distempers, that a continual Summer afflicts them withal, nothing being wanting as to the natural Ornaments and Blessings of a Country, that conduce to make reasonable Men happy. And for those that are otherwise, they are so much their own Enemies, where they are, that they will scarce ever be any one's Friends or their own, when they are transplanted so, it is much better for all sides, that they remain as they are. Not but that there are several good People that, upon just Grounds, may be uneasy under their present Burdens; and such I would advise to remove to the Place I have been treating of, where they may enjoy their Liberty and Religion, and peaceably eat the Fruits of their Labour, and drink the Wine of their own Vineyards, without the Alarms of a troublesome worldly Life. If a Man be a Botanist, here is a plentiful Field of Plants to divert him in. If he be a Gardner, and delight in that pleasant and happy Life, he will meet with a Climate and Soil that will further and promote his Designs, in as great a Measure, as any Man can wish for; and as for the Constitution of this Government, it is so mild and easy, in respect to the Properties and Liberties of a Subject, that without rehearsing the Particulars, I say once for all, it is the mildest and best established Government in the World, and the Place where any Man may peaceably enjoy his own without being invaded by another; Rank and Superiority ever giving Place to Justice and Equity, which is the Golden Rule that every Government ought to be built upon, and regulated by. Besides it is worthy our Notice, that this Province has been settled, and continued the most free from the Insults and Barbarities of the Indians of any Colony that was ever yet seated in America, which must be esteemed as a particular Providence of God, handed down from Heaven to these People, especially when we consider how irregularly they settled North-Carolina, and yet how undisturbed they have ever remained, free from any foreign Danger or Loss, even to this very Day. And what may well be looked upon for as great a Miracle, this is, a Place where no Malefactors are found deserving Death, or even a Prison for Debtors, there being no more than two Persons, as far as I have been able to learn, ever suffered as Criminals, although it has been a Settlement near sixty Years; One of whom was a Turk that committed Murder, the other an old Woman, for Witchcraft. These tis true, were on the Stage and acted many Years before I knew the Place, but as for the last, I wish it had been undone to this day, although they give a great many Arguments to justify the Deed which I had rather they should have had a Hand in than myself; seeing I could never approve of taking Life away upon such Accusations, the Justice whereof I could never yet understand.

But to return to the Subject in Hand, we there make extraordinary good Bricks throughout the Settlement. All sorts of Handicrafts, as Carpenters, Joiners, Masons, Plaisters, Shoemakers, Tanners, Taylors, Weavers, and most others, may with small Beginnings, and God's Blessing, thrive very well in this Place, and provide Estates for their Children, Land being sold at a much cheaper Rate there than in any other Place in America, and may, as I suppose, be purchased of the Lords Proprietors here in England, or of the Governour there for the time being, by any that shall have a mind to transport themselves to that Country. The Farmers that go thither (for which sort of Men it is a very thriving Place) should take with them some particular Seeds of Grass, as Trefoil, Clovergrass all sorts, Sanfoin, and Common Grass, or that which is a Rarity in Europe, especially, what has sprung and rose first from a warm Climate, and will endure the Sun without flinching. Likewise, if there be any extraordinary sort of Grain for Increase or Hardiness, and some Fruit-Trees of choice kinds, they will be both profitable and pleasant to have with you, where you may see the Fruits of your Labor in Perfection, in a few Years. The necessary Instruments of Husbandry I need not acquaint the Husbandman withal. Hoes of all sorts and Axes, must be had, with Saws, Wedges, Augurs, Nails, Hammers, and what other Things may be necessary for building with Brick, or Stone, which sort your Inclination and Conveniency lead you to.

For, after having looked over this Treatise, you must needs be acquainted with the Nature of the Country, and therefore cannot but be Judges, what it is that you will chiefly want. As for Land, none need want it for taking up, even in the Places there seated on the Navigable Creeks, Rivers, and Harbours, without being driven into remoter Holes and Corners of the Country for Settlements, which all are forced to do, who, at this day, settle in most or all of the other English Plantations in America; which are already become so populous that a New-Comer cannot get a beneficial and commodious Seat, unless he purchases, when, in most Places in Virginia and Maryland, a thousand Acres of good Land, seated on a Navigable Water, will cost a thousand Pounds; whereas, with us, it is at present obtained for the fiftieth Part of the Money. Besides our Land pays to the Lords but an easy Quit-Rent, or yearly Acknowledgement; and the other Settlements pay two Shillings per hundred. All these things duly weighed, any rational Man that has a mind to purchase Land in the Plantations for a Settlement of himself and Family, will soon discover the Advantages that attend the Settlers and Purchasers of Land in Carolina above all other Colonies in the English Dominions in America. And as there is a free Exercise of all Persuasions amongst Christians, the Lord's Proprietors to encourage Ministers of the Church of England have given free Land towards the Maintenance of a Church, and especially for the Parish of S. Thomas in Pampticough, over-against the Town is already laid out for a Glebe of two hundred and twenty-three Acres of rich well situated Land, that a Parsonage-House may be built upon. And now I shall proceed to give an Account of the Indians, their Customs and Ways of Living, with a short Dictionary of their Speech.

An Account of the Indians of N. Carolina

THE Indians, which were the Inhabitants of America when the Spaniards and other Europeans discovered the several Parts of that Country, are the People which we reckon the Natives thereof; as indeed they were, when we first found out those Parts and appeared therein. Yet this has not wrought in me a full Satisfaction to allow these People to have been the Ancient Dwellers of the New-World, or Tract of Land we call America. The Reasons that I have to think otherwise, are too many to set down here; but I shall give the Reader a few before I proceed, and some others he will find scattered in my Writings elsewhere.

In Carolina (the Part I now treat of) are the fairest Marks of a Deluge, (that at some time has probably made strange Alterations as to the Station that Country was then in) that ever I saw, or, I think, read of, in any History. Amongst the other Subterraneous Matters that have been discovered, we found, in digging of a Well that was twenty-six foot deep, at the Bottom thereof, many large Pieces of the Tulip-Tree, and several other sorts of Wood, some of which were cut and notched, and some squared, as the Joices of a House are, which appeared (in the Judgment of all that saw them) to be wrought with Iron Instruments; it seeming impossible for anything made of Stone, or what they were found to make use of, to cut Wood in that manner. It cannot be argued, that the Wood so cut, might float from some other Continent, because Hiccory and the Tulip-Tree are spontaneous in America, and in no other Places that I could ever learn. It is to be acknowledged that the Spaniards give us Relations of magnificent Buildings, which were raised by the Indians of Mexico and other Parts, which they discovered and conquered, amongst whom no Iron Instruments were found. But tis a great Misfortune that no Person in that Expedition was so curious as to take an exact Draught of the Fabricks of those People, which would have been a Discovery of great Value, and very acceptable to the Ingenius; for, as to the Politeness of Stones, it may be effected by Collision and Grinding, which is of a contrary Nature, on several Accounts, and disproves not my Arguments in the least.

The next is, the Earthern Pots that are often found under Ground, and at the Foot of the Banks where the Water has washed them away. They are, for the most part broken in pieces; but we find them of a different sort, in Comparison of those the Indians use at this day, who have had no other ever since the English discovered America. The Bowels of the Earth cannot have altered them, since they are thicker, of another Shape and Composition, and nearly approach to the Urns of the Ancient Romans.

Again, the Peaches, which are the only tame Fruit, or what is Foreign, that these People enjoy, which is an Eastern Product, and will keep and retain its vegetative and growing Faculty the longest of anything of that Nature, that I know of. The Stone, as I elsewhere have remarked, is thicker than any other sort of the Peaches in Europe, or of the European sort, now growing in America, and is observed to grow, if planted, after it has been for several Years laid by; and it seems very probable that these People might come from some Eastern Country; for when you ask them whence their Fore Fathers came, that first inhabited the Country, they will point to the Westward, and say, *Where the Sun sleeps our Forefathers came thence,* which, at that distance, may be reckoned amongst the Eastern Parts of the World. And, to this day, they are a shifting, wandering People; for I know some Indian Nations that have changed their Settlements many hundred Miles, sometimes no less than a thousand, as is proved by the Savanna Indians, who formerly lived on the Banks of the Messiasippi, and removed thence to the Head of one of the Rivers of South-Carolina; since which, (for some Dislike,) most of them are removed to live in the Quarters of the Iroquo or Sinnagars, which are on the Heads of the Rivers that disgorge themselves into the Bay of Chesapeak. I once met with a young Indian Woman that had been brought from beyond the Mountains, and was sold a Slave into Virginia. She spoke the same Language as

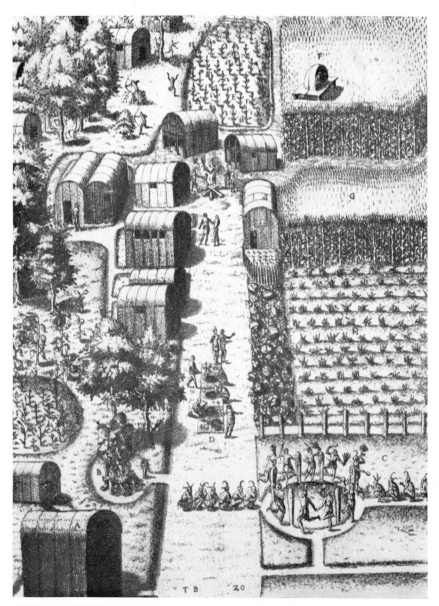

TOWN OF SECOTA: (A.) Wherein are the tombs of their kings and princes; (B.) Where they assemble themselves to make their solemn prayers; (C.) A broad plot in the town where they meet with their neighbors to celebrate their chief solemn feasts; (D.) Where after the feast they make merry together; (E.) Field of tobacco. Indian name for Uppowoc; (F.) Field of corn, with guard house in which a watchman sits making continual cries and noise to keep away the large flocks of birds and marauding animals; (G.) Shows the corn choked by its own growth when planted too close; (H.) Shows the broad furrows they use in planting their corn, otherwise its growth would be choked by its rapid spread; (I.) Garden wherein they sow their pompions. (Mentioned in Lawson's text. Ed.); (K.) A place where they make a fire for their solemn feasts. (All feasts are held at night.); (L.) The river outside the town from which they fetch their water.

"This people therefore voyde of all comforts lyve cherfullye and att their harts ease. Butt they solemnise their feasts in the night, and therefore they keepe verye great fyres to avoyde darkness, and to testifie their Joye." From *A Briefe and True Report of Virginia,* by Thomas Hariot.

the Coramine Indians, that dwell near Cape Lookout, allowing for some few Words, which were different, yet no otherwise than that they might understand one another very well.

The Indians of North-Carolina are a well shaped clean-made People, of different Statures, as the Europeans are, yet chiefly inclined to be tall. They are a very straight People, and never bend forwards or stoop in the Shoulders, unless much overpowered by old Age. Their Limbs are exceeding well shaped. As for their Legs and Feet, they are generally the handsomest in the World. Their Bodies are a little flat, which is occasioned by being laced hard down to a Board in their Infancy. This is all the Cradle they have, which I shall describe at large elsewhere. Their Eyes are black, or of a dark Hazel; The White is marbled with red Streaks, which is ever common to these People, unless when sprung from a white Father or Mother. Their Colour is of a tawny, which would not be so dark did they not dawb themselves with Bear's Oil, and a Colour like burnt Cork. This is begun in their Infancy and continued for a long time, which fills the Pores and enables them better to endure the Extremity of the Weather. They are never bald on their Heads, although never so old, which, I believe, proceeds from their Heads being always uncovered, and the greasing their Hair, so often as they do, with Bear's Fat, which is a great Nourisher of the Hair, and causes it to grow very fast. Amongst the Bear's Oil, (when they intend to be fine) they mix a certain red Powder, that comes from a Scarlet Root which they get in the hilly Country, near the Foot of the Ridge of Mountains, and it is no where else to be found. They have this Scarlet Root in great Esteem, and sell it for a very great Price one to another. The Reason of its Value is, because they not only go a long way for it but are in great Danger of the Sinnagers or Iroquois, who are mortal Enemies to all our Indians, and very often take them Captives or kill them before they return from this Voyage. The Tuskeruros and other Indians have often brought this Seed with them from the Mountains; but it would never grow in our Land. With this and Bear's Grease they anoint their Heads and

Temples, which is esteemed as ornamental, as sweet Powder to our Hair. Besides, this Root has the Virtue of Killing Lice, and suffers none to abide or breed in their Heads. For want of this Root, they sometimes use Pecoon-Root, which is of a Crimson Colour, but it is apt to die the Hair of an ugly Hue.

Their Eyes are commonly full and manly, and their Gate sedate and majestic. They never walk backward and forward as we do, nor contemplate on the Affairs of Loss and Gain, the things which daily perplex us. They are dexterous and steady, both as to their Hands and Feet, to Admiration. They will walk over deep Brooks and Creeks on the smallest Poles, and that without any Fear or Concern. Nay, an Indian will walk on the Ridge of a Barn or House and look down the Gable-end, and spit upon the Ground as unconcerned as if he was walking on Terra firma. In Running, Leaping or any such other Exercise, their Legs seldom miscarry and give them a Fall; and as for letting any thing fall out of their Hands, I never yet knew one Example. They are no Inventers of any Arts or Trades worthy mention; the Reason of which I take to be, that they are not possessed with that Care and Thoughtfulness, how to provide for the Necessaries of Life as the Europeans are; yet they will learn any thing very soon. I have known an Indian stock Guns better than most of our Joiners, although he never saw one stocked before; and besides, his Working-Tool was only a sorry Knife. I have also known several of them that were Slaves to the English, learn Handicraft-Trades very well and speedily. I never saw a Dwarf amongst them, nor but one that was Hump-backed. Their Teeth are yellow with Smoaking Tobacco, which both Men and Women are much addicted to. They tell us that they had Tobacco amongst them before the Europeans made any Discovery of that Continent. It differs in the Leaf from the sweet scented, and Oroonoko, which are the Plants we raise and cultivate in America. Theirs differs likewise much in the Smell, when green, from our Tobacco before cured. They do not use the same way to cure it as we do, and therefore the Difference must be very considerable in Taste; for all Men (that know Tobacco) must allow that it is the Ordering thereof which gives a Hogoo to that Weed rather than any Natural Relish it possesses when green. Although they are great Smokers, yet they never are seen to take it in Snuff or chew it.

They have no Hairs on their Faces, (except some few) and those but little, nor is there often found any Hair under their Arm-Pits. They are continually plucking it away from their Faces by the Roots. As for their Privities, since they wore Tail-Clouts to cover their Nakedness, several of the Men have a deal of Hair thereon. It is to be observed that the Head of the Penis is covered, (throughout all the Nations of the Indians I ever saw) both in Old and Young. Although we reckon these a very smooth People, and free from Hair; yet I once saw a middle aged Man that was hairy all down his Back; the Hairs being above an Inch long.

As there are found very few, or scarce any, Deformed or Cripples amongst them, so neither did I ever see but one blind Man; and then they would give me no Account how his Blindness came. They had a Use for him, which was to lead him with a Girl, Woman or Boy, by a String; so they put what Burdens they pleased upon his Back, and made him very servicable upon all such Occasions. No People have better Eyes, or see better in the Night or Day than the Indians. Some alledge that the Smoke of the Pitch-Pine which they chiefly burn, does both preserve and strengthen the Eyes; as, perhaps, it may do, because that Smoke never offends the Eyes, though you hold your Face over a great fire thereof. This is occasioned by the volatile Part of the Turpentine, which rises with the Smoke, and is of a friendly, balsamic Nature; for the Ashes of the Pine-Tree afford no fixed Salt in them.

They let their Nails grow very long, which, they reckon, is the Use Nails are designed for, and laugh at the Europeans for pairing theirs, which, they say disarms them of that which Nature designed them for.

They are not of so robust and strong Bodies as to lift great Burdens, and endure Labour and Slavish Work, as the Europeans are;

yet some that are Slaves, prove very good and laborious; But, of themselves, they never work as the English do, taking care for no farther than what is absolutely necessary to support Life. In Traveling and Hunting, they are very indefatigable, because that carries a Pleasure along with the Profit. I have known some of them very strong; and as for Running and Leaping, they are extraordinary Fellows, and will dance for several Nights together with the greatest Briskness imaginable, their Wind never failing them.

Their Dances are of different Natures; and for every sort of Dance they have a Tune, which, is allotted for that Dance; as, if it be a War-Dance, they have a war-like Song, wherein they express, with all the Passion and Vehemence imaginable, what they intend to do with their Enemies; how they will kill, roast, sculp, beat, and make Captive, such and such Numbers of them; and how many they have destroyed before. All these Songs are made new for every Feast; nor is one and the same Song sung at two several Festivals. Some one of the Nation, (which has the best Gift of expressing their Designs,) is appointed by their King and War-Captains to make these Songs.

Others are made for Feasts of another Nature; as, when several Towns, or sometimes different Nations have made Peace with one another; then the Song suits both Nations, and relates how the bad Spirit made them go to War and destroy one another; but it shall never be so again; but that their Sons and Daughters shall marry together, and the two Nations love one another, and become as one People.

They have a third sort of Feasts and Dances, which are always when the Harvest of Corn is ended and in the Spring. The one to return Thanks to the good Spirit for the Fruits of the Earth; the other, to beg the same Blessings for the succeeding Year. And to encourage the young Men to Labour stoutly in planting their Maiz and Pulse, they set a sort of an Idol in the Field, which is dressed up exactly like an Indian, having all the Indians Habit, besides abundance of Wampum and their Money, made of Shells, that hangs about his Neck. The Image none of the young Men dare approach; for the old ones will not suffer them to come near him, but tell them that he is some famous Indian Warriour that died a great while ago, and now is come amongst them to see if they work well, which if they do, he will go to the good Spirit and speak to him to send them Plenty of Corn, and to make the young Men all expert Hunters and mighty Warriours. All this while, the King and old Men sit round the Image and seemingly pay a profound Respect to the same. One great Help to these Indians in carrying on these Cheats, and inducing Youth to do what they please, is, the uninterrupted Silence which is ever kept and observed with all the Respect and Veneration imaginable.

At these Feasts which are set out with the Magnificence their Fare allows of, the Masquerades begin at Night and not before. There is commonly a Fire made in the middle of the House, which is the largest in the Town, and is very often the Dwelling of their King or War-Captain; where sit two Men on the Ground upon a Mat; one with a Rattle, made of a Gourd, with some Beans in it; the other with a Drum made of an earthern Pot, covered with a dressed-Deer-Skin, and one Stick in his Hand to beat thereon; and so they both begin the Song appointed. At the same time one drums and the other rattles, which is all the artificial Musick of their own making I ever saw amongst them. To these two Instruments they sing, which carries no Air with it, but is a sort of unsavory Jargon; yet their Cadences and Raising of their Voices are formed with that Equality and Exactness that, (to us Europeans) it seems admirable how they should continue these Songs without once missing to agree, each with the others Note and Tune.

As for their Dancing, were there Masters of that Profession amongst them as there are with us, they would dearly earn their Money; for these Creatures take the most Pains at it that Men are able to endure. I have seen thirty odd together a dancing, and every one dropped down with Sweat, as if Water had been poured down their Backs. They used those hard Labours to make them able to endure Fatigue and improve their Wind, which indeed is very long and durable, it being a hard matter in any Exercise to dispossess them of it.

At these Feasts, they meet from all the Towns within fifty or sixty Miles round, where they buy and sell several Commodities, as we do at Fairs and Markets. Besides they game very much, and often strip one another of all they have in the World; and what is more, I have known several of them play themselves away, so that they have remained the Winners Servants, till their Relations or themselves could pay the Money to redeem them; and when this happens, the Loser is never dejected or melancholy at the Loss, but Laughs and seems no less contented than if he had won. They never differ at Gaming, neither did I ever see a Dispute about the Legality thereof, so much as rise amongst them.

Their chiefest Game is a sort of Arithmetic, which is managed by a Parcel of small, split Reeds, the Thickness of a small Bent; these are made very nicely, so that they part and are tractable in their Hands. They are fifty-one in Number; their Length about seven Inches; when they play, they throw part of them to their Antagonist; the Art is, to discover upon sight, how many you have, and what you throw to him that plays with you. Some are so expert at their Numbers that they will tell ten times together, what they throw out of their Hands. Although the whole Play is carried on with the quickest Motion it is possible to use, yet some are so expert at this Game, as to win great Indian Estates by this Play. A good Sett of these Reeds, fit to play withal, are valued and sold for a dressed Doe-Skin.

They have several other Plays and Games, as, with the Kernels or Stones of Persimmons, which are in effect the same as our Dice, because Winning or Losing depend on which side appear uppermost, and how they happen to fall together.

Another Game is managed with a Batton and a Ball, and resembles our Trap-ball; besides, several Nations have several Games and Past-times, which are not used by others.

These Savages live in Wigwams, or Cabins, built of Bark, which are made round, like an Oven, to prevent any Damage by hard Gales of Wind. They make the Fire in the middle of the House, and have a Hole at the Top of the Roof right above the Fire to let out the Smoke. These Dwellings are as hot as Stoves, where the Indians sleep and sweat all Night. The Floors thereof are never paved nor swept, so that they have always a loose Earth on them. They are often troubled with a multitude of Fleas, especially near the Places where they dress their Deer-Skins, because that Hair harbours them; yet I never felt any ill, unsavory Smell in their Cabins, whereas, should we live in our Houses, as they do, we should be poisoned with our own Nastiness, which confirms these Indians to be, as they really are, some of the sweetest People in the World.

The Bark they make their Cabins withal, is generally Cypress, or red or white Cedar; and sometimes, when they are a great way from any of these Woods, they make use of Pine-Bark, which is the worser sort. In building these Fabricks, they get very long Poles of Pine, Cedar, Hiccory, or any other Wood that will bend; these are the Thickness of the Small of a Man's Leg, at the thickest end, which they generally strip of the Bark, and warm them well in the Fire, which makes them tough and fit to bend. Afterwards, they stick the thickest ends of them in the Ground, about two Yards asunder, in a Circular Form, the distance they design the Cabin to be (which is not always round, but sometimes oval) then they bend the Tops and bring them together, and bind their ends with Bark of Trees, that is proper for that use, as Elm is, or sometimes the Moss that grows on the Trees, and is a Yard or two long, and never rots; then they brace them with other Poles to make them strong; afterwards cover them all over with Bark, so that they are very warm and tight, and will keep firm against all the Weathers that blow. They have other sorts of Cabins without Windows, which are for their Granaries, Skins and Merchandizes, and others that are covered overhead; the rest left open for the Air. These have Reed-Hurdles, like Tables, to lie and sit on, in Summer, and serve for pleasant

Banqueting-Houses in the hot Season of the Year. The Cabins they dwell in have Benches all round, except where the Door stands on these they lay Beast-Skins, and Mats made of Rushes, whereon they sleep and loll. In one of these several Families commonly live, though all related to one another.

As to the Indian's Food, it is of several sorts, which are as follows:

Venison, and Fawns in the Bags, cut out of the Doe's Belly; Fish of all sorts, the Lamprey-Eel excepted, and the Sturgeon, our Salt-Water Indians will not touch; Bear, and Bever, Panther, Pole-cat, Wild-Cat, Possum, Raccoon, Hares, and Squirrels, roasted with their Guts in; Snakes, all Indians will not eat them, though some do; All wild Fruits, that are palatable, some of which they dry and keep against Winter, as all sort of Fruits, and Peaches, which they dry and make Quiddonies and Cakes, that are very pleasant, and a little tartish; young Wasps, when they are white in the Combs, before they can fly, this is esteemed a Dainty; All sorts of Tortois and Terebins, Shell-Fish, and Stingray, or scate, dried; Guords, Melons, Cucumbers, Squashes, Pulse of all sorts; Rockahomine Meal, which is their Maiz, parched and pounded into Powder; Fowl, of all sorts that are eatable; Ground-Nuts, or wild Potatoes; Acorns and Acorn Oil, Wild-Bulls, Beef, Mutton, Pork, &c., from the English; Indian Corn, or Maiz, made into several sorts of Bread; Ears of Corn roasted in the Summer, or preserved against Winter.

The Victuals is common throughout the whole Kindred Relations, and often to the whole Town; especially when they are in Hunting-Quarters, then they all fare alike, whichsoever of them kills the Game. They are very kind and charitable to one another, but more especially to those of their own Nation; for if any one of them has suffered any Loss, by Fire, or otherwise, they order the grieved Person to make a Feast, and invite them all thereto, which, on the day appointed, they come to, and after every Man's Mess of Victuals is dealt to him, one of their Speakers, or grave old Men, makes an Harrangue, and acquaints the Company, That that Man's

Their sitting at meate. XVI.

Heir manner of feeding is in this wise. They lay a matt made of bents one the grownde and sett their meate on the mids therof, and then sit downe Rownde, the men vppon one side, and the woemen on the other. Their meate is Mayz sodden, in suche sorte as I described yt in the former treatise of verye good taste, deers flesche, or of some other beaste, and fishe. They are verye sober in their eatinge, and trinkinge, and consequentlye verye longe liued becaufe they doe not oppress nature.

C

House has been burnt, wherein all his Goods were destroyed; That he and his Family very narrowly escaped; That he is every Man's Friend in that Company; and, That it is all their Duties to help him, as he would do to any of them had the like Misfortune befallen them. After this Oration is over, every Man, according to his Quality, throws him down upon the Ground some Present, which is commonly Beads, Ronoak, Peak, Skins, or Furs, and which very often amounts to treble the Loss he has suffered. The same Assistance they give to any Man that wants to build a Cabin, or make a Canoe. They say it is our Duty thus to do; for there are several Works that one Man cannot effect, therefore we must give him our Help, otherwise our Society will fall, and we shall be deprived of those urgent Necessities which Life requires. They have no Fence to part one anothers Lots in their Corn-Fields, but every Man knows his own, and it scarce ever happens that they rob one another of so much as an Ear of Corn, which, if any is found to do, he is sentenced by the Elders to work and plant for him that was robbed, till he is recompensed for all the Damage he has suffered in his Corn-Field; and this is punctually performed, and the Thief held in Disgrace that steals from any of his Country-Folks. It often happens that a Woman is destitute of her Husband, and has a great many Children to maintain; such a Person they always help, and make their young men plant, reap, and do every thing that she is not capable of doing herself; yet they do not allow any one to be idle, but to employ themselves in some Work or other.

They never fight with one another unless drunk, nor do you ever hear any Scolding amongst them. They say the Europeans are always rangling and uneasy, and wonder they do not go out of this World, since they are so uneasy and discontented in it. All their Misfortunes and Loses end in Laughter; for if their Cabins take Fire, and all their Goods are burnt therein (indeed, all will strive to prevent farther Damage whilst there is any Possibility) yet such a Misfortune ends in a hearty Fitt of Laughter, unless some of their Kinsfolks and Friends have lost their Lives; but then the Case is altered, and they become very pensive, and go into deep Mourning, which is continued for a considerable Time; sometimes longer or shorter, according to the Dignity of the Person, and the Number of Relations he had near him.

The Burial of their Dead is performed with a great deal of Ceremony, in which one Nation differs in some few Circumstances from another, yet not so much but we may, by a general Relation, pretty nearly account for them all.

When an Indian is dead the greater Person he was, the more expensive is his Funeral. The first thing which is done, is to place the nearest Relations near the Corps, who mourn and weep very much, having their Hair hanging down their Shoulders in a very forlorn manner. After the dead Person has lain a Day and a Night in one of their Hurdles of Canes, commonly in some Out-House made for that purpose, those that officiate about the Funeral go into the Town, and the first young Men they meet withal, that have Blankets or Match Coats on, whom they think fit for their Turn, they strip them from their Backs, who suffer them so to do without any Resistance. In these they wrap the dead Bodies. and cover them with two or three Mats which the Indians make of Rushes or Cane; and last of all, they have a long Web of woven Reeds or hollow Canes, which is the coffin of the Indians, and is brought round several times and tied fast at both ends, which, indeed, looks very decent and well. Then the Corps is brought out of the House into the Orchard of Peach-Trees, where another Hurdle is made to receive it, about which comes all the Relations and Nation that the dead Person belonged to, besides several from other Nations in Alliance with them; all which sit down on the Ground upon Mats spread there for that purpose; where the Doctor or Conjurer appears; and, after some time, makes a Sort of O-yes, at which all are very silent, then he begins to give an Account who the dead Person was, and how stout a Man he approved himself; how many Enemies and Captives he had killed and taken; how strong, tall, and nimble he was; that he was a great Hunter; a Lover of his Country, and possessed of a great many beautiful Wives and Children, esteemed the greatest of Blessings among these Savages, in which they have a true Notion. Thus this Orator runs on, highly extoling the Dead Man for his Valor, Conduct, Strength, Riches, and Good-Humour; and enumerating his Guns, Slaves, and almost everything he was possesed of when living. After which he addresses himself to the People of that Town or Nation, and bids them supply the dead Man's Place by following his steps, who, he assures them, is gone into the Country of Souls, (which they think lies a great way off in this World which the Sun visits in his ordinary Course,) and that he will have the Enjoyment of handsome young Women, great Store of Deer to hunt, never meet with Hunger, Cold or Fatigue, but everything to answer his Expectation and Desire. This is the Heaven they propose to themselves; but, on the contrary, for those Indians that are lazy, thievish amongst themselves, bad Hunters, and no Warriours, nor of much Use to the Nation, to such they allot, in the next World, Hunger, Cold, Troubles, old ugly Women for their Companions, with Snakes, and all sorts of nasty Victuals to feed on. Thus is marked out their Heaven and Hell. After all this Harangue, he diverts the People with some of their Traditions, as when there was a violent hot Summer, or very hard Winter; when any notable Distempers raged amongst them; when they were at War with such and such Nations; how victorious they were; and what were the Names of their War-Captains: To prove the times more exactly, he produces the Records of the Country, which are a Parcel of Reeds of different Lengths, with several distinct Marks, known to none but themselves, by which they seem to guess very exactly at Accidents that happened many Years ago; nay, two or three Ages or more. The Reason I have to believe what they tell me on this Account, is, because I have been at the Meetings of several Indian Nations, and they agreed, in relating the same Circumstances as to Time, very exactly; as for Example, they say there was so hard a Winter in Carolina 105 Years ago, that the great Sound was frozen over, and the Wild Geese came into the Woods to eat Acorns, and that they were so tame, (I suppose through Want) that they killed abundance in the Woods by knocking them on the Head with Sticks.

But to return to the dead Man. When this long Tale is ended, by him that spoke first; perhaps a second begins another long Story; so a third, and fourth, if there be so many Doctors present; which all tell one and the same thing. At last the Corps is brought away from that Hurdle to the Grave by four young Men, attended by the Relations, the King, old Men, and all the Nation. When they come to the Sepulcre, which is about six Foot deep and eight Foot long, having at each end (that is, at the Head and Foot) a Light-Wood or Pitch-Pine Fork driven close down the sides of the Grave firmly into the Ground; (these two Forks are to contain a Ridge-Pole, as you shall understand presently) before they lay the Corps into the Grave, they cover the bottom two or three times over with Bark of Trees, then they let down the Corps (with two Belts, that the Indians carry their Burdens withal) very Leisurely upon the said Barks; then they lay over a Pole of the same Wood in the two Forks, and having a great many Pieces of Pitch-Pine Logs, about two Foot and a half long, they stick them in the sides of the Grave down each End and near the Top thereof, where the other Ends lie on the Ridge-Pole, so that they are declining like the Roof of a House. These being very thick placed, they cover them (many times double) with Bark; then they throw the Earth thereon that came out of the Grave, and beat it down very firm; by this Means the dead Body lies in a Vault, nothing touching him; so that when I saw this way of Burial I was mightily pleased with it, esteeming it very decent and pretty, as having seen a great many Christians buried without the tenth Part of that Ceremony and Decency. Now, when the Flesh is rotted and moulded from the Bone, they take up the Carcass and clean the Bones and joint them together; afterwards they dress them up in pure white dressed Deer-Skins, and lay them amongst their Grandees and Kings in the Quiogonzon, which is their Royal Tomb or Burial-Place of their Kings and War-Captains. This is a very large magnificent Cabin, (according to their Building) which is raised at the Public Charge of the Nation, and maintained in a great deal of Form and Neatness. About seven Foot high is a Floor or Loft made, on which lie all their Princes and Great Men that have died for several hundred Years, all attired in the Dress I before told you of. No Person is to have his Bones lie here, and to be thus dressed, unless he gives a round Sum of their Money to the Rulers for Admittance. If they remove never so far, to live in a Foreign Country, they never fail to take all these dead Bones along with them, though the Tediousness of their short daily Marches keeps them never so long on their Journey. They reverence and adore this Quiogozon with all the Veneration and Respect that is possible for such a People to discharge, and had rather lose all than have any Violence or Injury offered thereto.

These Savages differ some small matter in their Burials; some burying right upwards, and otherwise, as you are acquainted with-al in my Journal from South to North Carolina; Yet they all agree in the Mourning, which is, to appear every Night at the Sepulchre, and howl and weep in a very dismal manner, having their Faces dawbed over with Light-Wood Soot, (which is the same as Lamp-black) and Bear's Oil. This renders them as black as it is possible to make themselves, so that theirs very much resemble the Faces of Executed Men boiled in Tar. If the dead Person was a Grandee, to carry on the Funeral Ceremonies, they hire People to cry and lament over the dead Man. Of this sort there are several that practice it for a Livelihood, and are very expert at Shedding abundance of Tears, and howling like Wolves, and so discharging their Office with abundance of Hypocrisy and Art. The Women are never accompanied with these Ceremonies after Death, and to what World they allot that Sex, I never understood, unless to wait on their dead Husbands: but they have more Wit than some of the other Eastern Nations, who sacrifice themselves to accompany their Husbands into the next World. It is the dead Man's Relations by Blood as his Uncles, Brothers, Sisters, Cousins, Sons and Daughters, that mourn in good earnest, the Wives thinking their Duty is discharged, and that they are become free, when their Husband is dead; so as fast as they can look out for another to supply his Place.

As for the Indian Women which now happen in my Way, when young, and at Maturity, they are as fine shaped Creatures, (take them generally,) as any in the Universe. They are of a tawny Complexion, their Eyes very brisk and amorous, their Smiles afford the finest Composure a Face can possess, their Hands are of the finest Make, with small, long Fingers, and as soft as their Cheeks, and their whole Bodies of a smooth Nature. They are not so uncouth or unlikely as we suppose them, nor are they Strangers or not Proficients in the soft Passion. They are, most of them, mercenary, except the married Women, who sometimes bestow their Favours also to some or other, in their Husband's Absence; for which they never ask any Reward. As for the Report, that they are never found unconstant, like the Europeans, it is wholly false; for were the old World and the new one put into a Pair of Scales (in point of constancy) it would be a hard Matter to discern which was the heavier. As for the Trading Girls, which are those designed to get Money by their Natural Parts, these are discernable by the Cut of their Hair; their tonsure differing from all others of that Nation, who are not of their Profession, which Method is intended to prevent Mistakes; for the Savages of America are desirous (if possible) to keep their Wives to themselves, as well as those in other Parts of the World. When any Addresses are made to one of these Girls, she immediately acquaints her Parents therewith, and they tell the King of it, (provided he that courts her be a Stranger) his Majesty commonly being the principal Bawd of the Nation he rules over, and there seldom being any of these Winchester-Weddings agreed on without his Royal Consent. He likewise advises her what Bargain to make, and if it happens to be an Indian Trader that wants a Bedfellow and has got Rum to sell, be sure the King must have a large Dram for a fee to confirm the Match. These Indians that are of the elder sort, when any such Question is put to them, will debate the

Matter amongst themselves with all the Sobriety and Seriousness imaginable, every one of the Girl's Relations arguing the Advantage or Detriment that may ensue such a Night's Encounter; all which is done with as much Steadiness and Reality as if it was the greatest Concern in the World, and not so much as one Person shall be seen to smile, so long as the Debate holds, making no Difference betwixt an Agreement of this Nature and a Bargain of any other. If they comply with the Men's Desire, then a particular Bed is provided for them, either in a Cabin by themselves or else all the young people turn out to another Lodging, that they may not spoil Sport, and if the old People are in the same Cabin along with them all Night, they lie as unconcerned as if they were so many Logs of Wood. If it be an Indian of their own Town or Neighborhood, that wants a Mistress, he comes to none but the Girl, who receives What she thinks fit to ask him, and so lies all Night with him, without the Consent of her Parents.

The Indian Traders are those which travel and abide amongst the Indians for a long space of time; sometimes for a Year, two or three. These Men have commonly their Indian Wives, whereby they soon learn the Indian Tongue, keep a Friendship with the Savages; and, besides the Satisfaction of a She-Bed-Fellow, they find these Indian Girls very servicable to them, on Account of dressing their Victuals, and instructing them in the Affairs and Customs of the Country. Moreover, such a Man gets a great Trade with the Savages; for when a Person that lives amongst them, is reserved from the Conversation of their Women, tis impossible for him ever to accomplish his Designs amongst that People.

But one great Misfortune which often times attends those that converse with these Savage Women, is, that they get Children by them, which are seldom educated any otherwise than in a State of Infidelity; for it is a certain Rule and Custom, amongst all the Savages of America, that I was ever acquainted withal, to let the Children always fall to the Woman's Lot; for it often happens, that two Indians that have lived together, as Man and Wife, in which

Time they have had several Children; if they part, and another Man possesses her, all the Children go along with the Mother, and none with the Father. And therefore, on this Score it ever seems impossible for the Christians to get their Children which they have by these Indian Women) away from them; whereby they might bring them up in the Knowledge of the Christian Principles. Nevertheless, we often find, that English Men, and other Europeans that have been accustomed to the Conversation of these Savage Women and their Way of Living, have been so allured with that careless sort of Life, as to be constant to their Indian Wife, and her Relations, so long as they lived, without ever desiring to return again amongst the English, although they had very fair Opportunities of Advantages amongst their Countrymen; of which sort I have known several.

As for the Indian Marriages, I have read and heard of a great deal of Form and Ceremony used, which I never saw; nor yet could learn in the Time I have been amongst them, any otherwise than I shall here give you an Account of, which is as follows:

When any young Indian has a Mind for such a Girl to his Wife, he, or some one for him, goes to the young Woman's Parents, if living; if not, to her nearest Relations, where they make Offers of the Match betwixt the Couple. The Relations reply, they will consider of it; which serves for a sufficient Answer, till there be a second Meeting about the Marriage, which is generally brought into Debate before all the Relations, (that are old People) on both Sides, and sometimes the King with all his great Men, give their Opinions therein. If it be agreed on, and the young Woman approve thereof, (for these Savages never give their Children in Marriage without their own Consent) the Man pays so much for his Wife; and the handsomer she is the greater Price she bears. Now, it often happens, that the Man has not so much of their Money ready as he is to pay for his Wife; but if they know him to be a good Hunter, and that he can raise the Sum agreed for, in some few Moons, or any little time they agree, she shall go along with

THEIR MANNER OF PRAYING WITH RATTLES ABOUT THE FIRE.

him as betrothed, but he is not to have any Knowledge of her till the utmost Payment is discharged; all which is punctually observed. Thus they lie together under one Covering for several Months, and the Woman remains the same as she was when she first came to him. I doubt our Europeans would be apt to break this Custom, but the Indian Men are not so vigorous and impatient in their Love as we are. Yet the Women are quite contrary, and those Indian Girls that have conversed with the English and other Europeans, never care for the Conversation of their own Countrymen afterwards.

They never marry so near as a first Cousin, and although there is nothing more coveted amongst them than to marry a Woman of their own Nation, yet when the Nation consists of a very few People, (as nowadays it often happens) so that they are all of them related to one another, then they look out for Husbands and Wives amongst Strangers. For if an Indian lies with his Sister, or any very near Relation, his Body is burnt, and his Ashes thrown into the River, as unworthy to remain on Earth; yet an Indian is allowed to marry two Sisters, or his Brother's Wife. Although these People are called Savages, yet Sodomy is never heard of amongst them, and they are so far from the Practice of that beastly and loathsome Sin, that they have no Name for it in their Language.

The Marriages of these Indians are no farther binding than the Man and Woman agree Together. Either of them has Liberty to leave the other upon any frivolous Excuse they can make, yet whosoever takes the Woman that was another Man's before, and bought by him, as they all are, must certainly pay to her former Husband whatsoever he gave for her. Nay, if she be a Widow, and her Husband died in Debt, whosoever takes her to Wife pays all her Husband's Obligations, though never so many; yet the Woman is not required to pay anything, (unless, she is willing) that was owing from her Husband, so long as she keeps Single. But if a Man courts her for a Night's Lodging and obtains it, the Creditors will make him pay her Husband's Debts, and he may, if he will take her for his Money, or sell her to another for his Wife. I have seen several of these Bargains driven in a day; for you may see Men selling their Wives as Men do Horses in a Fair, a Man being allowed not only to change as often as he pleases, but likewise to have as many Wives as he is able to maintain. I have often seen that very old Indian Men, (that have been Grandees in their own Nation) have had three or four very likely young Indian Wives, which I have much wandered at, because, to me, they seemed incapacitated to make good Use of one of them.

The young Men will go in the Night from one House to another to visit the young Women, in which sort of Rambles they will spend the whole Night. In their Addresses they find no Delays, for if she is willing to entertain the Man, she gives him Encouragement and grants him Admittance; otherwise she withdraws her Face from him, and says, I cannot see you, either you or I must leave this Cabin and sleep somewhere else this Night.

They are never to boast of their Intrigues with the Women. If they do, none of the Girls value them ever after, or admit of their Company in their Beds. This proceeds not on the score of Reputation, for there is no such thing, (on that account) known amongst them; and although we may reckon them the greatest Libertines and most extravagant in their Embraces, yet they retain and possess a Modesty that requires those Passions never to be divulged.

The Trading Girls, after they have led that Course of Life, for several Years, in which time they scarce ever have a Child; (for they have an Art to destroy the Conception, and she that brings a Child in this Station, is accounted a Fool, and her Reputation is lessened thereby) at last they grow weary of so many, and betake themselves to a married State, or to the Company of one Man; neither does their having been common to so many any wise lessen their Fortunes, but rather augment them.

The Woman is not punished for Adultery, but tis the Man that makes the injured Person Satisfaction, which is the Law of Nations practised amongst them all; and he that strives to evade such Satisfaction as the Husband demands, lives daily in Danger of his Life; yet when discharged, all Animosity is laid aside, and the Cuckold is very well pleased with his Bargain, whilst the Rival is laughed at by the whole Nation, for carrying on his intrigue with no better Conduct, than to be discovered and pay so dear for his Pleasure.

The Indians say, that the Woman is a weak Creature, and easily drawn away by the Man's Persuasion; for which Reason, they lay no Blame upon her, but the Man (that ought to be Master of his Passion) for persuading her to it.

They are of a very hale Constitution; their Breaths are as Sweet as the Air they breathe in, and the Woman seems to be of that tender Composition, as if they were designed rather for the Bed than Bondage. Yet their Love is never of that Force and Continuance, that any of them ever runs Mad, or makes away with themselves on that score. They never love beyond Retrieving their first Indifferency, and when slighted, are as ready to untie the Knot at one end, as you are at the other.

Yet I knew an European Man that had a Child or two by one of these Indian Women, and afterwards married a Christian, after which he came to pass away a Night with his Indian Mistress; but she made Answer that she then had forgot she ever knew him, and that she never lay with another Woman's Husband, so fell a crying and took up the Child she had by him, and went out of the Cabin (away from him) in great Disorder.

The Indian Women's Work is to cook the Victuals for the whole Family, and to make Mats, Baskets, Girdles, of Possum-Hair, and such like. They never plant the Corn amongst us, as they do amongst the Iroquois, who are always at War and Hunting; therefore, the Plantation Work is left for the Women and Slaves to perform, and look after; whilst they are wandering all over the Continent betwixt the two Bays of Mexico and St Laurence.

The Mats the Indian Women make, are of Rushes, and about five Foot high, and two Fathom long, and sewed double, that is, two together; whereby they become very commodious to lay under our

Beds, or to sleep on in the Summer Season in the Day-time, and for our Slaves in the Night.

There are other Mats made of Flags, which the Tuskeruro Indians make, and sell to the Inhabitants.

The Baskets our Neighboring Indians make are all made of a very fine sort of Bulrushes, and sometimes of Silk-grass, which they work with Figures of Beasts, Birds, Fishes, &c.

A great way up in the Country, both Baskets and Mats are made of the split Reeds, which are only the outward shining Part of the Cane. Of these I have seen Mats, Baskets, and Dressing-Boxes, very artificially done.

The Savage Women of America have very easy Travail with their Children; sometimes they bring Twins, and are brought to bed by themselves, when took at a Disadvantage; not but they have Midwives amongst them, as well as Doctors who make it their Profession (for Gain) to assist and deliver Women, and some of these Midwives are very knowing in several Medicines that Carolina affords, which certainly expedite, and make easy Births. Besides, they are unacquainted with those severe Pains which follow the Birth in our European Women. Their Remedies are a great Cause of this Easiness in that State; for the Indian Women will run up and down the Plantation the same day, very briskly, and without any sign of pain or Sickness; yet they look very meagre and thin. Not but that we must allow a great deal owing to the Climate and the natural Constitution of these Women, whose Course of Nature never visits them in such Quantities, as the European Women have. And though they never want Plenty of Milk, yet I never saw an Indian Woman with very large Breasts; neither does the youngest Wife ever fail of proving so good a Nurse as to bring her Child up free from the Rickets and Disasters that proceed from the Teeth, with many other Distempers which attack our Infants in England, and other Parts of Europe. They let their Children suck till they are well grown, unless they prove big with Child sooner. They always nurse their own Children themselves, unless Sickness or Death prevents. I once saw a Nurse hired to give Suck to an Indian Woman's Child, which you have in my Journal. After Delivery, they absent the Company of a Man for forty days. As soon as the Child is born, they wash it in cold Water at the next Stream and then bedawb it, as I have mentioned before. After which the Husband takes care to provide a Cradle, which is soon made, consisting of a Piece of flat Wood, which they hew with their Hatches to the likeness of a Board; it is about two Foot long, and a Foot broad; to this they brace and tie the Child down very close, having near the middle, a Stick fastened about two Inches from the Board, which is for the Child's Breech to rest upon, under which they put a Wad of Moss that receives the Child's Excrements, by which means they can shift the Moss and keep all clean and sweet. Some Nations have very flat Heads, as you have heard in my Journal, which is made whilst tied on this Cradle, as that Relation informs you. These Cradles are apt to make the Body flat; yet they are the most portable things that can be invented, for there is a String which goes from one Corner of the Board to the other, whereby the Mother flings her Child on her Back; so the Infant's Back is towards hers, and its Face looks up towards the Sky. If it rains, she throws her Leather or Woollen Match-coat, over her Head, which covers the Child all over, and secures her and it from the Injuries of rainy Weather. The Savage Women quit all Company, and dress not their own Victuals during their Purgations.

After they have had several Children, they grow strangely out of Shape in their Bodies; As for Barenness, I never knew any of their Women that have not Children when married.

The Women's Dress is, in severe Weather, a hairy Match-coat in the Nature of a Plad, which keeps out the Cold, and, (as I said before,) defends their Children from the Prejudices of the Weather. At other times they have only a sort of Flap or Apron containing two Yards in Length, and better than half a Yard deep. Sometimes it is a Deer-Skin dressed white, and pointed or slit at the bottom, like Fringe. When this is clean it becomes them very well. Others wear blue, or red Flaps, made of Bays and Plains, which they buy of the English, of both which they tuck in the Corners, to fasten the Garment, and sometimes make it fast with a Belt. All of them, when ripe, have a small String round the Waist, to which another is tied and comes between their Legs, where always is a Wad of Moss against the Ospubis, but never any Hair is there to be found. Sometimes they wear Indian Shooes or Moggizons, which are made after the same manner as the Men's are.

The Hair of their Heads is made into a long Roll like a Horses Tail, and bound round with Ronoak, or Porcelan, which is a sort of beads they make of the Conk-Shells. Others that have not this make a Leather-String serve.

The Indian Men have a Match-Coat of Hair, Furs, Feathers, or Cloth, as the Women have. Their Hair is rolled up on each Ear, as the Women's, only much shorter, and oftentimes a Roll on the Crown of the Head, or Temples, which is just as they fancy, there being no Strictness in their Dress. Betwixt their Legs comes a Piece of Cloth, that is tucked in by a Belt, both before and behind. This is to hide their Nakedness, of which Decency they are very strict Observers, although never practiced before the Christians came amongst them. They wear Shooes of Buck's and sometimes Bear's Skin, which they tan in an Hour or two, with the Bark of Trees boiled, wherein they put the Leather whilst hot, and let it remain a little while, whereby it becomes so qualified as to endure Water and Dirt, without growing hard. These have no Heels, and are made as Fit for the Feet as a Glove is for the Hand, and are very easy to travel in when one is a little used to them. When these Savages live near the Water, they frequent the Rivers in Summer-time very much, where both Men and Women very often in a day go in naked to wash themselves, though not both Sexes together.

Their Feather Match-Coats are very pretty, especially some of them, which are made extraordinary charming, containing several pretty figures wrought in Feathers, making them seem like a fine Flower Silk-Shag; and when new and fresh, they become a Bed very well, instead of a Quilt. Some of another sort are made of Hare, Raccoon, Bever, or Squirrel-Skins, which are very warm. Others again are made of the green Part of the Skin of a Mallard's Head, which they sew perfectly well together, their Thread being either the Sinews of a Deer divided very small, or Silk-grass. When these are finished, they look very finely, though they must needs be very troublesome to make. Some of their great Men, as Rulers and such, that have Plenty of Deer-Skins by them, will often buy the English-made Coats, which they wear on Festivals and other Days of Visiting. Yet none ever buy any Breeches, saying, that they are too much confined in them, which prevents their Speed in running, &c.

We have some Indians that are more civilized than the rest, which wear Hats, Shooes, Stockings, and Breeches, with very tolerable Linnen Shirts, which is not common amongst these Heathens. The Paspitank Indians did formerly keep Cattle and make Butter.

These are them that wear the English Dress. Whether they have Cattle now or no, I am not certain, but I am of the Opinion that such Inclinations in the Savages should meet with Encouragement, and every Englishman ought to do them Justice and not defraud them of their Land, which has been allotted them formerly by the Government; for if we do not show them Examples of Justice and Vertue, we can never bring them to believe us to be a worthier Race of Men than themselves.

The Dresses of these People are so different, according to the Nation that they belong to, that it is impossible to recount all the whimsical Figures that they sometimes make by their Antick Dresses. Besides, Carolina is a warm Country, and very mild in its Winters to what Virginia, Maryland, Pennsylvania, New York, the Jersies, and New England are; wherefore our Indian's Habit very much differs from the Dresses that appear amongst the Savages who inhabit those cold Countries; in regard their chiefest Cloathing for the Winter-Seasons is made of the Furs of Bever, Roccoon and other Northern Furs, that our Climate is not acquainted withal, they producing some Furs as the Monack, Moor, Marten, Black Fox, and others to us unknown.

Their Dress in Peace and War is quite different. Besides, when they go to War, their Hair is combed out by the Women and done over very much with Bear's Grease and red Root, with Feathers, Wings, Rings, Copper, and Peak, or Wampum in their Ears. Moreover, they buy Vermillion of the Indian Traders, wherewith they paint their Faces all over red, and commonly make a Circle of Black about one Eye and another Circle of White about the other, whilst others bedawb their Faces with Tobacco-Pipe Clay, Lamp-black, black Lead, and divers other Colours, which they make with the several sorts of Minerals and Earths that they get in different Parts of the Country, where they hunt and travel. When these Creatures are thus painted, they make the most frightful Figures that can be imitated by Men, and seem more like Devils than Human Creatures. You may be sure that they are about some Mischief when you see them thus painted; for in all the Hostilities which have ever been acted against the English at any time in several of the Plantations of America, the Savages always appeared in this Disguize, whereby they might never after be discovered or known by any of the Christians that should happen to see them after they had made their Escape; for it is impossible ever to know an Indian under these Colours, although he has been at your House a thousand times, and you know him at other times as well as you do any Person living. As for their Women, they never use any Paint on their Faces; neither do they ever carry them along with them into the Field, when they intend any Expedition, leaving them at home with the old Men and Children.

Some of the Indians wear great Bobs in their Ears, and sometimes in the Holes thereof they put Eagles and other Birds, Feathers, for a Trophy. When they kill any Fowl, they commonly pluck off the downy Feathers, and stick them all over their Heads. Some (both Men and Women) wear great Necklaces of their Money made of Shells. They often wear Bracelets made of Brass, and sometimes of Iron Wire.

Their Money is of different sorts, but all made of Shells, which are found on the Coast of Carolina, which are very large and hard, so that they are very difficult to cut. Some English Smiths have tried to drill this sort of Shell-Money, and there by thought to get an Advantage; but it proved so hard, that nothing could be gained. They oftentimes make, of this Shell, a sort of Gorge, which they wear about their Neck in a string; so it hangs on their Collar, whereon sometimes is engraven a Cross, or some odd sort of Figure, which comes next in their Fancy. There are other sorts valued at a Doe-Skin, yet the Gorges will sometimes sell for three or four Buck-Skins ready dressed. There be others, that eight of them go readily for a Doe Skin; but the general and current Species of all the Indians in Carolina, and, I believe, all over the Continent, as far as the Bay of Mexico, is that which we call Peak and Ronoak; but Peak more especially. This is that which at New York, they call Wampum, and have used it as current Money amongst the Inhabitants for a great many Years. This is what many Writers call Porcelan, and is made in New York in great Quantities, and with us in some measure. Five Cubits of this purchase a dressed Doe-Skin, and seven or eight purchase a dressed Buck-Skin. An Englishman could not afford to make so much of this Wampum for five or ten times the Value; for it is madè out of a vast great Shell, of which that Country affords Plenty; where it is ground smaller than the small End of a Tobacco-Pipe, or a large Wheat Straw. Four or five of these make an Inch, and every one is to be drilled through, and made as smooth as Glass, and so strung, as Beads are, and a Cubit of the Indian Measure contains as much in Length, as will reach from the Elbow to the End of the little Finger. They never stand to question, whether it is a tall Man or a short one, that measures it; but if this Wampum Peap be black or purple, as some Part of that Shell is, then it is twice the Value. This the Indians grind on Stones and other things, till they make it current but the Drilling is the most difficult to the Englishmen, which the Indians manage with a Nail stuck in a Cane or Reed. Thus they roll it continually on their Thighs, with their Right-Hand holding the Bit of Shell with their Left, so in time they drill a Hole quite through it, which is a very tedious Work; but especially in making their Ronoak, four of which will scarce make one Length of Wampum. The Indians are a People that never value their time, so that they can afford to make them, and never need to fear the English will take the Trade out of their Hands. This is the Money with which you may buy Skins, Furs, Slaves, or any thing the Indians have; it being the Mammon (as our Money is to us) that entices and persuades them to do any thing, and part with every thing they possess, except their Children for Slaves. As for their Wives, they are often sold, and their Daughters violated for it. With this they buy off Murders; and whatsoever a Man can do that is ill, this Wampum will quit him of, and make him, in their Opinion, good and Vertuous, though never so black before.

All the Indians give a Name to their Children, which is not the same as the Father or Mother, but what they fancy. This Name they keep, (if Boys) till they arrive to the Age of a Warriour, which is sixteen or seventeen Years; then they take a Name to themselves, sometimes, Eagle, Panther, Allegator, or some such wild Creature, esteeming nothing on Earth worthy to give them a Name, but these Wild-Fowl, and Beasts. Some again take the Name of a Fish, which they keep as long as they live.

The King is the Ruler of the Nation, and has others under him, to assist him, as his War-Captains, and Counsellors, who are picked out and chosen from among the ancientest Men of the Nation he is King of. These meet him in all general Councils and Debates, concerning War, Peace, Trade, Hunting, and all the Adventures and Accidents of Human Affairs, which appear within their Verge; where all Affairs are discoursed of and argued pro and con, very deliberately (without making any manner of Parties or Divisions) for the Good of the Publick; for, as they meet there to treat, they discharge their Duty with all the Integrity imaginable, never looking towards their Own Interest, before the Publick Good. After every Man has given his Opinion, that which has most Voices, or, in Summing up, is found the most reasonable, that they make use of without any Jars and Wrangling, and put it in Execution, the first Opportunity that offers.

The Succession falls not to the King's Son, but to his Sister's Son, which is a sure way to prevent Imposters in the Succession. Sometimes they poison the Heir to make way for another, which is not seldom done, when they do not approve of the Youth that is to succeed them. The King himself is commonly chief Doctor in that Cure.

They are so well versed in Poison, that they are often found to poison whole Families, nay, most of a Town; and which is most to be admired, they will poison a running Spring or Fountain of Water, so that whosoever drinks thereof, shall infallibly die. When the Offender is discovered, his very Relations urge for Death, whom nothing will appease, but the most cruel Torment imaginable which is executed in the most publick Manner that it is possible to act such a Tragedy in. For all the whole Nation, and all the Indians within a hundred Miles, (if it is possible to send for them), are summoned to come and appear at such a Place and Time, to see and rejoice at the Torments and Death of such a Person, who is the common and professed Enemy to all the friendly Indians thereabouts, who now lies under the Condemnation of the whole Nation, and accordingly is to be put to Death. Then all appear, (young and old) from all the adjacent Parts, and meet, with all the Expressions of Joy, to consummate this horrid and barbarous Feast, which, is carried on after this dismal Manner. First, they bring the Prisoner to the Place appointed for the Execution, where he is set down on his Breech on the Ground. Then they all get about him and you shall not see one sorrowful or dejected Countenance amongst them, but all very merrily disposed, as if some Comedy was to be acted instead of a Tragedy. He that is appointed to be the chief Executioner, takes a Knife and bids him hold out his Hands, which he does, and then cuts round the Wrist through the Skin, which is drawn off like a Glove, and flead quite off at the Fingers' Ends, then they break his Joints and Bones, and buffet and torment him after a very inhuman

Manner, till some violent Blow perhaps ends his Days; then they burn him to Ashes and throw them down the River. Afterwards they eat, drink and are merry, repeating all the Actions of the Tormentors and the Prisoner, with a great deal of Mirth and Satisfaction. This Accusation is laid against an Indian Heroe sometimes wrongfully, or when they have a mind to get rid of a Man that has more Courage and Conduct than his neighboring Kings or great Men; then they alledge the Practice of poisoning Indians against him, and make a Rehearsal of every Indian that died for a year or two, and say that they were poisoned by such an Indian; which Reports stir up all the Relations of the deceased against the said Person, and by such means make him away presently. In some Affairs, these Savages are very reserved and politick, and will attend a long time with a great deal of Patience to bring about their Designs; they being never impatient or hasty in executing any of their Designs or Revenge.

Now I am gone so far in giving an Account of the Indian's Temper, I will proceed, and can give you no other Character of them, but that they are a very wary People, and are never hasty or impatient. They will endure a great many Misfortunes, Loses, and Disappointments without showing themselves, in the least, vexed or uneasy. When they go by Water, if there proves a Head-Wind, they never vex and fret as the Europeans do, and let what Misfortune come to them as will or can happen, they never relent. Besides, there is one Vice very common everywhere, which I never found amongst them, which is, Envying other Men's Happiness, because their Station is not equal to, or above their Neighbors. Of this Sin I cannot say I ever saw an Example, though they are a People that set as great a Value upon themselves, as any sort of Men, in the World, upon which Account they find something Valuable in themselves above Riches. Thus, he that is a good Warriour is the proudest Creature living; and he that is an expert Hunter, is esteemed by the People and himself; yet all these are natural Vertues and Gifts, and not Riches, which are as often in the

Possession of a Fool as a Wise-Man. Several of the Indians are possessed of a great many Skins, Wampums, Ammunition, and what other things are esteemed Riches amongst them; yet such an Indian is no more esteemed amongst them, than any other ordinary Fellow, provided he has no personal Endowments which are the Ornaments that must gain him an Esteem among them; for a great Dealer amongst the Indians, is no otherwise respected and esteemed than as a Man that strains his Wits and fatigues himself to furnish others with Necessaries of Life that live much easier and enjoy more of the World than he himself does with all his Pelf. If they are taken Captives and expect a miserable Exit, they sing; if Death approach them in Sickness, they are not afraid of it; nor are ever heard to say, Grant me some time. They know by Instinct, and daily Example, that they must die; wherefore they have that great and noble Gift to submit to everything that happens, and value nothing that attacks them.

Their Cruelty to their Prisoners of War is what they are seemingly guilty of an Error in, (I mean as to a natural Failing) because they strive to invent the most inhuman Butcheries for them that the Devils themselves could invent or hammer out of Hell; they esteeming Death no Punishment, but rather an Advantage to him, that is exported out of this into another World.

Therefore, they inflict on them Torments, wherein they prolong Life in that miserable state as long as they can, and never miss Skulping of them as they call it, which is, to cut off the Skin from the Temples and taking the whole Head of Hair along with it, as if it was a Night-cap. Sometimes they take the Top of the Skull along with it; all which they preserve and carefully keep by them, for a Trophy of their Conquest over their Enemies. Others keep their Enemies Teeth which are taken in War, whilst other split the Pitch-Pine into Splinters, and stick them into the Prisoner's Body yet alive. Thus they light them which burn like so many Torches; and in this manner they make him dance round a great Fire, every one buffeting and deriding him, till he expires, when every one strives to get a Bone or some Relick of this unfortunate Captive. One of the young Fellows that has been at the Wars, and has had the Fortune to take a Captive, returns the proudest Creature on Earth, and sets such a Value on himself, that he knows not how to contain himself in his Senses. The Iroquois, or Sinnagars, are the most Warlike Indians that we know of, being always at war, and not to be persuaded from that Way of Living by any Argument that can be used. If you go to persuade them to live peaceably with the Tuskeruros, and let them be one People, and in case those Indians desire it and will submit to them, they will answer you that they cannot live without War, which they have ever been used to; and that if Peace be made with the Indians they now war withal, they must find out some others to wage War against; for them to live in Peace is to live out of their Element, War, Conquest, and Murder, being what they delight in, and value themselves for. When they take a Slave and intend to keep him to Work in their Fields, they flea the Skin from the Setting on his Toes to the middle of his Foot, so cut off one half of his Feet, wrapping the Skin over the Wounds, and healing them. By this cruel Method, the Indian Captive is hindered from making his Escape, for he can neither run fast or go anywhere, but his Feet are more easily traced and discovered. Yet I know one Man who made his Escape from them, though they had thus disabled him, as you may see in my Journal.

The Indians ground their Wars on Enmity, not on Interest, as the Europeans generally do; for the Loss of the meanest person in the Nation, they will go to War and lay all at Stake, and prosecute their Designs to the utmost, till the Nation they were injured by, be wholly destroyed, or make them that Satisfaction which they demand. They are very politick in waging and carrying on their War: first, by advising with all the ancient Men of Conduct and Reason, that belong to their Nation; such as superannuated War-Captains, and those that have been Counsellors for many years, and whose Advice has commonly succeeded very well. They have likewise their Field Counsellors, who are accustomed to Ambuscades and Surprises, which Methods are commonly used by the Savages, for I scarce ever heard of a Field-Battle fought amongst them.

One of their Expeditions afforded an Instance, worthy mention, which was thus; Two Nations of Indians here in Carolina were at War together, and a Party of each were in the Forest ranging to see what Enemies they could take. The lesser Number found they were discovered, and could not well get over a River, (that lay between them and their home) without engaging the other Party, whose Numbers were much the greater; so they called a Council, which met, and having weighed their present Circumstances with a great deal of Argument and Debate, for a considerable time, and found their Enemies Advantage, and that they could expect no success in Engaging such an unequal Number; they, at last, concluded on this Stratagem, which, in my Opinion, carried a great deal of Policy along with it. It was; That the same Night, they should make a great Fire, which they were certain would be discovered by the adverse Party, and there dress up Logs of Wood in their Cloaths, and make them exactly seem like Indians, that were asleep by the Fireside; (which is their Way, when in the Woods) so, said they, our enemies will fire upon these Images, supposing them to be us, who will lie in Ambuscade, and, after their Guns are unloaded, shall deal well enough with them. This Result was immediately put in Execution, and the Fire was made by the side of a Valley, where they lay perdu very advantageously. Thus, a little before Break of Day, (which commonly is the Hour they surprise their Enemies in) the Indians came down to their Fire, and at once fired in upon those Logs in the Indians Cloaths, and run up to them, expecting they had killed every Man dead; but they found themselves mistaken, for then the other Indians, who had lain all the Night stark-naked in the Bottom, attacked them with their loaded Pieces, which so surprised them, that every Man was taken Prisoner, and brought in bound to their Town.

Another Instance was betwixt the Machapunga Indians and the

Coranine's on the Sand-Banks; which was as follows. The Macha-pungas were invited to a Feast, by the Coranines; (which two Nations had been a long time at War together, and had lately con-cluded a Peace.) Thereupon, the Machapunga Indians took the Advantage of coming to the Coranines' Feast, which was to avoid all Suspicion, and their King, who, of a Savage, is a great Politician and very stout, ordered all his Men to carry their Tomakawks along with them, hidden under their Match-Coats, which they did; and being acquainted when to fall on, by the Word given, they all (upon this Design) set forward for the Feast, and came to the Cora-nine Town, where they had gotten Victuals, Fruits, and such things as make an Indian Entertainment, all ready to make these new Friends welcome, which they did; and, after Dinner, towards the Evening, (as it is customary amongst them) they went to Danc-ing, all together; so when the Machapunga King saw the best op-portunity offer, he gave the Word, and his Men pulled their toma-hawks or hatchets from under their Match-Coats, and killed sev-eral, and took the rest Prisoners, except some few that were not present, and about four or five that escaped. The Prisoners they sold Slaves to the English. At the time this was done, those In-dians had nothing but Bows and Arrows, neither side having Guns.

The Indians are very revengeful, and never forget an Injury done, till they have received Satisfaction. Yet they are the freest from Heats and Passions (which possess the Europeans) of any I ever heard of. They never call any Man to account for what he did, when he was drunk; but say, it was the Drink that caused his Mis-behaviour, therefore he ought to be forgiven. They never frequent a Christian's House that is given to Passion, nor will they ever buy or sell with him, if they can get the same Commodities of any other Person; for they say, such Men are mad Wolves, and no more Men.

They know not what Jealousy is, because they never think their Wives are unconstant, unless they are Eye-witnesses thereof. They are generally very bashful, especially the young Maids, who when

THEIR DANCES WHICH THEY USE ATT THEIR HIGH FEASTS. "At a Certayne tyme of the yere they make a great and soleme feaste wherunto their neighbours of the townes adjoining repayre from all parts, every man attyred in the most strange fashion they can devise having certayne marks on the backs to declare of what place they bee. The place where they meet is a broade playne, above the which are planted in the grownde certayne posts carved with heads like to the faces of Nonnes covered with theyr vayles. Then being sett in order they dance, singe, and use the strangest gestures they can possibly devise. Three of the fayrest Virgins, of the companie are in the mydds, which imbrassinge one another doe as yt wear turne abowt in their dancinge." From *A Briefe and True Report of Virginia* by Thomas Hariot.

they come into a strange Cabin, where they are not acquainted, never ask for any thing, though never so hungry or thirsty, but sit down, without speaking a Word, (be it never so long) till some of the House asks them a Question, or falls into Discourse, with the Stranger. I never saw a Scold amongst them, and to their Children they are extraordinary tender and indulgent; neither did I ever see a Parent correct a Child, excepting one Woman, that was the King's Wife, and she (indeed) did possess a Temper that is not commonly found amongst them. They are free from all manner of Compliments, except Shaking of Hands and scratching on the Shoulder, which two are the greatest Marks of Sincerity and Friendship, that can be shewed one to another. They cannot express *fare-you-well;* but when they leave the House, will say, *I go straightway,* which is to intimate their Departure; and if the Man of the House has any Message to send by the going Man, he may acquaint him therewith. Their Tongue allows not to say, *Sir, I am your Servants;* because they have no different Titles for Man, only King, War-Captain, Old Man, or Young Man, which respect the Stations and Circumstances Men are employed in, and arrived to, and not Ceremony. As for Servants, they have no such thing, except Slave, and their Dogs, Cats, tame or domestic Beasts, and Birds, are called by the same Name. For the Indian Word for Slaves includes them all. So when an Indian tells you he has got a Slave for you, it may (in general Terms, as they use) be a young Eagle, a Dog, Otter, or any other thing of that Nature, which is obsequiously to depend on the Master for its Sustenance.

They are never fearful in the Night, nor do the Thoughts of Spirits ever trouble them; such as the many Hobgoblins and Bugbears that we suck in with our Milk, and the Foolery of our Nurses and Servants suggests to us; who by their idle Tales of Fairies, and Witches, make such Impressions on our tender years, that at Maturity, we carry Pigmies' Souls in Giants' Bodies and ever after, are thereby so much deprived of Reason, and unmaned, as never to be Masters of half the Bravery Nature designed for us.

Not but that the Indians have as many Lying Stories of Spirits and Conjurers, as any People in the World; but they tell it with no Disadvantage to themselves; for the great Esteem which the Old Men bring themselves to, is by making the others believe their Familiarity with Devils and Spirits, and how great a Correspondence they ever after are held in the greatest Veneration imaginable, and whatever they after impose upon the People, is received as infallible, They are so little startled at the Thoughts of another World, that they not seldom murder themselves; as for Instance, a Bear-River Indian, a very likely young Fellow, about twenty Years of Age, whose Mother was angry at his drinking of too much Rum, and chid him for it, thereupon replied, he would have her satisfied, and he would do the like no more; upon which he made his Words good; for he went aside, and shot himself dead. This was a Son of the Politick King of the Machupunga, I spoke of before, and has the most Cunning of any Indian I ever met withal.

Most of the Savages are much addicted to Drunkenness, a Vice they never were acquainted with, till the Christians came amongst them. Some of them refrain drinking strong Liquors, but very few of that sort are found amongst them. Their chief Liquor is Rum, without any Mixture. This the English bring amongst them, and buy Skins, Furs, Slaves and other of their Commodities therewith. They never are contented with a little, but when once begun, they must make themselves quite drunk; otherwise they will never rest, but sell all they have in the Wold, rather than not have their full Dose. In these drunken Frolicks, (which are always carried on in the Night) they sometimes murder one another, fall into the fire, fall down Precipices, and break their Necks, with several other Misfortunes which this drinking of Rum brings upon them; and though they are sensible of it, yet they have no Power to refrain this Enemy. About five years ago, when Landgrave Daniel was Governor, he summoned in all the Indian Kings, and Rulers to meet, and in a full Meeting of the Government and Council, with those Indians, they agreed upon a firm Peace, and the Indian Rulers desired no Rum might be sold to them, which was granted, and a Law made, that inflicted a Penalty on those that sold Rum to the Heathens; but it was never strictly observed, and besides the young Indians were so disgusted at that Article, that they threatened to kill the Indians that made it, unless it was laid aside, and they might have Rum sold them, when they went to the Englishmens' Houses to buy it.

Some of the Heathens are so very poor that they have no Manner of Cloaths, save a Wad of Moss to hide their Nakedness. These are either lusty and will not work; otherwise they are given to Gaming or Drunkenness; yet these get Victuals as well as the rest, because that is common amongst them, If they are caught in theft they are Slaves till they pay the Person, (as I mentioned before) but to steal from the English they reckon no Harm. Not but that I have known some few Savages that have been as free from Theft as any of the Christians. When they have a Design to lie with a Woman, which they cannot obtain any otherwise than by a larger Reward than they are able to give, they then strive to make her drunk, which a great many of them will be; then they take the Advantage to do with them what they please, and sometimes in their Drunkenness, cut off their Hair and sell it to the English, which is the greatest Affront can be offered to them. They never value Time; for if they be going out to hunt, fish, or any other indifferent Business, you may keep them in talk as long as you please, so you but keep them in Discourse, and seemed pleased with their Company; yet none are more expeditous and safer Messengers than they, when any extraordinary Business that they are sent about requires it.

When they are upon traveling the Woods, they keep a constant Pace, neither will they stride over a Tree that lies cross the Path, but always go round it, which is quite contrary to the Custom of the English and other Europeans. When they cut with a Knife, the Edge is towards them, whereas we always cut and whittle from us. Nor did I ever see one of them left-handed. Before the Christians came amongst them, not knowing the Use of Steel and Flints, they got their Fire with Sticks, which by vehement Collision or Rubbing together, take Fire. This Method they will sometimes practice now, when it has happened through rainy Weather, or some other Accident, that they have wet their Spunk, which is a sort of soft, corky Substance, generally of a Cinnamon Colour, and grows in the concave part of an Oak, Hiccory, and several other Woods, being dug out with an Ax and always kept by the Indians, instead of Tinder or Touch-Wood, both which it exceeds. You are to understand that the two Sticks they use to strike Fire withal are never of one sort of Wood, but always differ from each other.

They are expert Travelers, and though they have not the Use of our artificial Compass, yet they understand the North-point exactly, let them be in never so great a Wilderness. One Guide is a short Moss, that grows upon some Trees, exactly on the North-Side thereof.

Besides, they have Names for eight of the thirty-two Points, and call the Winds by their several Names, as we do; but indeed more properly; for the North-West Wind is called the cold Wind; the North-East, the wet Wind; the South, the warm Wind, and so agreeable of the rest. Sometimes it happens that they have a large River or Lake to pass over, and the Weather is very foggy, as it often happens in the Spring and Fall of the Leaf; so that they cannot see which Course to steer; In such a Case, they being on one side of the River or Lake, they know well enough what Course such a Place, (which they intend for) bears from them. Therefore, they get a great many Sticks and Chunks of Wood in their Canoe and then set off directly for their Port, and now and then throw over a Piece of Wood, which directs them, by seeing how the Stick bears from the Canoe Stern, which they always observe to keep right aft; and this is the Indian Compass, by which they will go over a broad Water ten or twenty Leagues wide. They will find the Head of any River, though it is five, six, or seven hundred miles off, and they never were there in their Lives before, as is often proved by their appointing to meet on the Head of such a River, where, perhaps, none of them ever was before, but where they shall rendezvous exactly at the prefixed time; and if they meet with any Obstruction, they leave certain Marks in the Way where they that come after, will understand how many have passed by already, and which way they are gone. Besides, in their War-Expeditions, they have very certain Hieroglyphicks, whereby each Party informs the other of the Success or Losses they have met withal; all which is so exactly performed by their *Sylvian* Marks and Characters, that they are never at a Loss to understand one another. Yet there was never found any Letters amongst the Savages of *Carolina*; nor I believe, among any other Natives in *America*, that were possessed with any manner of Writing, or Learning throughout all the Discoveries of the *New-World*. They will draw Maps very exactly of all the Rivers, Towns, Mountains and Roads, or what you shall enquire of them, which you may draw by their Directions, and come to a small matter of Latitude, reckoned by their Day's Journeys. These Maps they will draw in the Ashes of the Fire, and sometimes upon a Mat or piece of Bark. I have put a Pen and Ink into a Savage's Hand, and he has drawn me the Rivers Bays, and other Parts of a Country, which afterwards I have found to agree with a great deal of Nicety. But you must be very much in their Favor, otherwise they will never make these Discoveries to you, especially if it be in their own Quarters. And as for Mines of Silver and other Metals, we are satisfied we have enough, and those very rich, in *Carolina* and its adjacent Parts, some of which the *Indians* are acquainted withal, although no Enquirers thereafter, but what came and were discovered by Chance; yet they say it is this Metal that the *English* covet, as they do their Peak and Ronoak, and that we have gained Ground of them wherever we have come. Now, say they, if we should discover these Minerals to the *English*, they would settle at or near these Mountains, and bereave us of the best Hunting-Quarters we have, as they have already done wherever they have inhabited; so by that means we shall be driven to some unknown Country, to live, hunt, and get our Bread in. These are the Reasons that the Savages give for not making known what they are acquainted withal of that Nature. And, indeed, all Men that have ever gone upon those Discoveries, allow them to be good; more especially my ingenious Friend, Mr. Francis Louis Mitchell, of Bern in Switzerland, who has been for several Years, very indefatigable and strict in his Discoveries amongst those vast Ledges of Mountains and spacious Tracts of Land, lying towards the Heads of the great Bays and Rivers of Virginia, Maryland and Pensylvania, where he has discovered a spacious Country inhabited by none but the Savages, and not many of them, who yet are of a very friendly Nature to the Christians. This Gentleman has been employed by the Canton of Bern to find out a Tract of Land in the English America, where that Republick might settle some of their People; which Proposal, I believe, is now in a fair way towards a Conclusion between her Majesty of Great Britain and that Canton. Which must needs be of great Advantage to both; and as for ourselves, I believe no Man that is in his Wits, and understands the situation and Affairs of America, but will allow, nothing can be of more Security and Advantage to the Crown and Subjects of Great Britain, than to have our Frontiers secured by a warlike People, and our Friends, as the Switzers are; especially when we have more Indians than we can civilize, and so many Christian Enemies lying on the back of us, that we do know not how long or short a time it may be before they visit us. Add to these the Effects and Produce that may be expected from those Mountains; which may hereafter prove of Advantage to the British Monarchy: and none more fit than an industrious People, bred in a mountainous Country, and inured to all the Fatigues of War and Travel, to improve a Country. Thus we have no room to doubt, but as soon as any of those Parts are seated by the Switzers, a great many Britains will strive to live amongst them, for the Benefit of the sweet Air and healthful Climate which that Country affords, were it only for the Cultivating of Hemp, Flax, Wine, and other valuable Staples which those

People are fully acquainted withal. Not to mention the Advantages already discovered by that worthy Gentleman I just now spoke of, who is highly deserving of the Conduct and Management of such an Affair, as that wise Canton has intrusted him withal.

When these Savages go a hunting, they commonly go out in great Numbers, and oftentimes a great many Days' Journey from home, beginning at the coming in of the Winter; that is, when the Leaves are fallen from the Trees and are become dry. Tis then they burn the Woods by setting Fire to the Leaves and withered Bent and Grass, which they do with a Match made of the black Moss that hanks on the Trees in Carolina, and is sometimes above six Foot long. This, when dead, becomes black, (though of an Ash-Colour) and will then hold Fire as well as the best Match we have in Europe. In Places where this Moss is not found, (as towards the Mountains) they make Lintels of the Bark of cypress beaten, which serve as well. Thus they go and fire the Woods for many Miles, and drive the Deer and other Game into small Necks of Land and Isthmuses where they kill and destroy what they please. In these Hunting-Quarters they have their Wives and Ladies of the Camp, where they eat all the Fruits and Dainties of that Country, and live in all the Mirth and Jollity which it is possible for such People to entertain themselves withal. Here it is that they get their Complement of Deer-Skins and Furs to trade with the English, (the Deer-Skins being in Season in Winter which is contrary to England.) All small Game, as Turkies, Ducks and small Vermine, they commonly kill with Bow and Arrow, thinking it not worth throwing Powder and Shot after them. Of Turkies they have abundance, especially in Oak-Land, as most of it is that lies any distance backwards. I have been often in their Hunting-Quarters where a roasted or barbakued Turkey, eaten with Bear's Fat, is held a good Dish, and indeed I approve of it very well; for the Bear's Grease is the sweetest and less offensive to the Stomach, (as I said before) of any Fat of Animals I ever tasted. The Savage Men never beat their Corn to make Bread; but that is the Women's Work, especially the Girls, of whom you shall see four beating with long great Pestils in a narrow wooden Mortar; and every one keeps her Stroke so exactly, that tis worthy of Admiration. Their Cookery continues from Morning till Night. The Hunting makes them hungry, and the Indians are a People that always eat very often, not seldom getting up at Midnight to eat. They plant a great many sorts of Pulse, Part of which they eat green in the Summer, keeping great Quantities for their Winter-Store, which they carry along with them into the Hunting-Quarters and eat them.

The small red Pease is very common with them, and they eat a great deal of that and other sorts boiled with their Meat, or eaten with Bear's Fat, which Food makes them break Wind backwards, which the Men frequently do and laugh heartily at it, it being accounted no ill Manners amongst the Indians; Yet the Women are more modest than to follow that ill Custom. At their setting out, they have Indians to attend their Hunting Camp that are not good and expert Hunters; therefore are employed to carry Burdens, to get Bark for the Cabins, and other Servile Work; also to go backward and forward to their Towns, to carry News to the old People, whom they leave behind them. The Women are forced to carry their Loads of Grain and other Provisions and get Fire-Wood; for a good Hunter or Warriour in these Expeditions, is employed in no other Business than the Affairs of Game and Battle. The wild Fruits which are dried in the Summer, over Fires, on Hurdles and in the Sun, are now brought into the Field; as are likewise the Cakes and Quiddonies of Peaches and that Fruit and Bilberries dried, of which, they stew and make Fruit-Bread and Cakes. In some parts where Pigeons are plentiful, they get of their Fat enough to supply their Winter Stores. Thus they abide in these Quarters all the Winter long, till the Time approach for planting their Maiz and other Fruits. In these quarters, at Spare-hours, the Women make Baskets and Mats to lie upon, and those that are not extraordinary Hunters, make Bowls, Dishes and Spoons, of Gum-wood, and the Tulip-Tree, others (where they find a Vein of white Clay, fit for their purpose) make Tobacco-pipes, all which are often transported to other Indians, that perhaps have greater Plenty of Deer and other Game; so they buy, with these Manufactures, their raw Skins, with the Hair on, which our neighboring Indians bring to their Towns, and in the Summertime, make the Slaves and sorry Hunters dress them, the Winter-Sun being not strong enough to dry them; and those that are dried in the Cabins are black and nasty with the Light-Wood Smoke, which they commonly burn. Their way of Dressing their Skins is, by soaking them in Water, so they get the Hair off with an Instrument made of the Bone of a Deer's Foot; yet some use a sort of Iron Drawing-Knife, which they purchase of the English, and after the Hair is off they dissolve Deer's Brains, (which before hand are made in a Cake and baked in the Embers) in a Bowl of Water, so soak the Skins therein till the Brains have sucked up the Water; then they dry it gently, and keep working it with an Oyster-Shell, or some such thing, to scrape withal till it is dry; whereby it becomes soft and pliable. Yet these so dressed will not endure wet, but become hard thereby; which to prevent, they either cure them in the Smoke or tan them with Bark, as before observed; not but that young Indian Corn beaten to a Pulp, will effect the same as the Brains. They are not only good Hunters of the wild Beasts and Game of the Forest, but very expert in taking the Fish of the Rivers and Waters near which they inhabit, and are acquainted withal. Thus they that live a great way up the Rivers practice Striking Sturgeon and Rock-fish, or Bass, when they come up the Rivers to spawn; besides the vast Shoals of Sturgeon which they kill and take with Snares, as we do Pike in Europe. The Herrings, in March and April, run a great way up the Rivers and fresh Streams to spawn, where the Savages make great Wares with Hedges that hinder their Passage only in the Middle, where an artificial Pound is made to take them in, so that they cannot return. This Method is in use all over the Fresh Streams, to catch Trout and the other Species of Fish which those Parts afford. Their taking of Craw-fish is so pleasant, that I cannot pass it by without mention; When they have a mind to get these

Shell-fish, they take a Piece of Venison and half barbekue or roast it, then they cut it into thin Slices, which Slices they stick through with Reeds about six Inches asunder betwixt Piece and Piece; then the Reeds are made sharp at one end; and so they stick a great many of them down in the bottom of the Water, (thus baited) in the small Brooks and Runs, which the Craw-fish frequent. Thus the Indians sit by and tend those baited Sticks, every now and then taking them up to see how many are at the Bait; where they generally find abundance, so take them off and put them in a Basket for the Purpose, and stick the Reeds down again. By this Method, they will, in a little time, catch several Bushels, which are as good as any I ever eat. Those Indians that frequent the Salt-Waters, take abundance of Fish, some very large and of several sorts, which to perserve, they first barbakue, then pull the Fish to pieces, so dry it in the Sun, whereby it keeps for Transportation; as for Scate, Oysters, Cockles, and several sorts of Shell-fish, they open and dry them upon Hurdles, having a constant Fire under them. The Hurdles are made of Reeds of Canes in the shape of a Gridiron. Thus they dry several Bushels of these Fish and keep them for their Necessities. At the time when they are on the Salts, and Sea-Coasts, they have another Fishery, that is for a little Shell-Fish, which those in England call Blackmoors Teeth. These they catch by tying Bits of Oysters to a long String, which they lay in such Places, as they know, those Shell-Fish haunt. These Fish get hold of the Oysters, and suck them in, so that they pull up those long Strings, and take great Quantities of them, which they carry a great way into the main Land, to trade with the remote Indians, where they are of great Value; but never near the Sea, by reason they are common, therefort not esteemed. Besides, the Youth and Indian Boys go in the Night, and one holding a Light-Wood Torch, the other has a Bow and Arrows, and the Fire directing him to see the Fish, he shoots them with the Arrows; and thus they kill a great many of the smaller Fry, and sometimes pretty large ones. It is an established Custom amongst all these Natives, that the young Hunter never eats of that Buck,

Bear, Fish, or any other Game, which happens to be the first they kill of that sort; because they believe, if he should eat thereof, he would never after be fortunate in Hunting. The like foolish Ceremony they hold, when they have made a Ware to take Fish withal; if a big bellied Woman eat of the first Dish that is caught in it, they say, that Ware will never take much Fish; and as for killing of Snakes, they avoid it, if they lie in their way, because their Opinion is, that some of the Serpents Kindred would kill some of the Savages' Relations, that should destroy him. They have thousand of these foolish Ceremonies and Beliefs, which they are strict Observers of. Moreover, several Customs are found in some Families, which others keep not; as for Example, two Families of the Machapunga Indians, use the Jewish Custom of Circumcision, and the rest do not, neither did I ever know any others amongst the Indians that practiced any such things, and perhaps, if you ask them, what is the Reason they do so, they will make you no manner of Answer; which is as much as to say, I will not tell you. Many other Customs they have, for which they will render no Reason or Account; and to pretend to give a true Description of their Religion, it is impossible; for there are a great many of their Absurdities, which, for some Reason, they reserve as a Secret amongst themselves; or otherwise, they are jealous of their Weakness in the practicing them; so that they never acquaint any Christian with the Knowledge thereof, let Writers pretend what they will; for I have known them amongst their Idols and dead Kings in their Quiogozon for several Days, where I could never get Admittance, to see what they were doing, though I was at great Friendship with the King and great Men; but all my Persuasions availed me nothing. Neither were any but the King, with the Conjurer, and some few old Men, in that House; as for the young Men, and chiefest Numbers of the Indians, they were kept as ignorant of what the Elders were doing, as myself.

They all believe, that this World is round, and that there are two Spirits; The one good, the other bad. The good one they reckon to be the Author and Maker of every thing, and say, that it is he, that gives them the Fruits of the Earth, and has taught them to hunt, fish, and be wise enough to overpower the Beasts of the Wilderness, and all other Creatures, that they may be assistant, and beneficial to Man; to which they add, that the Quera, or good Spirit, has been very kind to the English Men, to teach them to make Guns, and Ammunition, besides a great many other Necessaries, that are helpful to Man, all which, they say will be delivered to them, when that good Spirit sees fit. They do not believe that God punishes any Man either in this Life, or that to come; but that he delights in doing good, and in giving the Fruits of the Earth, and instructing us in making several useful and ornamental things. They say, it is a bad Spirit, (who lives separate from the good one) that torments us with Sicknesses, Disappointments, Losses, Hunger, Travel, and all the Misfortunes, that Human Life is incident to. How they are treated in the next World, I have already mentioned, and, as I said before, they are very resolute in dying, when in the Hands of Savage Enemies; yet I saw one of their young Men, a very likely Person, condemned, on a Sunday, for Killing a Negro, and burning the House. I took good Notice of his Behavior, when he was brought out of the House to die, which was the next Morning after Sentence, but he changed his Countenance with Trembling, and was in the greatest Fear and Agony. I never saw any Person under his Circumstances, which perhaps, might be occasioned by his being delivered up by his own Nation, (which was the Tuskeruros) and executed by us, that are not their common Enemies, though he met with more Favour than he would have received at the Hands of Savages; for he was only hanged on a Tree near the Place where the Murder was committed; and the three Kings, that but the day before shewed such a Reluctancy to deliver him up, (but would have given another in his Room) when he was hanged, pulled him by the Hand, and said: *Thou wilt never play any more Rogue's Tricks in this World; whither art thou gone to show thy Tricks now?* Which shews these Savages to be what they really are, viz: a People that will save their own Men if they can, but if the Safety of all the People lies at Stake, they will deliver up the most innocent Person living, and be so far from Concern, when they have made themselves easy thereby, that they will laugh at their Misfortunes, and never pity or think of them more.

Their Priests are the Conjurers and Doctors of the Nation. I shall mention some of their Methods and Practices, and so leave them to the Judgment of the Reader. As I told you before, the Priests make their Orations at every Feast, or other great Meeting of the Indians. I happened to be at one of these great Meetings, which was at the Funeral of a Tuskeruro Indian, that was slain with Lightning at a Feast the day before, where I was amongst the rest. It was in July, and a very fair day, where, in the Afternoon, about six or seven a Clock, as they were dealing out their Victuals, there appeared a little black cloud to the North West, which spread and brought with it Rain, Wind and Lightning; so we went out from the Place where we were all at Victuals, and went down to the Cabins where I left the Indians and went to lie in my Canoe, which was convenient enough to keep me dry. The Lightning came so terrible and down in long Streams, that I was afraid it would have taken hold of a Barrel of Powder I had in my Vessel, and so blown me up; but it pleased God that it did me no Harm; yet the Violence of the Wind had blown all the Water away, where I rid at Anchor, so that my Canoe lay dry, and some Indian Women came with Torches in their Hands to the side of the Canoe, and told me an Indian was killed with Lightning. The next day, (I think) he was buried, and I staid to see the Ceremony, and was very tractable to help the Indians to trim their Reeds and make the Coffin, which pleased them very much, because I had a mind to see the Interment. Before he was Interred, according to their Custom, they dealt every one some hot Victuals, which he took and did what he would with. Then the Doctor began to talk, and told the People what Lightning was, and that it killed every thing that dwelt upon the Earth; nay the very Fishes did not escape; for it often reached the Porpoises and other Fish, and destroyed them; that everything strove to shun it except the Mice, who, he said, were the busiest in eating their Corn in the Fields when it lightened the most. He added, that no Wood or Tree could withstand it, except the black Gum, and that it would run round that Tree a great many times to enter therein, but could not effect it. Now you must understand that sort of Gum will not split or rive; therefore, I suppose, the Story might arise from thence. At last he began to tell the most ridiculous, absurd Parcel of Lyes about Lightning that could be; as that an Indian of that Nation had once got Lightning in the Likeness of a Partridge; That no other Lightning could harm him whilst he had that about him; and that after he had kept it for several Years it got away from him; so that he then became as liable to be struck with Lightning as any other Person. There was present at the same time an Indian that had lived from his Youth chiefly in an English House; so I called to him and told him what a Parcel of Lyes the Conjurer told, not doubting but he thought so as well as I, but I found to the contrary; for he replied, that I was much mistaken, for that old Man, (who I believe was upwards of an hundred Years old) did never tell Lyes; and as for what he said, it was very true, for he knew it himself to be so. Thereupon seeing the Fellow's Ignorance, I talked no more about it. Then the Doctor proceeded to tell a long Tale of a great Rattle Snake, which, a great while ago, lived by a Creek in that River, which was Neus, and that it killed abundance of Indians; but at last a bald Eagle killed it and they were rid of a Serpent that used to devour whole Canoes full of Indians at a time. I have been something tedious upon this Subject, on purpose to show what strange, ridiculous Stories these Wretches are inclinable to believe. I suppose these Doctors understand a little better themselves, than to give Credit to any such Fooleries; for I reckon them the cunningest Knaves in all the Pack. I will therefore begin with their Physic and Surgery, which is next: You must know that the Doctors or Conjurers, to gain a greater Credit amongst these People, tell them that all Distempers are the Effects of evil Spirits, or the bad Spirit, which has struck them with this or that Malady, therefore none of these Physicians undertake any Distemper but that he comes to an Exorcism to effect the Cure, and acquaints the sick Party's Friends, that he must converse with the good Spirit, to know whether the Patient will recover or not, if so, then he will drive out the bad Spirit, and the Patient will become well. Now, the general way of their Behavior in curing the Sick, (a great deal of which I have seen, and shall give some Account thereof, in as brief a manner as possible) is, when an Indian is sick, if they think there is much Danger of Life, and that he is a great Man or hath good Friends, the Doctor is sent for. As soon as the Doctor comes into the Cabin, the sick Person is set on a Mat or Skin stark-naked, lying on his Back and all uncovered, except some small Trifle that covers their Nakedness when ripe, otherwise, in very young Children, there is nothing about them. In this manner the Patient lies, when the Conjurer appears, and the King of that Nation comes to attend him with a Rattle made of a Gourd with Pease in it. This the King delivers into the Doctor's Hands, whilst another brings a Bowl of Water, and sets it down. Then the Doctor begins, and utters some few Words very softly; afterwards he smells of the Patient's Navel and Belly, and sometimes scarifies him a little with a Flint, or an Instrument made of Rattle-Snake's Teeth for that purpose; then he sucks the Patient and gets out a Mouthful of Blood and Serum, but serum chiefly, which, perhaps, may be a better Method in many Cases than to take away great Quantities of Blood, as is commonly practiced, which he spits in the Bowl of Water. Then he begins to mutter, and talk apace, and at last to cut Capers and clap his Hands on his Breech and Sides, till he gets into a Sweat, so that a Stranger would think he was running mad, now and then sucking the Patient, and so, at times, keeps sucking, till he has got a great quantity of very ill coloured Matter out of the Belly, Arms, Breast, Forehead, Temples, Neck, and most Parts, still continuing his Grimaces, and antick postures, which are not to be matched in Bedlam. At last you will see the Doctor all over of a dropping Sweat, and scarce able to utter one Word, having quite spent himself, then he will cease for a while, and so begin again till he comes in the same Pitch of Raving and seeming Madness, as before, (all this time the sick Body never so much as moves, although, doubtless, the Lancing and Sucking must be a great Punishment to them, but they certainly are the patientest and most steady people under any Burden that I ever saw in my Life.) At last, the Conjurer makes an end, and tells the Patient's Friends, whether the Person will live or die; and then one that waits at this Ceremony, takes the Blood away, (which remains in a Lump, in the middle of the Water) and buries it in the Ground, in a Place unknown to anyone, but he that inters it. Now, I believe a great deal of Imposture in these Fellows; yet I never knew their Judgment fail, though I have seen them give their Opinion after this Manner, several times: Some affirm, that there is a smell of Brimstone in the Cabins, when they are Conjuring, which I cannot contradict, which way it may come, I will not argue, but proceed to a Relation or two, which I have from a great many Persons, and some of them worthy of Credit.

The first is, of a certain Indian, that one rainy Night, underminded a House made of Logs, (such as the Swedes in America very often make, and are very strong) which belonged to Seth Southwell, Esq., governor of North Carolina, and one of the Proprietors. There was but one place the Indian could get in at, which was very narrow; the rest was secured, by having Barrels of Pork and other Provisions set against the side of the House, so that if this Indian had not exactly hit the very Place he underminded, it had been impossible for him to have got therein, because of the full Barrels that stood round the House, and barricadoed it within. The Indian stole sixty or eighty dressed Deer-Skins, besides Blankets, Powder, Shot and Rum, (this being the Indian Store-House, where the Trading Goods were kept.) Now, the Indian had made his Escape, but dropped some of the Skins by the way and they tracked his Foot-steps, and found him to be an Indian; then they guessed who it was, because none but that Indian had lately been near the House. Thereupon, the Governor sent to the Indian Town that he

EIR IDOL KIWASSA. "The people of this cuntrie have an Idol, which they call Kiwassa: yt is
ved of woode in lengthe 4 foote whose heade is like the heades of the people of Florida, the
e is of a flesh colour, the brest white, the rest is all blacke, the thighes are also spotted with whitte.
. . This Idol is placed in the temple of the towne of Secotam, as the keper of the kings dead
pses." Thomas Hariot, ib.

belonged to, which was the Tuskeruros, and acquainted them that if they did not deliver up the Indian, who had committed the Robbery, he would take a Course with them, that would not be very agreeable. Upon this, the Indians of the Town he belonged to, brought him in bound, and delivered him up to the Governor, who laid him in Irons. At the same time, it happened that a Robbery was committed amongst themselves, at the Indian Town, and this Prisoner was one of their Conjurers; so the Indians came down to the Governor's House, and acquainted him with what had happened amongst them, and that a great Quantity of Peak was stolen away out of one of their Cabins, and no one could find out the Thief, unless he would let the Prisoner conjure for it, who was the only Man they had at making such Discoveries. The Governor was content he should try his kill for them, but not to have the Prisoner's Irons taken off, which was very well approved of. The Indian was brought out in his Fetters where were the Governor's Family, and several others of the Neighborhood, now living, to see this Experiment; which he performed thus.

The Conjurer ordered three Fires to be made in a triangular Form, which was accordingly done; then he was hoodwinked very securely, with a dressed Deer-Skin, two or three doubles, over his Face. After he had made some Motions, as they always do, he went directly out of one of the three Gaps, as exactly as if he had not been blindfolded, and kept muttering to himself, having a Stick in his Hand, with which, after some time, he struck two Strokes very hard, upon the Ground, and made thereon a Cross, after which he told the Indian's Name that had stolen the Goods, and said, that he would have a Cross of his Back; which proved true; for when they took and searched him, there appeared two great Wheals, on his Back, one Cross the other; for the Theif was at Governor Southwell's House, and was under no Apprehension of being discovered. The Indians proffered to sell him as a Slave to the Governor, but he refused to buy him; so they took him bound away.

Another Instance of the like Nature happened at the same

House. One of the Tuskeruro Kings had brought in a Slave to the same Governor, to whom he had sold him; and before he returned fell sick at the Governor's House; upon which the Doctor that belonged to this King's Nation was sent for, being a Man that was held to be the greatest Conjurer amongst them. It was three Days before he could arrive, and he appeared, (when he came) to be a very little Man, and so old, that his Hair was as white as ever was seen. When he approached the sick King, he ordered a Bowl of Water to be brought him and three Chuncks of Wood, which was immediately done. Then he took the Water and set it by him, and spurted a little on him, and with the three Pieces of Wood he made a Place to stand on, whereby he was raised higher; (he being a very low statured Man); then he took a String of Ronoak, which is the same as a String of small Beads; this he held by one End between his Fingers; the other End touched the King's Stomach, as he stood on the Logs. Then he began to talk, and, at length, the By-stand-ers thought really that they heard somebody talk to him, but saw no more than what first came in. At last, this String of Beads, which hung thus perpendicular, turned up as an Eel would do, and without any Motion of his, they came all up, (in a lump) under his Hand, and hung so for a considerable time, he never closing his Hand, and at length returned to their pristine Length and Shape, at which the Spectators were much frightened. Then he told the Company that he would recover, and that his Distemper would remove into his Leg, all which happened to be exactly as the Indian Doctor had told. These are Matters of Fact, and, I can, at this day, prove the Truth thereof by several substantial Evidences that are Men of Reputation, there being more than a dozen People present when this was performed; most of whom are now alive.

There are a great many other Stories of this Nature, which are seemingly true, being told by Persons that affirm they were Eye-Witnesses thereof; as, that they have seen one Roncommock, a Chu-wou Indian, and a great Conjurer, take a Reed about two Foot long in his Mouth, and stand by a Creek-Side, where he called twice or thrice with the Reed in his Mouth, and, at last, has opened his Arms and fled over the Creek, which might be near a quarter of a Mile wide or more; but I shall urge no Man's Belief, but tell my own; which is, that I believe the two first Accounts which were acted at Mr. Southwell's Plantation, as firmly as any Man can believe any thing of that which is Told him by honest Men, and he has not seen; not at all doubting the Credit of my Authors.

The Cures I have seen performed by the Indians, are too many to repeat here; so I shall only mention some few, and their Method. they cure Scald-heads infallibly, and never miss. Their chief Remedy, as I have seen them make use of, is, the Oil of Acorns, but from which sort of Oak I am not certain. They cure Burns beyond Credit. I have seen a Man burnt in such a manner, (when drunk) by falling into a Fire, that I did not think he could recover; yet they cured him in ten Days so that he went about. I knew another blown up with Powder, that was cured to Admiration. I never saw an Indian have an Ulcer, or foul Wound in my life; neither is there any such thing to be found amongst them. They cure the Pox by a Berry that salivates as Murcury does; yet they use Sweating and Decoctions very much with it, as they do almost on every Occasion; and when they are thoroughly heated, they leap into the River. The Pox is frequent in some of the Nations; amongst which I knew one Woman die of it; and they could not, or would not cure her. Before she died she was worn away to a Skeleton, yet walked up and down to the last. We had a Planter in Carolina who had got an Ulcer in his Leg, which had troubled him a great many Years; at last he applied himself to one of these Indian Conjurers, who was a Pamticough Indian, and was not to give the Value of fifteen Shillings for the Cure. Now, I am not positive whether he washed the Ulcer with any thing before he used what I am now going to speak of, which was nothing but the rotten, doated Grains of Indian Corn, beaten to Powder and the soft Down growing on a Turkey's Rump. This Dried the Ulcer up immediately, and no other Fontanel was made to discharge the Matter, he remaining a healthful Man till the time he had the Misfortune to be drowned, which was many Years after. Another Instance, (not of my own Knowledge, but I had it confirmed by several dwellers in Maryland, where it was done) was, of an honest Planter that had been possessed with a strange, Lingering Distemper, not usual amongst them, under which he emaciated and grew every Month worse than another, it having held him several Years, in which time he had made tryal of several Doctors, as they call them, which, I suppose, were Ship-Surgeons. In the beginning of this Distemper, the Patient was very well to pass, and was possessed of several Slaves, which the Doctors purged all away, and the poor Man was so far from mending that he grew worse and worse every day. But it happened that one day as his Wife and he were commiserating his miserable Condition, and that he could not expect to recover, but looked for Death very speedily, and condoling the Misery he should leave his Wife and Family in, since all his Negroes were gone. At that time, I say, it happened that an Indian was in the same Room, who had frequented the House for many Years, and so was become as one of the Family, and would sometimes be at this Planter's House and at other times amongst the Indians.

This Savage, hearing what they talked of, and having a great Love for the Sick Man, made this Reply to what he had heard: *Brother, you have been a long time Sick, and I know you have given away your Slaves to your English Doctors. What made you do so, and now become poor? They do not know how to cure you; for it is an Indian Distemper, which your People know not the Nature of. If it had been an English Disease, probably they could have cured you; and had you come to me at first I would have cured you for a small matter, without taking away your Servants that made Corn for you and your Family to eat; and yet, if you will give me a Blanket to keep me warm, and some Powder and Shot to kill Deer withal, I will do my best to make you well still.* The Man was low in Courage and Pocket too, and made the Indian this Reply: *Jack, my Distemper is past Cure, and if our English Doctors cannot cure it I am sure the Indians cannot.* But his Wife accosted her Husband in very mild terms, and told him, he did not know but God might be pleased to give a Blessing to that Indian's Undertaking more than he had done to the English; and further added, *if you die I cannot be much more miserable, by giving this small matter to the Indian; so I pray you, my Dear, take my Advice, and try him;* to which, by her persuasions, he consented. After the Bargain was concluded, the Indian went into the Woods and brought in both Herbs and Roots, of which he made a Decoction, and gave it the Man to drink, and bade him go to bed, saying, it should not be long before he came again, which the Patient performed as he had ordered; and the Potion he had administered made him sweat after the most violent manner that could be, whereby he smelled very offensively both to himself, and they that were about him; but in the Evening, towards Night, Jack came, with a great Rattle-Snake in his Hand alive, which frightened the People almost out of their Senses; and he told his Patient that he must take that to Bed to him; at which the Man was in a great Consternation, and told the Indian he was resolved to let no Snake come into his Bed, for he might as well die of the Distemper he had, as be killed with the Bite of that Serpent. To which the Indian replied, he could not bite him now nor do him any harm, for he had taken out his Poison-Teeth, and shewed him that they were gone. At last, much with Persuasion, he admitted the Snake's Company, which the Indian put about his Middle, and ordered no body to take him away upon any account, which was strictly observed, although the Snake girdled him as hard for a great while, as if he had been drawn in by a Belt which one pulled at with all his strength. At last the Snake's Twitches grew weaker and weaker, till, by degrees, he felt him not; and opening the Bed he was found dead, and the Man thought himself better. The Indian came in the Morning, and seeing the Snake dead, told the Man that his Distemper was dead along with that Snake, which proved so as he said, for the Man speedily recovered his Health and became perfectly well.

They cure the Spleen, (which they are much addicted to) by burning with a Reed. They lay the Patient on his Back, so put a hollow Cane into the Fire, where they burn the End thereof till it is very hot, and on Fire at the end. Then they lay a Piece of thin Leather on the Patient's Belly, between the Pit of the Stomach and the Navel, so press the hot Reed on the Leather, which burns the Patient so that you may ever after see the Impression of the Reed where it was laid on, which Mark never goes off so long as he lives. This is used for the Belly-Ach sometimes. They can colour their Hair black, though sometimes it is reddish, which they do with the Seed of a Flower that grows commonly in their Plantations. I believe this would change the reddest Hair into perfect black. They make use of no Minerals in their Physick, and not much of Animals; but chiefly rely on Vegetables. They have several Remedies for the Tooth-ache, which often drive away the Pain: but if they fail, they have Recourse to punching out the Tooth with a small Cane set against the same on a Bit of Leather. Then they strike the Reed and so drive out the Tooth; and howsoever it may seem to the Europeans, I prefer it before the common way of drawing Teeth by those Instruments that endanger the Jaw, and a Flux of Blood often follows which this Method of a Punch never is attended withal: neither is it half the Pain. The Spontaneous Plants of America the Savages are well acquainted withal, and a Flux of Blood never follows any of their Operations. They are wholly Strangers to Amputation, and for what natural Issues of Blood happen immoderately, they are not to seek for a certain and speedy Cure. Tears, Rozins, and Gums, I have not discovered that they make much use of; And as for Purging and Emeticks, so much in fashion with us, they never apply themselves to, unless in drinking vast Quantities of their Yaupon or Tea, and vomiting it up again as clear as they drink it. This is a Custom amongst all those that can procure that Plant, in which manner they take it every other Morning or oftener, by which Method they keep their Stomachs clean without pricking the Coats, and straining Nature, as every Purge is an Enemy to. Besides the great Diuretick Quality of their Tea carries off a great deal that perhaps might prejudice their Health by Agues and Fevers, which all watery Countries are addicted to; for which reason I believe it is that the Indians are not so much addicted to that Distemper as we are, they preventing its siezing upon them by this Plant alone. Moreover, I have remarked that it is only those places bordering on the Ocean and great Rivers that this Distemper is frequent in, and only on and near the same Places this Evergreen is to be found, and none up towards the Mountains, where these Agues seldom or never appear. Nature having provided suitable Remedies in all Countries, proper for the Maladies that are common thereto. The Savages of Carolina have this Tea in Veneration above all the Plants they are acquainted withal, and tell you the Discovery thereof was by an infirm Indian, that labored under the Burden of many rugged Distempers, and could not be cured by all their Doctors: so one day he fell asleep and dreamed that if he took a Decoction of the Tree that grew at his Head, he would certainly be cured. Upon which he awoke, and saw the Yaupon or Caffena-Tree, which was not there when he fell asleep. He followed the Direction of his Dream and became perfectly well in a short time. Now, I suppose no Man has so little Sense as to believe this Fable, yet it lets us see what they intend thereby, and that it has, doubtless, worked Feats enough to gain it such an Esteem amongst these Savages who are too well versed in Vegetables to be brought to a continual use of any one of them, upon a mere Conceit or Fancy, without some apparent Benefit they found thereby; especially when we are sensible they drink the Juices of Plants to free Nature of her Burdens, and not out of Foppery and Fashion as the other Nations are oftentimes found to do. Amongst all the Discoveries of America by the Missionaries of the French and Spaniards I wonder none of them was so kind to the World as to have kept a Catalogue of the Distempers they found the Savages capable of curing, and their Method of Cure, which might have been of some Advantage to our *Materia Medica* at home, when delivered by Men of Learning and other Qualifications, as most of them are. Authors generally tell us that the Savages are well enough acquainted with those Plants which their Climate affords, and that some of them effect great Cures, but by what Means and in what Form, we are left in the dark. The Bark of the Root of the Sassafras-Tree I have observed is much used by them. They generally torrefy it in the Embers, so strip off the Bark from the Root, beating it to a Consistence fit to spread, so lay it on the grieved Part, which both cleanses a fowl Ulcer, and after Scarification being applied to a Contusion or Swelling, draws forth the Pain and reduces the Part to its pristine State of Health, as I have often seen effected. Fats and Unguents never appear in their Chirurgery when the Skin is once broken. The Fats of Animals are used by them to render their Limbs pliable, and when wearied, to relieve the Joints, and this not often, because they approve of the Sweating House (in such cases) above all things. The Salts they mix with their Bread and Soup, to give them a Relish, are Alkalis, viz: Ashes, and calcined Bones of Deer, and other Animals. Sallads, they never eat any, as for Pepper and Mustard, they reckon us little better than Madmen, to make use of it amongst our Victuals. They are never troubled with the Scurvey, Dropsy, nor Stone. The Phtisick, Ashma, and Diabetes, they are wholly Strangers to. Neither do I remember I ever saw one Paralytick amongst them. The Gout, I cannot be certain whether they know what it is, or not. Indeed, I never saw any Nodes or Swellings, which attend the Gout in Europe; yet they have a sort of Rheumatism or Burning of the Limbs, which tortures them grievously, at which time their Legs are so hot, that they employ the young People continually to pour Water down them. I never saw but one or two thus afflicted. The Struma is not uncommon amongst these Savages, and another Distemper, which is, in some respects, like the Pox, but is attended with no gonorrhaea. This not seldom bereaves them of their Nose. I have seen three or four of them rendered most miserable Spectacles by this Distemper. Yet, when they have been so negligent, as to let it run on so far without curbing of it; at last, they make shift to patch themselves up, and live for many years after; and such Men commonly turn Doctors. I have known two or three of these no-nose Doctors in great Esteem amongst these Savages. The Juice of the Tulip-Tree is used as a proper Remedy for this Distemper. What knowledge they have in Anatomy, I cannot tell, neither did I ever see them employ themselves therein, unless as I told you before, when they make the Skeletons of their Kings and great Men's Bones.

The Indians are very careless and negligent of their Health; as, by Drunkness,' Wading in the Water, irregular Diet and Lodging, and a thousand other Disorders, (that would kill an European) which they daily use. They boil and roast their Meat extraordinary much, and eat abundance of Broth, except the Savages whom we call the naked Indians, who never eat any Soupe. They travel from the Banks of the Messiasippi, to war against the Sinnagars or Iroquois, and are, (if equal Numbers) commonly too hard for them. They will lie and sleep in the Woods without Fire, being inured thereto. They are the hardiest of all Indians, and run so fast, that they are never taken, neither do any Indians outrun them, if they are pursued. Their Savage Enemies say, their Nimbleness and Wind proceeds from their never eating any Broth. The Small-Pox has been fatal to them, they do not often escape, when they are seized with that Distemper, which is a contrary Fever to what they ever knew. Most certain, it had never visited America, before the Discovery thereof by the Christians. Their running into the Water, in the Extremity of this Disease, strikes it in, and kills all that use it. Now they are become a little wiser; but formerly it destroyed whole Towns, without leaving one Indian alive in the Village. The Plague was never known amongst them, that I could learn by what Enquiry I have made. These Savages use Scarification almost in all Distempers. Their chief Instruments for that Operation is the Teeth of Rattle-Snakes, which they poison withal. They take them out of the Snake's Head, and suck out the Poison with their

Mouths, (and so keep them for use) and spit out the Venom which is green, and are never damaged thereby. The Small-Pox and Rum, have made such a Destruction amongst them that, on good Grounds, I do believe, there is not the sixth Savage living within two hundred Miles of all our Settlements, as there were fifty Years ago. These poor Creatures have so many Enemies to destroy them, that it is a wonder one of them is alive near us. The Small-Pox I have acquainted you withal above, and so I have of Rum, and shall only add, that they have got away to carry it back to the Westward Indians, who never knew what it was, till within very few Years. Now they have it brought them by the Tuskeruros, and other Neighbour Indians, but the Tuskeruros chiefly, who carry it in Rundlets several hundred Miles, amongst other Indians. Some times they cannot forbear breaking their Cargo, but sit down in the Woods, and drink it all up, and then hollow and shout like so many Bedlamites. I accidentally once met with one of the drunken Crews, and was amazed to see a Parcel of drunken Savages so far from any Englishman's House; but the Indians I had in Company informed me, that they were Merchants, and had drunk all their Stock, as is very common for them to do. But when they happen to carry it safe, (which is seldom, without drinking some part of it, and filling it up with Water) and come to an Indian Town, those that buy Rum of them have so many Mouthfuls for a Buck-Skin, they never using any other Measure; and for this purpose, the Buyer always makes Choice of his Man, which is one that has the greatest Mouth, whom he brings to the Market with a Bowl to put it in. The Seller looks narrowly to the Man's Mouth that measures it, and if he happens to swallow any down, either through Wilfulness or other wise, the Merchant or some of his Party does not scruple to knock the Fellow down, exclaiming against him for false Measure. Thereupon, the Buyer finds another mouthpiece to measure the Rum by, so that this Trading is very agreeable to the Spectators, to see such a deal of Quarrelling and Controversy as often happens about it, and is very diverting.

Another Destroyer of them, is, the Art they have, and often practice, of poisoning one another; which is done by a large white spongy Root, that grows in the Fresh-Marshes, which is one of their Poisons, not but that they have many other Drugs, which they poison one another withal.

Lastly, the continual Wars these Savages maintain, one Nation against another, which sometimes hold for some Ages, killing and making Captives, till they become so weak thereby, that they are forced to make Peace for want of Recruits, to supply their Wars; and the Difference of Languages, that is found amongst these Heathens, seems altogether strange. For it often appears, that every dozen Miles, you meet with an Indian Town, that is quite different from the others you last parted withal, and what a little supplies this Defect is, that the most powerful Nation of these Savages scorns to treat or trade with any others, (of fewer Numbers and less Power) in any other Tongue, but their own, which serves for the Lingua of the Country, with which we travel and deal; as for Example, we see that the Tuskeruros are most numerous in North Carolina, therefore their Tongue is understood by some in every Town of all the Indians near us. And here I shall insert a small Dictionary of every Tongue, though not Alphabetically digested:

English.	Tuskeruro.
One,	Unche,
Two,	Necte,
Three,	Ohs-sah,
Four,	Untoc,
Five,	Ouch-whe,
Six,	Houeyoc,
Seven,	Chauh-noc,
Eight,	Nec-kara,
Nine,	Wearah,
Ten.	Wartsauh,
Eleven,	Unche scauwhau,
Twelve,	Nectec Scaukhau,
Twenty,	Wartsau scauhau,
Thirty,	Ossa te wartsau,
Hundred,	Touch se,
Thousand,	Ki you se,
Rum,	Oonaquod,
Blankets,	Oorewa,
White,	Ware-occa,
Red,	Cotcoo-rea,
Black or Blue, *idem*	Caw-hunshe,
Gunpowder,	Ou-ken,
Shot,	Cauna,
Axe,	Au-nuka,
Knife,	Oosocke nauh,
Tobacco,	Charho,
Shirt,	Ough-tre's,
Shoes,	Oo-ross-soo,
Hat,	Trossa,

Pampticough.
Weembot,
Neshinnauh,
Nish-wonner,
Yau-Ooner,
Umperren,
Who-yeoc,
Top-po-osh,
Nau-haush-shoo,
Pach-ic-conk,
Cosh,

Woccon.
Tonne,
Num-perre,
Nam-mee,
Punnum-punne,
Webtau,
Is-sto,
Nommis-sau,
Nupsau,
Wiehere,
Soone noponne,
Tonne hauk pea,
Soone nomme,
Winnop,

Weesaccon,
Mattosh,
Wop-poshaumosh,
Mish-cosk,
Mow-cottowosh,
Pungue,
Ar-rounser,
Tomma-hick,
Rig-cosq,
Hoohpau,

Mottau-quahan,

Yup-see,
Roo-iune,
Waurraupa,
Yauta,
Yah-testea,
Rooeyam,
Week,
Tau-unta winnik,
Wee,
Un-coone,
Tacca-pitteneer,
Wee-kessoo,
Intome-posswa,

English.	Tuskeruro.
Fire,	Utchar,
Water,	Awoo,
Goat,	Ouswox,
	Kawhitchra,
Awl or Needle,	Oose-waure,
A Hoe,	Wauche-wocnoc,
Salt,	Cheek-ha,
Paint,	Quaunt,
Ronoak,	Nauh-houyeot,
Peak,	Chu-teche,
Gun,	Auk-noc,
Gun-lock,	Oo-teste,
Flints,	Ou-negh-ra,
A Flap,	Oukhaure,
Belt,	Ona-teste,
Scissors and Tobacco	
tongues,	Cheh-ra,
A Kettle,	Oowaiana,
A Pot,	Ocnock,
Acorns,	Kooawa,
A Pine Tree,	Heigta,
Englishman,	Nickreruroh,
Indians,	Unqua,

Pampticough.
Tinda,
Umpe,
Taus-won,

Moc-cose,
Rosh-shocquon,

Chuwon,
Mis-kis-'su,
Ronoak,
Gau hooptop,
Gun tock seike,
Hinds,
Rappatoc,
Maachone,

Onnossa,
Tosh-shonte,
Nuppin,

Woccon.
Yau,
Ejau,
Rummissau,

Wonsh-shee,
Rooe-pau,

Whooyeonne,
Rummaer,
Erroco,
Wittape,
Noonkosso,
Matt-teer,
Rhooeyau,
Weekau,
Tockoor,

Tooseawau,

Roosome,
Hooheh,
Wintsohore,
Yauh-he,

English.	Tuskeruro.
A Horse,	A Hots,
Swine,	Watsquerre,
Moss.	Auoona hau,
Raw skin, undrest,	Ootahawa,
Buckskin,	Ocques,
Fawn skin,	Ottea,
Bear skin,	Oochehara,
Fox skin,	Che-chou,
Raccoon skin,	Roo-sotto,
Squirrel skin,	Sost,
Wildcat skin,	Cauhauweana,
Panther skin,	Caunerex,
Wolf,	Squarrena,
Min,	Chac-kauene,
Otter,	Chaunoc,
A Mat,	Ooyethne,
Basket,	Ooyaura,
Feathers,	Oosnooqua,
Drest skin,	Cotcoo,
A Turkey,	Coona,
A Duck,	Sooeau,
A King,	Teethha,
Fat,	Ootsaure,
Soft,	Utsauwanne,
Hard or heavy,	Waucots ne,
A Rope,	Utsera,
A Possum,	Che-ra,
Day,	Ootauh-ne,
A Pestal,	Tic-caugh-ne,
A Mortar,	Ootic caugh-ne,
Stockings,	Way haushe,
A Creek,	Wackena,
A River,	Ahunt wackena,

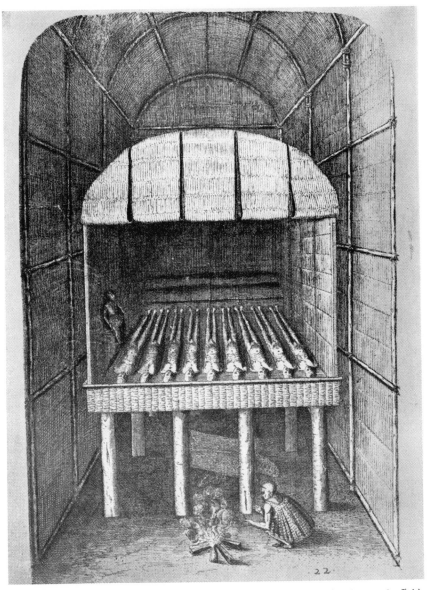

THE TOMB OF THEIR WARRIORS OR CHIEF LORDS. ". . . Under the . . . Scaffolde some of their priests hath his lodginge, which Mumbleth his prayers nighte and day, and hath charge of the corpses. For his bedd he hath two deares skinnes spredd on the grownde, if the wether bee cold hee maketh a fyre to warme by withall." Thomas Hariot, ib.

English.	*Tuskeruro.*
A Man,	Entequos,
Old Man,	Occooahawa,
Young Man,	Quottis,
Woman,	Con-noowa,
Old Woman,	Cusquerre,
Wife,	Kateocca,
A Child,	Woccanookne,
A Boy,	Wariaugh,
Infant,	Utserosta,
Ears,	Ooethnat,
Fishgig,	Ootosne,
A Comb,	Oonaquitchra,
A cake baked,	Ooneck,
A Head,	Ootaure,
Hair,	Oowaara,
Brother,	Caunotka,
I,	Ee,
Thou,	Eets,
There,	Ka,
Homine,	Cotquerre,
Bread,	Ootacnare,
Broath,	Oook-hoo,
	Oonaha,
	Oonave,
Corn,	Oosare,
	Oosha,
Peas,	Saugh-he,
A Bag,	Uttaqua,
Fish,	Cunshe,
A Louse,	Cheecq,
A Flea,	Nauocq,
Potatos,	Untone,
A Stick,	Chinqua,

English.	Tuskeruro.
Wood,	Ouyunkgue,
House,	Ounouse,
A Cow,	Ous-sarunt,
A Snake,	Us-quauh-ne,
A Bat,	Rusquiane,
A Goose,	Au-hoohaha,
A Swan,	Oorhast,
Allegator,	Utsererauh,
A Crab,	Rouare cou,
A Canoe,	Ooshunnawa,
A Box,	Ooanoo,
A Bowl,	Ortse,
A Spoon,	Oughquere,
A Path,	Wauh-hanhne,
Sun or Moon,	Heita,
Wind,	Hoonoch,
A Star,	Uttewiraratse,
Rain,	Untuch,
	Auhuntwood,
Night,	Oosottoo,
A Rundlet,	Oohunawa,
An Eel,	Cuhn-na,
A Cable,	Utquichra,
Small ropes,	Utsera utquichra,
A Button,	Tic-hah,
Breeches,	Wahunshe,
Stockings,	Oowissera,
Day,	Wauwoc-hook,
Mad,	Cosserunte,
Angry,	Cotcheroore,
Afraid,	Werricauna,
Smoak,	Oo-teighne,
A Thief or Rogue,	Katichhei,

English.	*Tuskeruro.*
A Dog,	Cheeth,
A Reed,	Cauna,
Lightwood,	Kkaoo,
To morrow,	Jureha,
Now,	Kahunk,
To-day,	Kawa,
A little while ago,	Kakoowa,
Yesterday,	Oousotto,
How manny,	Ut-tewots,
How far,	Untateawa,
Will you go along with me,	Unta-hah,
Go you,	Its warko,
Give it me,	Cotshu,
That's all,	Ut shat,
A Cubit length,	Kihoosocca,
Dead,	Whaharia,
A Gourd or Bottle,	Utchaawa,
A lazy fellow,	Wattattoo watse,
Englishman is thirsty,	Oukwockaninniwock,
I will sell you goods,	
very cheap,	Wausthanocha,
All the Indians are drunk,	Connaugh jost twane,
Have you any thing to eat,	Utta-ana-wox,
I am sick,	Connauwox,
A Fish-hook,	Oos-skinna,
Don't lose it,	Oon est nonne it quost,
A Tobacco-pipe,	Oosquaana,
I remember it,	Oonutsauka,
Let it alone,	Tnotsaurauweek,
Peaches,	Roo-ooe,
Walnuts,	Rootau-ooe,
Hickerynuts,	Rootau,
A Jew's-harp,	Ooratsa,

English.	Tuskeruro.
I forget it,	Merrauka,
North-west wind,	Hothooka,
Snow,	Acaunque.

English.	Woccon.
A Horse,	Yenwetoa,
Swine,	Nommewarraupa u,
Moss,	Itto,
Raw skin, undrest,	Teep,
Buckskin,	Rookau,
Fawn skin,	Wisto,
Bear skin,	Ourka,
Fox skin,	Hannatockore,
Raccoon skin,	Auher,
Squirrel skin,	Yehau,
Panther skin,	Wattau,
Wolf,	Tire kiro,
Min,	Soccon,
Otter,	Wetkes,
A Mat,	Soppepepor,
Basket,	Rookeppa,
Feathers,	Soppe,
Drest skin,	Rauhau,
A Turkey,	Yauta,
A Duck,	Welka,
A King,	Roamore,
Fat,	Yendare,
Soft,	Roosomme,
Hard or heavy,	Itte teraugh,
A Rope,	Trawhe,
A Pestel,	Miyau,
A Mortar,	Yossoo,
Old Woman,	Yicau,

English.	*Woccon.*
Wife,	Yecauau,
Fishgig,	Weetipsa,
A Comb,	Sacketoome possma,
A Head,	Poppe,
Hair,	Tumme,
Brother,	Yenxauhe,
Homine,	Roocauwa,
Bread,	Ikettau,
Corn,	Cose,
Pease,	Coosauk,
A Bag,	Ekoocromon,
Fish,	Yacunne,
A Louse,	Eppesyau,
Potatos,	Wauk,
Wood,	Yonne,
House,	Ouke,
A Cow,	Noppinjure,
A Snake,	Yau-hauk,
A Rat,	Wittau,
A Goose,	Auhaun,
A Swan,	Atter,
Allegator,	Monwittetau,
A Crab,	Wunneau,
A Canoe,	Watt,
A Box,	Yopoonitsa,
A Bowl,	Cotsoo,
A Spoon,	Cotsau,
A Path,	Yauh,
Sun or Moon,	Wittapare,
Wind,	Yuncor,
A Star,	Wattapi untakeer,
Rain,	Yawowa,
Night,	Yantoha,

English.	Woccon.
A Rundlet,	Ynpyupseunne,
A Button,	Rummissauwoune,
Breeches,	Rooeyaukitte,
Stockings,	Rooesoo possoo,
Day,	Waukhaway,
Mad,	Rockcumne,
Angry,	Roocheha,
Afraid,	Reheshiwau,
Smoak,	Too-she,
A Dog,	Tauh-he,
A Reed,	Weekwonne,
Lightwood,	Sek,
To-morrow,	Kittape,
A little while ago,	Yauka,
Yesterday,	Yottoha,
How many,	Tontarinte,
Will you go along with me,	Quauke,
Go you,	Yuppa me,
Give it me,	Mothei,
That is all,	Cuttaune,
A cubit length,	Ishewounaup,
Dead,	Caure,
A gourd or bottle,	Wattape,
A lazy fellow,	Tontaunette,
I will sell you goods very cheap,	Nau hou hoore-ene,
All the Indians are drunk, very cheap,	Nonnupper, Noccoo eraute,
I am sick,	Waurepa,
A tobacco pipe,	Intom,
I remember it,	Aucummato,
Let it alone,	Sauhau,
Peaches,	Yonne,

English.	*Woccon.*
Hickerynuts,	Nimmia,
A Jew's-Harp,	Wottiyau,
Snow,	Wawawa.

To repeat more of this Indian Jargon, would be to trouble the Reader; and as an Account how imperfect they are in their Moods and Tenses, has been given by several already, I shall only add, that their Languages, or Tongues are so deficient, that you cannot suppose the Indians ever could express themselves in such a Flight of Stile, as Authors would have you believe. They are so far from it, that they are but just able to make one another understand readily what they talk about. As for the two Consonants L. and F. I never knew them in any Indian Speech I have met withal; yet I must tell you, that they have such a Way of abbreviating their Speech, when in their great Councils and Debates, that the young Men do not understand what they treat about, when they hear them argue; It is wonderful, what has occasioned so many different Speeches as the Savages have. The three Nations I now mentioned, do not live above ten Leagues distant, and two of them, viz: the Tuskeruros and the Woccon, are not two Leagues asunder; yet their Speech differs in every Word thereof, except one, which is Tsaure, Cockles, which is in both Tongues the same, and nothing else. Now this Difference of Speech causes Jealousies and Fears amongst them, which bring Wars, wherein they destroy one another; otherwise the Christians had not, (in all Probability) settled America so easily, as they have done, had these Tribes of Savages united themselves into one People or general Interest, or were they so but every hundred Miles. In short, they are an odd sort of People, under the Circumstances they are at present, and have some such uncouth Ways in their Management and Course of Living, that it seems a Miracle to us, how they bring about their Designs, as they do, when their Ways are commonly quite contrary to ours. I believe they are, (as to this Life,) a very happy

People; and were it not for the Feuds amongst themselves they would enjoy the happiest State, (in this World) of all Mankind. They met with Enemies when we came amongst them; for they are no nearer Christianity now, than they were at the first Discovery, to all Appearance. They have learned several Vices of the Europeans, but not one Vertue, as I know of. Drunkenness was a Stranger, when we found them out, and Swearing their Speech cannot express; yet those that Speak English, learn to swear the first thing they talk of. It's true, they have some Vertues and some Vices; but how the Christians can bring these People into the Bosom of the Church, is a Proposal that ought to be formed and followed by the wisest Heads and best Christians. After I have given one Remark or two farther, of some of their strange Practices and Notions, I will give my Opinion, how I think, in all probability it may be, if possible, effected, and so shall conclude this Treatise of Carolina.

They are a very craving People, and if a Man give them any thing of a Present, they think it obliges him to give them another; and so on, till he has given them all he has; for they have no Bounds of Satisfaction in that way; and if they give you any thing, it is to receive twice the Value of it, They have no Consideration that you will want what you give them; for their way of Living is so contrary to ours, that neither we nor they can fathom one another's Designs and Methods. They call Rum and Physick by one Name, which implies that Rum make People sick, as when they have taken any poisonous Plant; yet they cannot forbear Rum. They make Offerings of their First Fruits, and the most serious sort of them throw into the Ashes, near the Fire, the first Bit or Spoonful of every Meal they sit down to, which they say, is the same to them as the pulling off our Hats and talking when we go to Victuals, is to us. They name the Months very agreeably, as one is the Herring-Month, another the Strawberry-Month, another the Mulberry-Month. Others name them by the Trees that blossom, especially the Dog-Wood Tree; or they say, we will return when Turkey-Cocks gobble, that is in March and April. The Age of the Moon they understand, but know no different Name for Sun and Moon. They can guess well at the time of the Day by the Sun's Height. Their Age they number by Winters, and say, such a Man or Woman is so many Winters old. They have no Sabbath or Day of Rest. Their Slaves are not overburdened with Work, and so not driven by Severity to seek for that Relief. Those that are acquainted with the English, and speak the Tongue, know when Sunday comes; besides the Indians have a distinct Name for Christmas, which they call Winnick Keshuse, or the Englishman's God's Moon. There is one most abominable Custom amongst them, which they call Husquenawing their young Men, which I have not made any Mention of as yet, so will give you an Account of it here. You must know, that most commonly, once a Year, at farthest once in two Years, these People take up so many of their young Men, as they think are able to undergo it, and Husquenaugh them, which is to make them obedient and respective to their Superiors, and, (as they say) is the same to them as it is to us to send our Children to School, to be taught good Breeding and Letters. This House of Correction is a large, strong Cabin, made on purpose for the Reception of the young Men and Boys, that have not passed this Graduation already; and it is always at Christmas that they husquenaugh their Youth, which is by bringing them into this House and keeping them dark all the time, where they more than half starve them. Besides, they give them Pellitory Bark, and several intoxicating Plants, that make them go raving mad as ever were any People in the World; and you may hear them make the most dismal and hellish Cries and Howlings that ever human Creatures expressed; all which continues about five or six Weeks, and the little Meat they eat, is the nastiest, loathsome stuff, and mixt with all manner of Filth it is possible to get. After the Time is expired, they are brought out of the Cabin, which never is in the Town, but always a distance off, and guarded by a Jayler or two, who watch by Turns. Now when they first come out, they are as poor as ever any Creatures were: for you must know several die under this diabolical Purgation. Moreover, they either really are, or pretend to be dumb, and do not speak for several Days; I think, twenty or thirty, and look so ghastly, and are so changed, that it is next to an Impossibility to know them again, although you was never so well acquainted with them before. I would fain have gone into the mad House, and have seen them in their time of Purgatory, but the King would not suffer it, because, he told me they would do me or any other white Man an Injury, that ventured in amongst them, so I desisted. They play this Prank with Girls as well as Boys, and I believe it a miserable Life they endure, because I have known several of them run away at that time to avoid it. Now the Savages say if it was not for this, they could never keep their Youth in Subjection, besides that it hardens them ever after to the Fatigues of War, Hunting, and all manner of Hardship, which their way of living exposes them to. Besides, they add, that it carries off those infirm weak Bodies, that would have been only a Burden and Disgrace to their Nation, and saves the Victuals and Cloathing for better People that would have been expended on such useless Creatures. These Savages are described in their proper Colours, but by a very few; for those that generally write Histories of this new World, are such as Interest Preferment and Merchandize, drew thither, and know no more of that People than I do of the Laplanders, which is only by Hear-say. And if we will make just Remarks how near such Relations generally approach Truth and Nicety, we shall find very few of them worthy of Entertainment; and as for the other part of the Volume, it is generally stuffed with Invectives against the Government they lived under, on which Stage is commonly acted greater Barbarities, in Murdering worthy Men's Reputations, than all the Savages in the New World are capable of equalizing or so much as imitating.

And since I hinted at a Regulation of the Savages, and to propose a way to convert them to Christianity, I will first particularize the several Nations of Indians that are our Neighbours, and then proceed to what I promised.

Tuskeruro Indians are fifteen Towns, viz: Haruta Waqui, Con-tah-nah, Anna Ooka, Conauh-Kare Harooka, Una Nauhan, Kentanuska, Chunaneets, Kenta, Eno, Naur-hegh-ne, Oonossoora, Tosneoc, Nonawharitse, Nursoorooka, Fighting-Men, 1200; Woccon, Towns, 2; Yupwauremau, Tooptatmeer, Fighting-Men, 120; Machapunga, Town, 1, Maramiskeet, Fighting Men, 30; Bear River, Town, 1, Raudauqua-quank, Fighting Men 50; Maherring Indians, Town 1, Maherring River, Fighting Men, 50; Chuwon Indians, Town 1; Bennett's Creek, Fighting Men, 15; Paspatank Indians, Town, 1; Paspatank River, Fighting Men, 10; Poteskeit, Town, 1; North River, Fighting Men, 30; Nottoway Indians, Town 1; Winoack Creek, Fighting Men, 30; Hatteras Town 1; Sand Banks, Fighting Men, 16; Connamox Indians, Towns 2; Coranine, Raruta, Fighting Men, 25; Neus Indians, Towns, 2; Chattooka, Rouconk, Fighting Men, 15; Pampticough Indians, Town, 1; Island, Fighting Men, 15; Jaupin Indians, 6 People. These five Nations of the Totero's, Sapona's, Keiauwee's, Aconechos, and Schoccories, are lately come amongst us, and may contain in all, about 750 Men, Women and Children; Total, 4780.

Now there appears to be one thousand six hundred and twelve Fighting Men, of our Neighbouring Indians, and probably there are three-fifths of Women and Children, not including Old Men, which amounts to four thousand and thirty Savages besides the five Nations lately come. Now, as I before hinted, we will see what grouds there are to make these People serviceable to us, and better themselves thereby.

On a fair Scheme, we must first allow these Savages what really belongs to them, that is, what good qualities and natural Endowments they possess, whereby they being in their proper Colours, the Event may be better guessed at and fathomed.

First, they are as apt to learn any Handicraft, as any People that the World affords; I will except none, as is seen by their Canoes and Stauking Heads, which they make of themselves; but to my purpose, the Indian Slaves in South Carolina and elsewhere, make my Argument good.

Secondly, we have no disciplined Men in Europe but what have, at one time or other been branded with Mutining and Murmuring against their Chiefs. These Savages are never found guilty of that great Crime in a Soldier. I challenge all Mankind to tell me of one Instance of it; besides, they never prove Traitors to their Native Country, but rather chuse Death than partake and side with the Enemy.

They naturally possess the Righteous Man's Gift; they are Patient under all Afflictions, and have a great many other Natural Vertues, which I have slightly touched throughout the Account of these Savages.

They are really better to us than we are to them, they always give us Victuals at their Quarters, and take care we are armed against Hunger and Thrist: We not do so by them, (generally speaking) but let them walk by our Doors Hungry and do not often relieve them. We look upon them with Scorn and Disdain, and think them little better than Beasts in Human Shape, though if well examined, we shall find that, for all our Religion and Education, we possess more Moral Deformities and Evils than these Savages do, or are acquainted withal.

We reckon them Slaves in Comparison to us, and Intruders, as oft as they enter our Houses, or hunt near our Dwellings. But if we will admit Reason to be our Guide, she will inform us that these Indians are the freest People in the World, and so far from being Intruders upon us that we have abandoned our own Native Soil, to drive them out, and possess theirs, neither have we any true Balance in Judging of these poor Heathens, because we neither give Allowance for their Natural Disposition, nor the Sylvian Education, and strange Customs (uncouth to us) they lie under and have ever been trained up to; these are false Measures for Christians to take, and indeed no Man can be reckoned a Moralist only, who will not make choice and use of better Rules to walk and act by. We trade with them, it is true, but to what End? Not to show them the Steps of Vertue, and the Golden Rule, to do as we would be done by. No, we have furnished them with the Vice of Drunkenness, which is the open Road to all others, and daily cheat them in every thing we sell, and esteem it a Gift of Christianity not to sell them so cheap as we do to the Christians, as we call ourselves. Pray, let me know where is there to be found one Sacred Command or Precept of our Master, that counsels us to such Behavior? Besides, I believe it will not appear but that all the Wars which we have had with the Savages, were occasioned by the unjust Dealings of the Christians towards them. I can name more than a few, which my own Enquiry has given me a right Understanding of, and I am afraid the remainder (if they come to the test) will prove themselves Birds of the same Feather.

As we are in Christian Duty bound, so we must act and behave ourselves to these Savages, if we either intend to be servicable in converting them to the Knowledge of the Gospel, or discharge the Duty which every Man, within the Pale of the Christian Church, is bound to do. Upon this Score, we ought to show a Tenderness for these Heathens under the weight of Infidelity; let us cherish their good Deeds, and, with Mildness and Clemency, make them sensible and forwarn them of their ill ones; let our Dealings be just to them in every Respect, and show no ill Example, whereby they may think we advise them to practice that which we will not be conformable to ourselves. Let them have cheap Penniworths, (without Guile in our Trading with them) and learn them the Mysteries of our Handicrafts, as well as our Religion, otherwise we deal unjustily by them. But it is highly necessary to be brought in Practice, which is, to give Encouragement to the ordinary People, and those of a lower Rank, that they might marry with these Indians, and come into Plantations, and Houses, where so many Acres of Land and some Gratuity of Money, (out of a publick Stock) are given to the new-married Couple; and that the Indians might have Encouragement to send their Children Apprentices to proper Masters, that would be kind to them and make them Masters of a Trade, whereby they would be drawn to live amongst us, and become Members of the same Eclesiastical and Civil government we are under; then we should have great Advantages to make daily Conversions amongst them, when they saw that we were kind and just to them in all our Dealings. Moreover, by the Indians Marrying with the Christians, and coming into Plantations with their English Husbands, or Wives, they would become Christians, and their Idolatry would be quite forgotten, and in all probability, a better Worship come in its Stead; for were the Jews engrafted thus, and alienated from the Worship and Conversation of Jews, their Abominations would vanish, and be no more.

Thus we should be let into a better Understanding of the Indian Tongue, by our new Converts; and the whole Body of these People would arrive to the Knowledge of our Religion and Customs, and become as one People with us. By this Method, also, we should have a true Knowledge of all the Indian's Skill in Medicine and Surgery; they would inform us of the Situation of our Rivers, Lakes and Tracts of Land in the Lord's Dominions, where, by their Assistance, greater Discoveries may be made than has been hitherto found out, and by their Accompanying us in our Expeditions, we might civilize a great many other Nations of the Savages, and daily add to our Strength in Trade, and Interest; so that we might be sufficiently enabled to conquer, or maintain our Ground, against all the Enemies to the Crown of England in America, both Christian and Savage.

What Children we have of theirs to learn Trades, &c., ought to be put into those Hands that are Men of the best Lives and Characters, and that are not only strict Observers of their Religion, but also of a mild, winning, and sweet Disposition, that these Indian Parents may often go and see how well their Children are dealt with, which would much win them to our Ways of Living, Mildness being a Vertue the Indians are in love withal, for they do not practice beating and correcting their Children as we do. A general

Complaint is, that it seems impossible to convert these People to Christianity, as, at first sight it does; and as for those in New Spain, they have the Prayer of that Church in Latin by Rote, and know the external Behavior at Mass and Sermons; yet scarce any of them are steady and abide with constancy in good Works and the Duties of the Christian Church. We find that the Fuentes and several other of the noted Indian Families about Mexico, and in other parts of New Spain, had given several large Gifts to the Altar, and outwardly seemed fond of their new Religion; yet those that were the greatest Zealots outwards, on a strict Enquiry, were found guilty of Idolatry and Witchcraft; and this seems to proceed from their Cohabiting, which, as I have noted before, gives opportunities of Cabals to recall their ancient pristine Infidelity and Superstitions. They never argue against our Religion, but with all imaginable Indifference own, that it is most proper for us that have been brought up in it.

In my opinion, it is better for Christians of a mean Fortune to marry with the Civilized Indians than to suffer the Hardships of four or five years' Servitude, in which they meet with Sickness and Seasonings amidst a Crowd of other Afflictions, which the Tyranny of a bad Master lays upon such poor Souls, all which those acquainted with our Tobacco Plantations are not Strangers to.

This seems to be a more reasonable Method of converting the Indians than to set up our Christian Banner in a Field of Blood, as the Spaniards have done in New Spain, and baptize one hundred with the Sword for one at the Font. Whilst we make way for a Christian Colony through a Field of Blood and defraud, and make away with those that one day may be wanted in this World, and in the next appear against us, we make way for a more potent Christian Enemy to invade us hereafter, of which we may repent, when too late.

THE END.